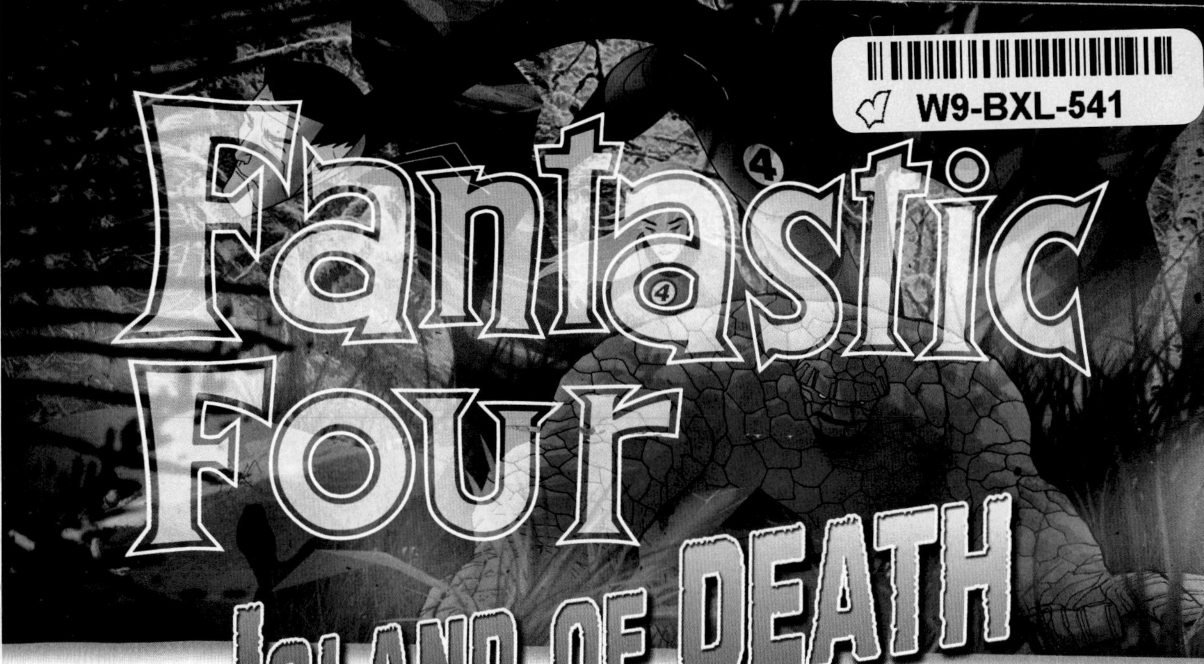

Fantastic Four

FANTASTIC FOUR ISLAND OF DEATH

WRITER **TOM BELAND** ARTIST **JUAN DOE**

LETTERERS **DAVE LANPHEAR** & **BLAMBOT'S NATE PIEKOS**

EDITOR **ALEJANDRO ARBONA**

SUPERVISING EDITOR **STEPHEN WACKER**

EXECUTIVE EDITOR **TOM BREVOORT**

SPECIAL THANKS TO **BRAD BOWERSOX, SUSAN HOMAR, MITCHELL JOACHIM, LARA GREDEN, JAVIER ARBONA, MARK MARTIN** AND **THE VIEQUES CONSERVATION AND HISTORICAL TRUST**

COLLECTION EDITOR & DESIGN **CORY LEVINE**
ASSISTANT EDITORS **ALEX STARBUCK** & **NELSON RIBEIRO**
EDITORS, SPECIAL PROJECTS **JENNIFER GRÜNWALD** & **MARK D. BEAZLEY**
SENIOR EDITOR, SPECIAL PROJECTS **JEFF YOUNGQUIST**
SVP OF PRINT & DIGITAL PUBLISHING SALES **DAVID GABRIEL**

EDITOR IN CHIEF **AXEL ALONSO** CHIEF CREATIVE OFFICER **JOE QUESADA**
PUBLISHER **DAN BUCKLEY** EXECUTIVE PRODUCER **ALAN FINE**

FANTASTIC FOUR: ISLAND OF DEATH. Contains material originally published in magazine form as FANTASTIC FOUR: ISLA DE LA MUERTE!, SPIDER-MAN & THE HUMAN TORCH IN...BAHIA DE LOS MUERTOS! and FANTASTIC FOUR IN ATAQUE DEL M.O.D.O.K.!. First printing 2013. ISBN# 978-0-7851-4410-6. Published by MARVEL WORLDWIDE, INC., a subsidiary of MARVEL ENTERTAINMENT, LLC. OFFICE OF PUBLICATION: 135 West 50th Street, New York, NY 10020.

Printed in the U.S.A. ALAN FINE, EVP - Office of the President, Marvel Worldwide, Inc. and EVP & CMO Marvel Characters B.V.; DAN BUCKLEY, Publisher & President - Print, Animation & Digital Divisions; JOE QUESADA, Chief Creative Officer; TOM BREVOORT, SVP of Publishing; DAVID BOGART, SVP of Operations & Procurement, Publishing; RUWAN JAYATILLEKE, SVP & Associate Publisher, Publishing; C.B. CEBULSKI, SVP of Creator & Content Development; DAVID GABRIEL, SVP of Print & Digital Publishing Sales; JIM O'KEEFE, VP of Operations & Logistics; DAN CARR, Executive Director of Publishing Technology; SUSAN CRESPI, Editorial Operations Manager; ALEX MORALES, Publishing Operations Manager; STAN LEE, Chairman Emeritus. For information regarding advertising in Marvel Comics or on Marvel.com, please contact Niza Disla, Director of Marvel Partnerships, at ndisla@marvel.com. For Marvel subscription inquiries, please call 800-217-9158. **Manufactured between 12/20/2012 and 1/22/2013 by QUAD/GRAPHICS, DUBUQUE, IA, USA.**

10 9 8 7 6 5 4 3 2 1

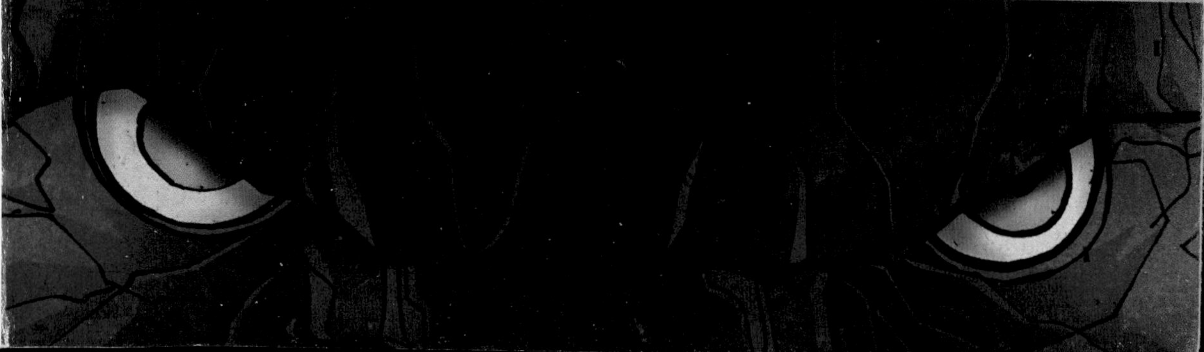

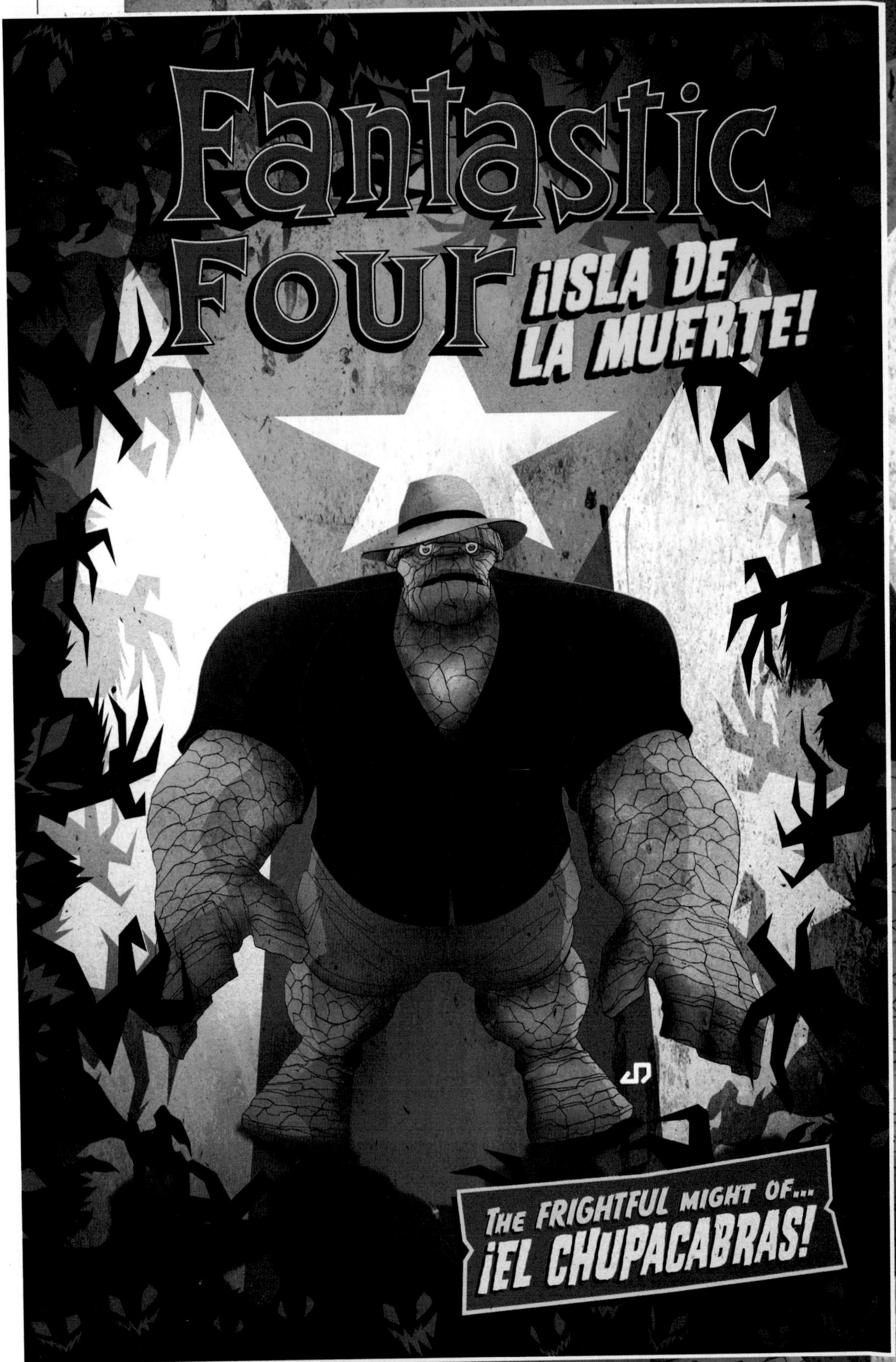
Fantastic Four
¡ISLA DE LA MUERTE!
The FRIGHTFUL MIGHT OF...
¡EL CHUPACABRAS!

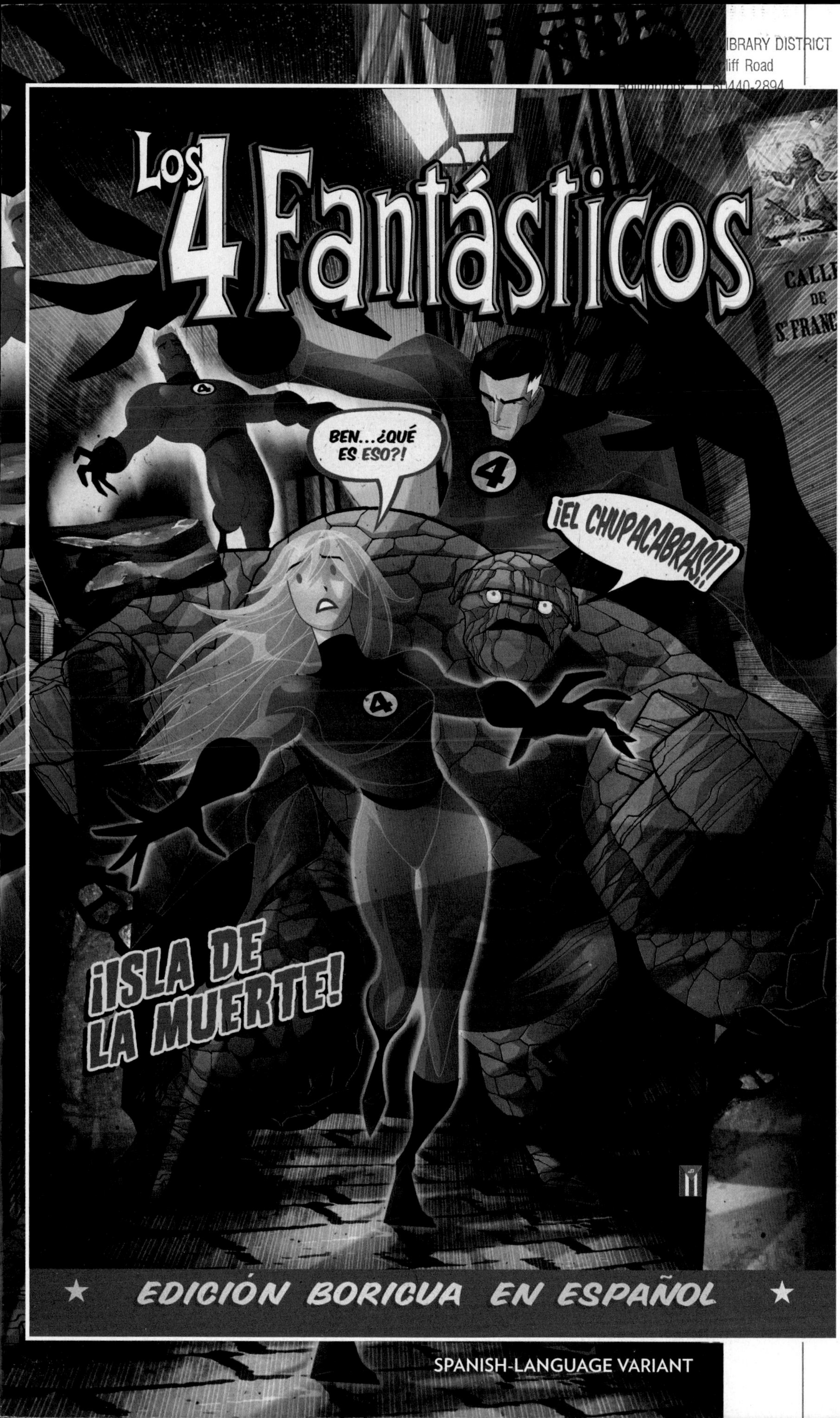
Los 4 Fantásticos
BEN...¿QUÉ ES ESO?!
¡EL CHUPACABRAS!!
CALLE DE S. FRANC
¡ISLA DE LA MUERTE!
★ EDICIÓN BORICUA EN ESPAÑOL ★
SPANISH-LANGUAGE VARIANT

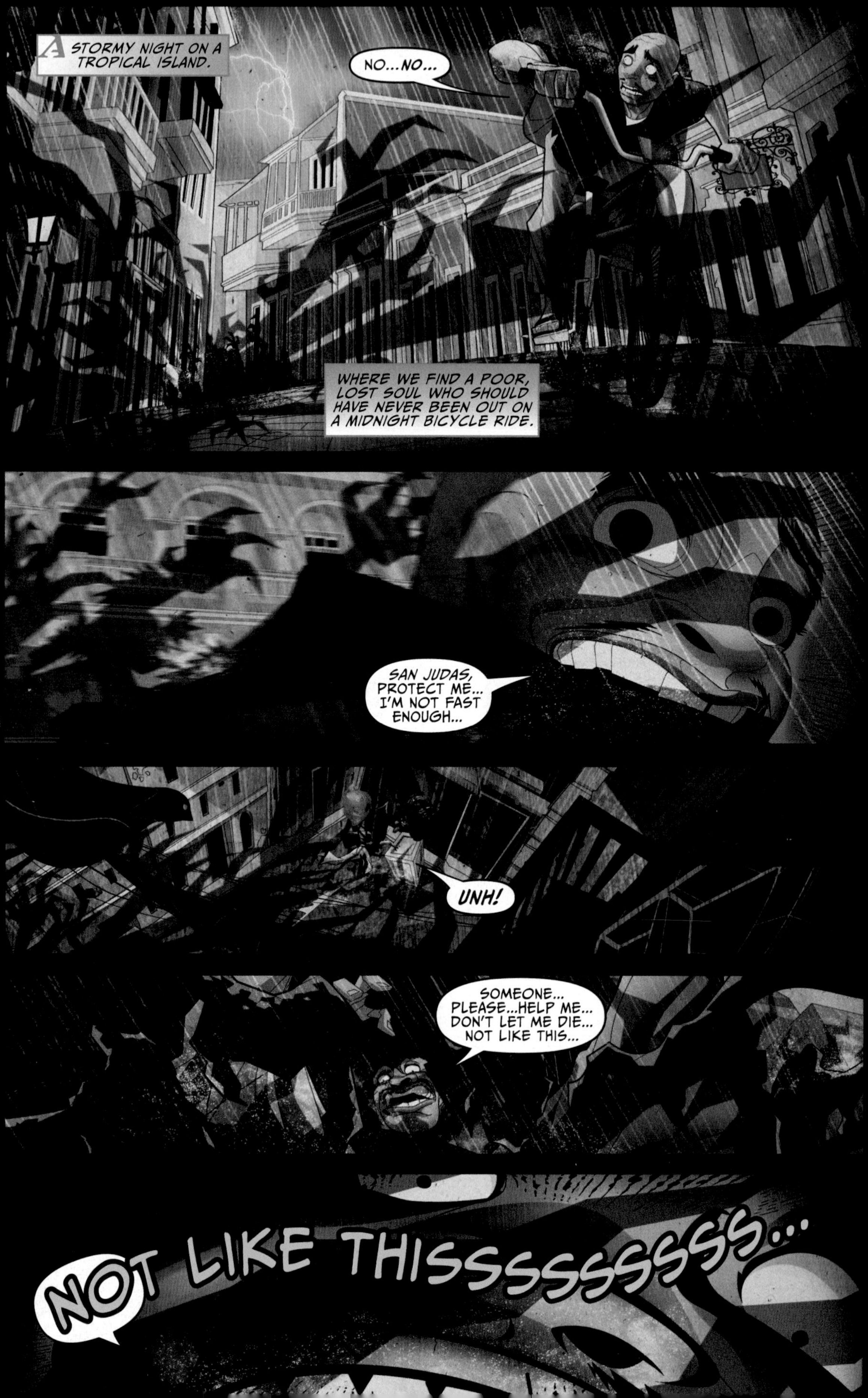
A STORMY NIGHT ON A TROPICAL ISLAND.
NO...NO...
WHERE WE FIND A POOR, LOST SOUL WHO SHOULD HAVE NEVER BEEN OUT ON A MIDNIGHT BICYCLE RIDE.
SAN JUDAS, PROTECT ME... I'M NOT FAST ENOUGH...
UNH!
SOMEONE... PLEASE...HELP ME... DON'T LET ME DIE... NOT LIKE THIS...
NOT LIKE THISSSSSSSSS...

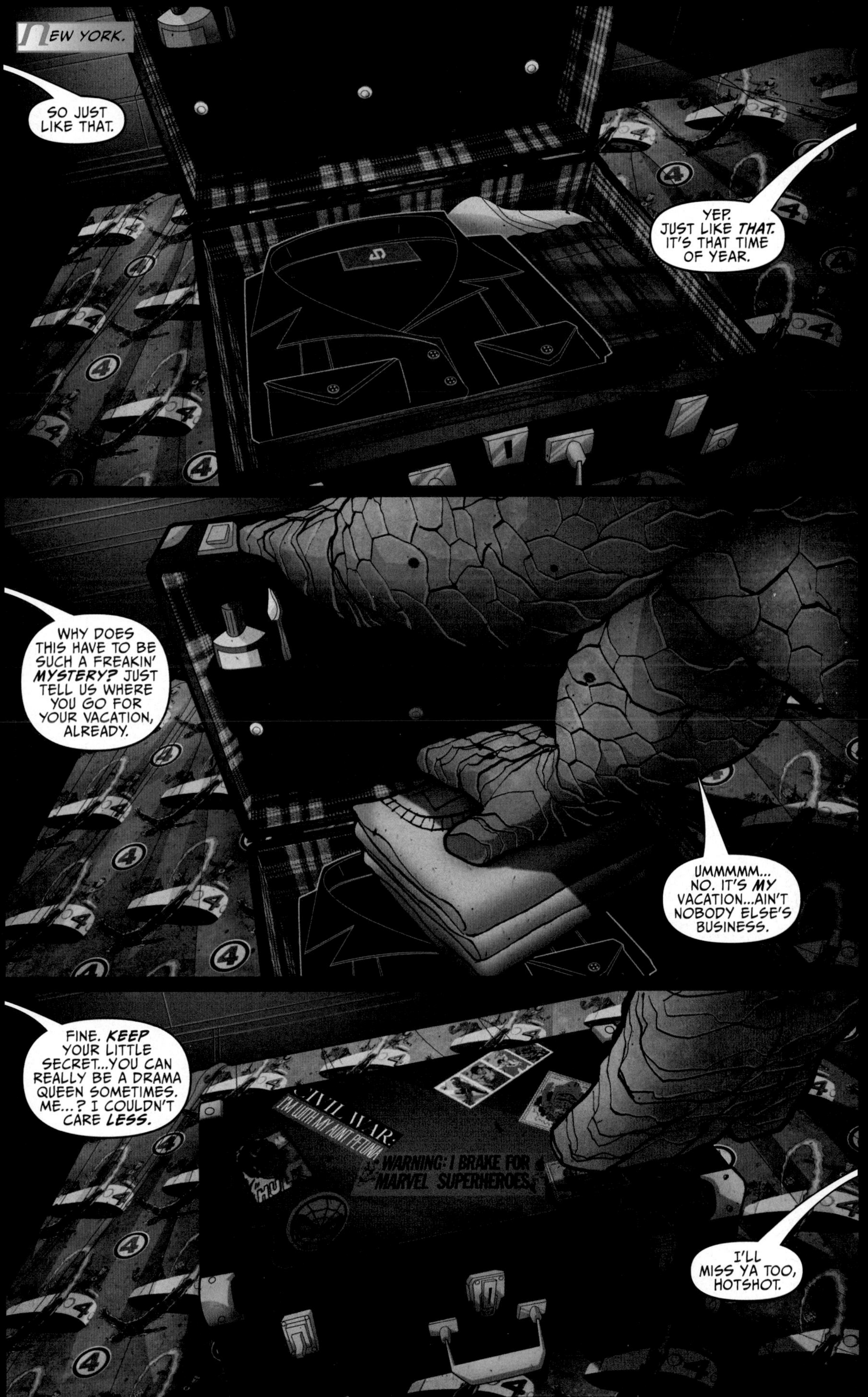
NEW YORK.
SO JUST LIKE THAT.
YEP. JUST LIKE *THAT.* IT'S THAT TIME OF YEAR.
WHY DOES THIS HAVE TO BE SUCH A FREAKIN' *MYSTERY?* JUST TELL US WHERE YOU GO FOR YOUR VACATION, ALREADY.
UMMMMM... NO. IT'S *MY* VACATION...AIN'T NOBODY ELSE'S BUSINESS.
FINE. *KEEP* YOUR LITTLE SECRET...YOU CAN REALLY BE A DRAMA QUEEN SOMETIMES. ME...? I COULDN'T CARE *LESS.*
CIVIL WAR:
I'M WITH MY AUNT PETUNIA
WARNING: I BRAKE FOR MARVEL SUPERHEROES
I'LL MISS YA TOO, HOTSHOT.

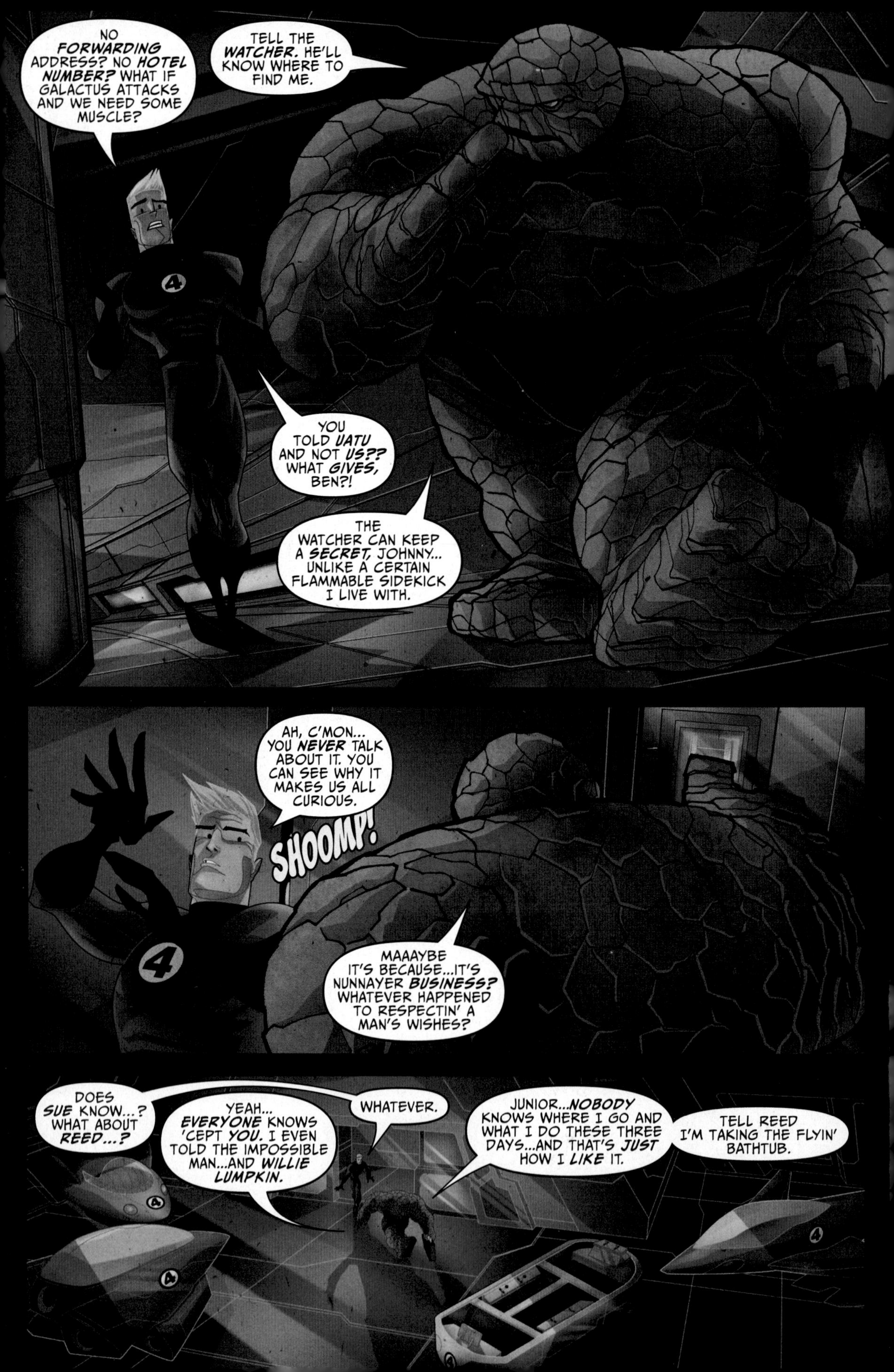

NO FORWARDING ADDRESS? NO HOTEL NUMBER? WHAT IF GALACTUS ATTACKS AND WE NEED SOME MUSCLE?
TELL THE WATCHER. HE'LL KNOW WHERE TO FIND ME.
YOU TOLD UATU AND NOT US?? WHAT GIVES, BEN?!
THE WATCHER CAN KEEP A SECRET, JOHNNY... UNLIKE A CERTAIN FLAMMABLE SIDEKICK I LIVE WITH.
AH, C'MON... YOU NEVER TALK ABOUT IT. YOU CAN SEE WHY IT MAKES US ALL CURIOUS.
SHOOMP!
MAAAYBE IT'S BECAUSE...IT'S NUNNAYER BUSINESS? WHATEVER HAPPENED TO RESPECTIN' A MAN'S WISHES?
DOES SUE KNOW...? WHAT ABOUT REED...?
YEAH... EVERYONE KNOWS 'CEPT YOU. I EVEN TOLD THE IMPOSSIBLE MAN...AND WILLIE LUMPKIN.
WHATEVER.
JUNIOR...NOBODY KNOWS WHERE I GO AND WHAT I DO THESE THREE DAYS...AND THAT'S JUST HOW I LIKE IT.
TELL REED I'M TAKING THE FLYIN' BATHTUB.

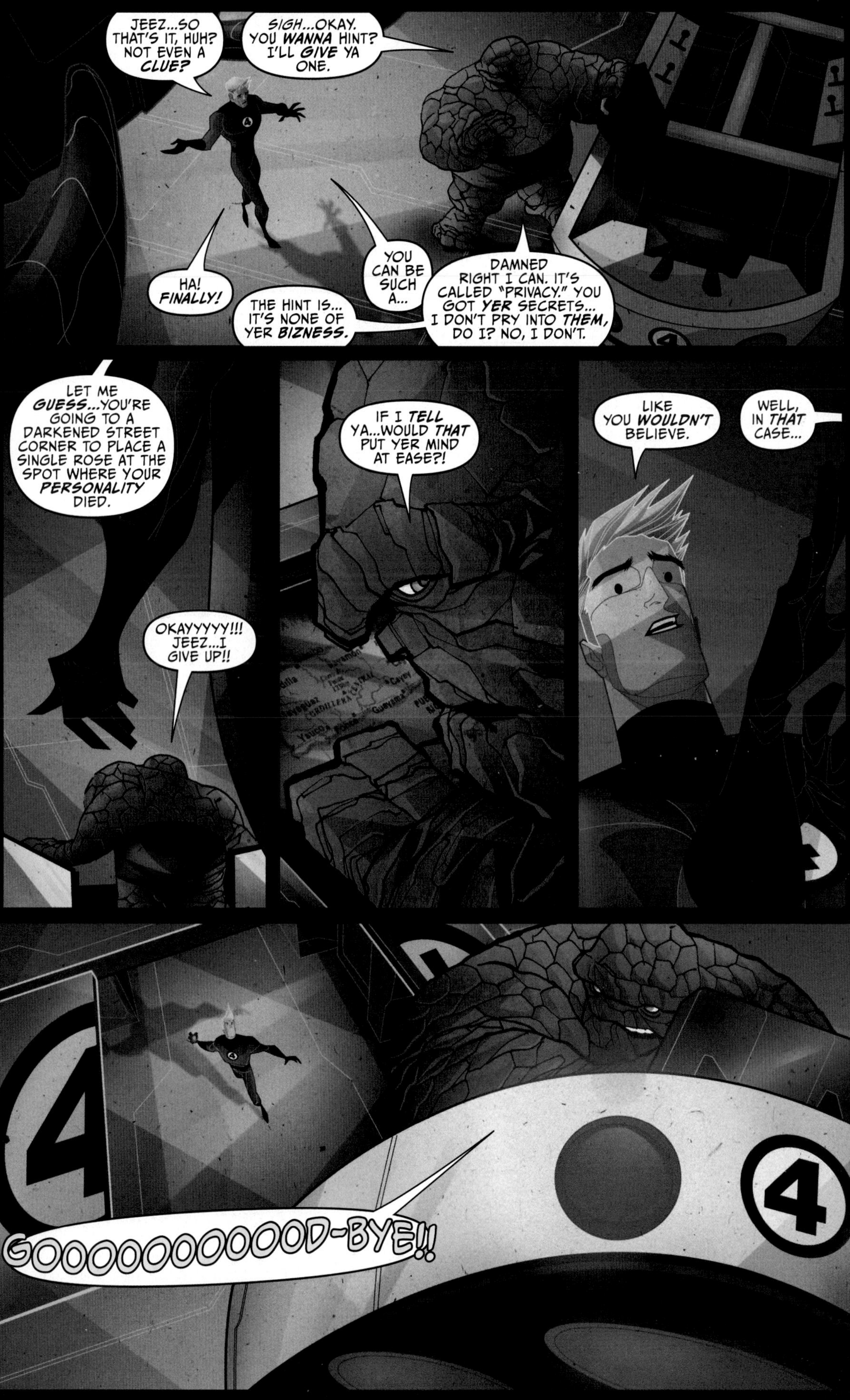
JEEZ...SO THAT'S IT, HUH? NOT EVEN A CLUE?
SIGH...OKAY. YOU WANNA HINT? I'LL GIVE YA ONE.
HA! FINALLY!
THE HINT IS... IT'S NONE OF YER BIZNESS.
YOU CAN BE SUCH A...
DAMNED RIGHT I CAN. IT'S CALLED "PRIVACY." YOU GOT YER SECRETS... I DON'T PRY INTO THEM, DO I? NO, I DON'T.
LET ME GUESS...YOU'RE GOING TO A DARKENED STREET CORNER TO PLACE A SINGLE ROSE AT THE SPOT WHERE YOUR PERSONALITY DIED.
OKAYYYYY!!! JEEZ...I GIVE UP!!
IF I TELL YA...WOULD THAT PUT YER MIND AT EASE?!
LIKE YOU WOULDN'T BELIEVE.
WELL, IN THAT CASE...
GOOOOOOOOOOD-BYE!!

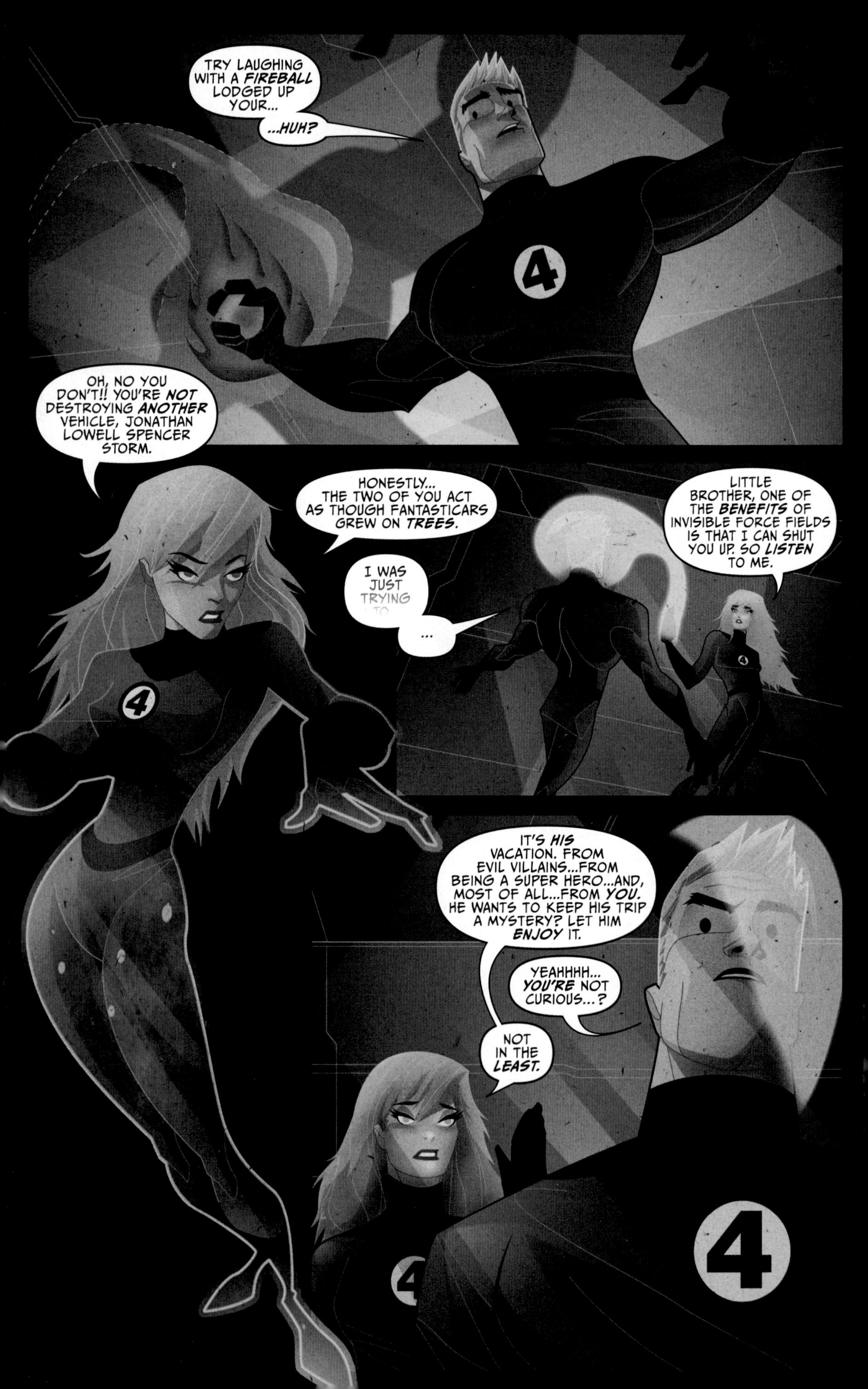
TRY LAUGHING WITH A FIREBALL LODGED UP YOUR...
...HUH?
OH, NO YOU DON'T!! YOU'RE NOT DESTROYING ANOTHER VEHICLE, JONATHAN LOWELL SPENCER STORM.
HONESTLY... THE TWO OF YOU ACT AS THOUGH FANTASTICARS GREW ON TREES.
I WAS JUST TRYING TO
...
LITTLE BROTHER, ONE OF THE BENEFITS OF INVISIBLE FORCE FIELDS IS THAT I CAN SHUT YOU UP. SO LISTEN TO ME.
IT'S HIS VACATION. FROM EVIL VILLAINS...FROM BEING A SUPER HERO...AND, MOST OF ALL...FROM YOU. HE WANTS TO KEEP HIS TRIP A MYSTERY? LET HIM ENJOY IT.
YEAHHHH... YOU'RE NOT CURIOUS...?
NOT IN THE LEAST.

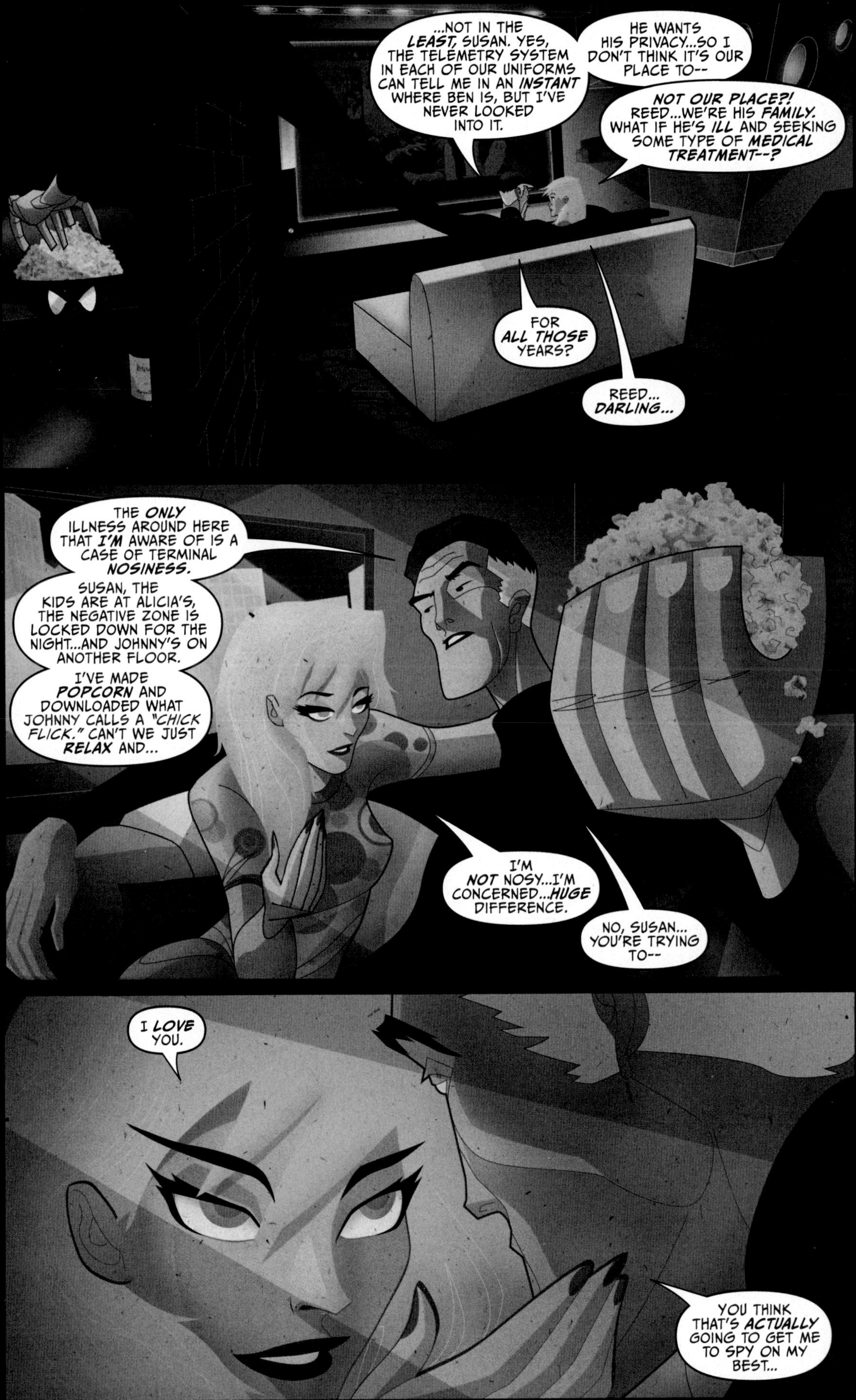
...NOT IN THE LEAST, SUSAN. YES, THE TELEMETRY SYSTEM IN EACH OF OUR UNIFORMS CAN TELL ME IN AN INSTANT WHERE BEN IS, BUT I'VE NEVER LOOKED INTO IT.
HE WANTS HIS PRIVACY...SO I DON'T THINK IT'S OUR PLACE TO--
NOT OUR PLACE?! REED...WE'RE HIS FAMILY. WHAT IF HE'S ILL AND SEEKING SOME TYPE OF MEDICAL TREATMENT--?
FOR ALL THOSE YEARS?
REED... DARLING...
THE ONLY ILLNESS AROUND HERE THAT I'M AWARE OF IS A CASE OF TERMINAL NOSINESS.
SUSAN, THE KIDS ARE AT ALICIA'S, THE NEGATIVE ZONE IS LOCKED DOWN FOR THE NIGHT...AND JOHNNY'S ON ANOTHER FLOOR.
I'VE MADE POPCORN AND DOWNLOADED WHAT JOHNNY CALLS A "CHICK FLICK." CAN'T WE JUST RELAX AND...
I'M NOT NOSY...I'M CONCERNED...HUGE DIFFERENCE.
NO, SUSAN... YOU'RE TRYING TO--
I LOVE YOU.
YOU THINK THAT'S ACTUALLY GOING TO GET ME TO SPY ON MY BEST...

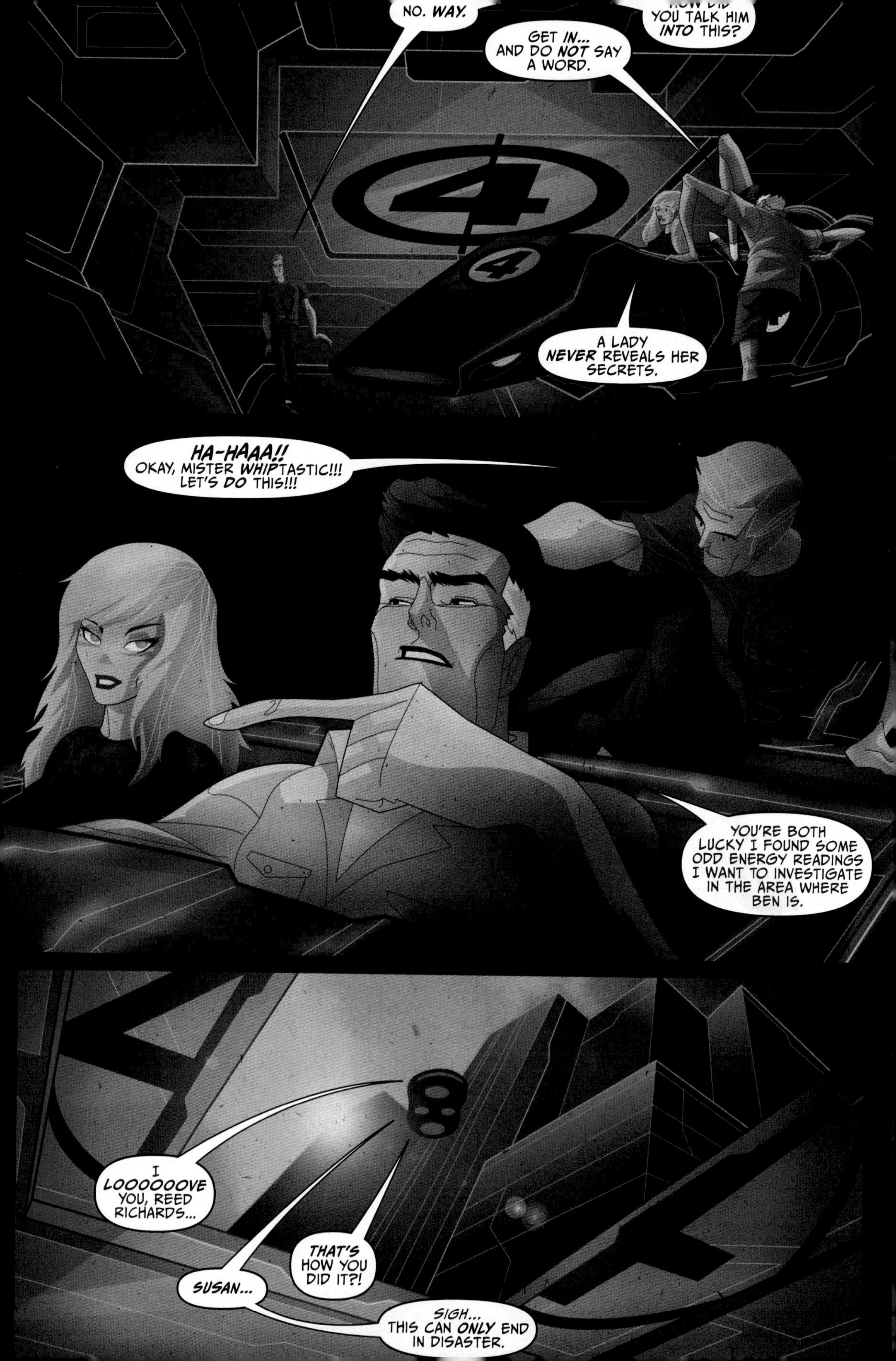
NO. WAY.
YOU TALK HIM INTO THIS?
GET IN... AND DO NOT SAY A WORD.
A LADY NEVER REVEALS HER SECRETS.
HA-HAAA!! OKAY, MISTER WHIPTASTIC!!! LET'S DO THIS!!!
YOU'RE BOTH LUCKY I FOUND SOME ODD ENERGY READINGS I WANT TO INVESTIGATE IN THE AREA WHERE BEN IS.
I LOOOOOOVE YOU, REED RICHARDS...
THAT'S HOW YOU DID IT?!
SUSAN...
SIGH... THIS CAN ONLY END IN DISASTER.

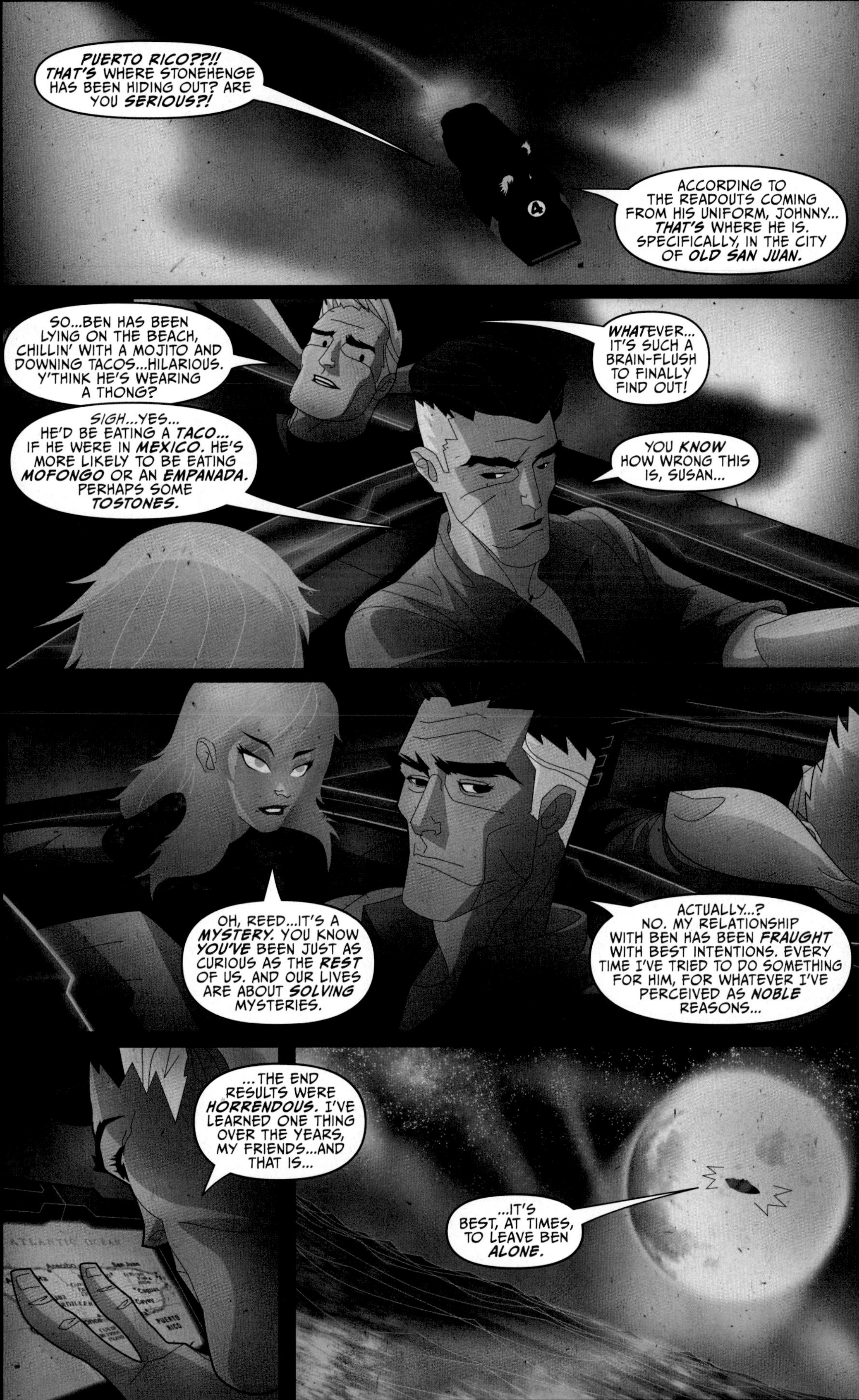
PUERTO RICO??!! THAT'S WHERE STONEHENGE HAS BEEN HIDING OUT? ARE YOU SERIOUS?!
ACCORDING TO THE READOUTS COMING FROM HIS UNIFORM, JOHNNY... THAT'S WHERE HE IS. SPECIFICALLY, IN THE CITY OF OLD SAN JUAN.
SO...BEN HAS BEEN LYING ON THE BEACH, CHILLIN' WITH A MOJITO AND DOWNING TACOS...HILARIOUS. Y'THINK HE'S WEARING A THONG?
WHATEVER... IT'S SUCH A BRAIN-FLUSH TO FINALLY FIND OUT!
SIGH...YES... HE'D BE EATING A TACO... IF HE WERE IN MEXICO. HE'S MORE LIKELY TO BE EATING MOFONGO OR AN EMPANADA. PERHAPS SOME TOSTONES.
YOU KNOW HOW WRONG THIS IS, SUSAN...
OH, REED...IT'S A MYSTERY. YOU KNOW YOU'VE BEEN JUST AS CURIOUS AS THE REST OF US. AND OUR LIVES ARE ABOUT SOLVING MYSTERIES.
ACTUALLY...? NO. MY RELATIONSHIP WITH BEN HAS BEEN FRAUGHT WITH BEST INTENTIONS. EVERY TIME I'VE TRIED TO DO SOMETHING FOR HIM, FOR WHATEVER I'VE PERCEIVED AS NOBLE REASONS...
...THE END RESULTS WERE HORRENDOUS. I'VE LEARNED ONE THING OVER THE YEARS, MY FRIENDS...AND THAT IS...
...IT'S BEST, AT TIMES, TO LEAVE BEN ALONE.

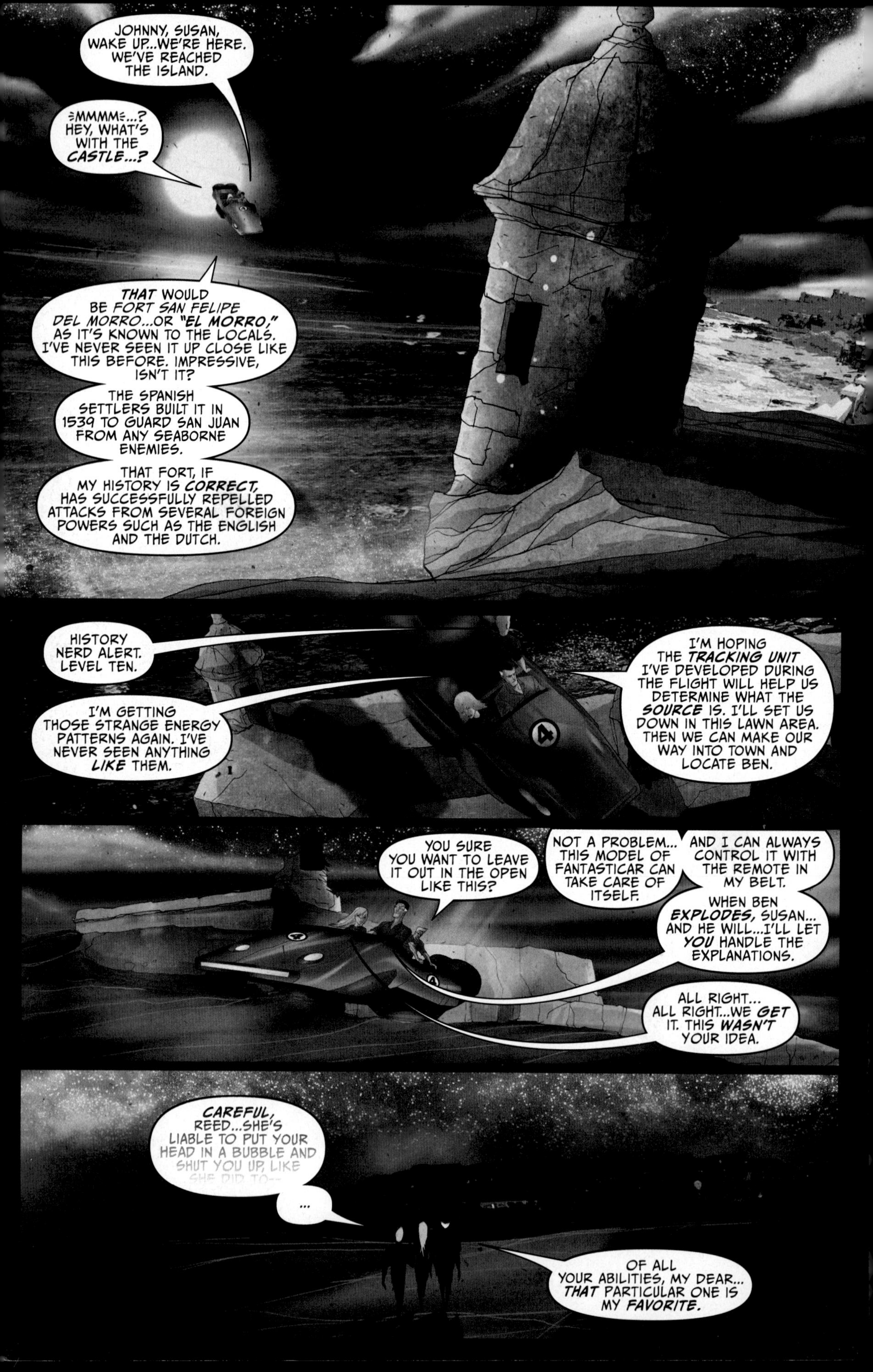
JOHNNY, SUSAN, WAKE UP...WE'RE HERE. WE'VE REACHED THE ISLAND.
MMMMM...? HEY, WHAT'S WITH THE *CASTLE...?*
THAT WOULD BE *FORT SAN FELIPE DEL MORRO*...OR *"EL MORRO,"* AS IT'S KNOWN TO THE LOCALS. I'VE NEVER SEEN IT UP CLOSE LIKE THIS BEFORE. IMPRESSIVE, ISN'T IT?
THE SPANISH SETTLERS BUILT IT IN 1539 TO GUARD SAN JUAN FROM ANY SEABORNE ENEMIES.
THAT FORT, IF MY HISTORY IS *CORRECT,* HAS SUCCESSFULLY REPELLED ATTACKS FROM SEVERAL FOREIGN POWERS SUCH AS THE ENGLISH AND THE DUTCH.
HISTORY NERD ALERT. LEVEL TEN.
I'M GETTING THOSE STRANGE ENERGY PATTERNS AGAIN. I'VE NEVER SEEN ANYTHING *LIKE* THEM.
I'M HOPING THE *TRACKING UNIT* I'VE DEVELOPED DURING THE FLIGHT WILL HELP US DETERMINE WHAT THE *SOURCE* IS. I'LL SET US DOWN IN THIS LAWN AREA. THEN WE CAN MAKE OUR WAY INTO TOWN AND LOCATE BEN.
YOU SURE YOU WANT TO LEAVE IT OUT IN THE OPEN LIKE THIS?
NOT A PROBLEM... THIS MODEL OF FANTASTICAR CAN TAKE CARE OF ITSELF.
AND I CAN ALWAYS CONTROL IT WITH THE REMOTE IN MY BELT.
WHEN BEN *EXPLODES,* SUSAN... AND HE WILL...I'LL LET *YOU* HANDLE THE EXPLANATIONS.
ALL RIGHT... ALL RIGHT...WE *GET* IT. THIS *WASN'T* YOUR IDEA.
CAREFUL, REED...SHE'S LIABLE TO PUT YOUR HEAD IN A BUBBLE AND SHUT YOU UP, LIKE SHE DID TO--
...
OF ALL YOUR ABILITIES, MY DEAR... *THAT* PARTICULAR ONE IS MY *FAVORITE.*

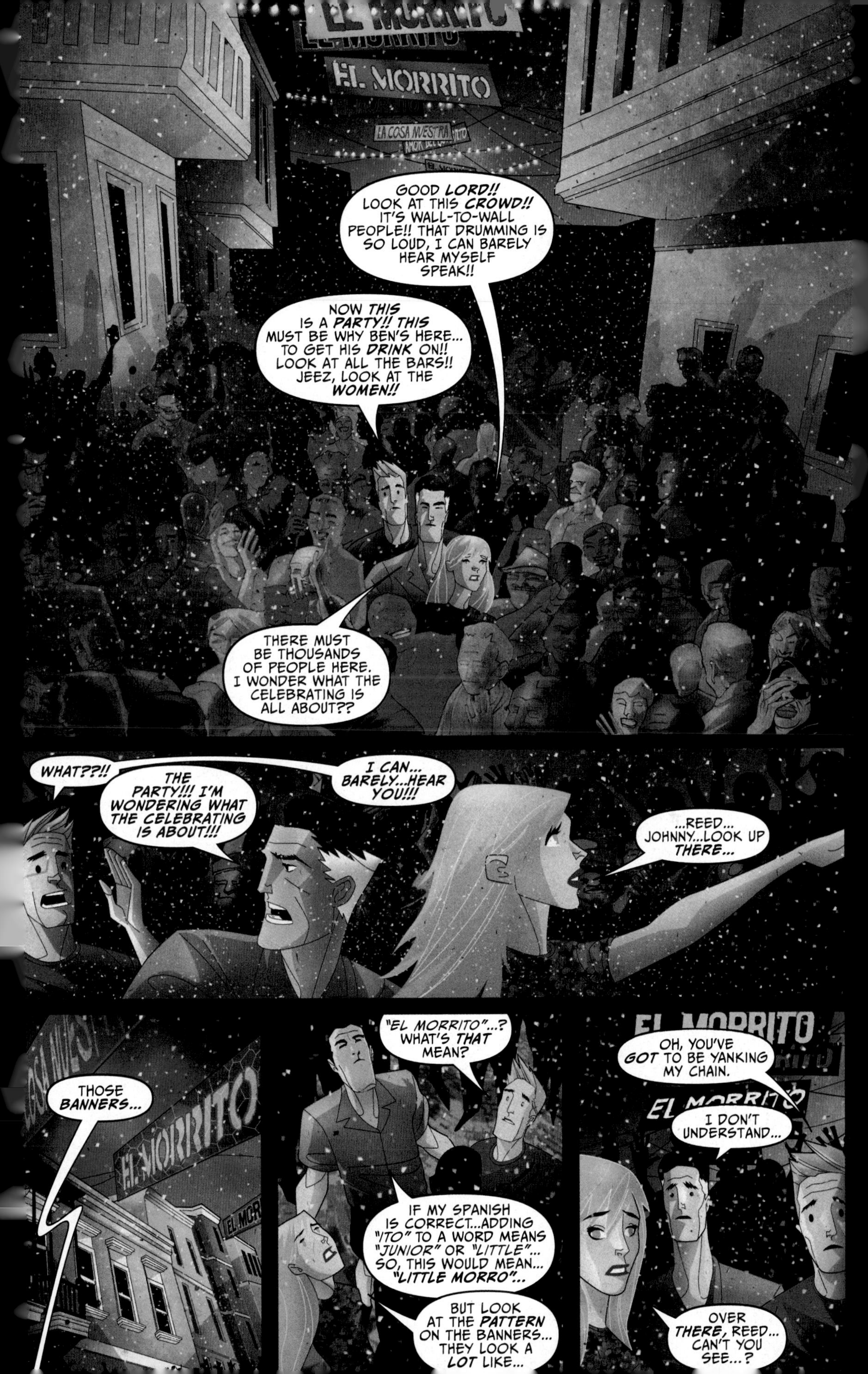
EL MORRITO
EL MORRITO
LA COSA NUESTRA
GOOD LORD!! LOOK AT THIS CROWD!! IT'S WALL-TO-WALL PEOPLE!! THAT DRUMMING IS SO LOUD, I CAN BARELY HEAR MYSELF SPEAK!!
NOW THIS IS A PARTY!! THIS MUST BE WHY BEN'S HERE... TO GET HIS DRINK ON!! LOOK AT ALL THE BARS!! JEEZ, LOOK AT THE WOMEN!!
THERE MUST BE THOUSANDS OF PEOPLE HERE. I WONDER WHAT THE CELEBRATING IS ALL ABOUT??
WHAT??!!
THE PARTY!!! I'M WONDERING WHAT THE CELEBRATING IS ABOUT!!!
I CAN... BARELY...HEAR YOU!!!
...REED... JOHNNY...LOOK UP THERE...
THOSE BANNERS...
EL MORRITO
EL MOR
"EL MORRITO"...? WHAT'S THAT MEAN?
IF MY SPANISH IS CORRECT...ADDING "ITO" TO A WORD MEANS "JUNIOR" OR "LITTLE"... SO, THIS WOULD MEAN... "LITTLE MORRO"...
BUT LOOK AT THE PATTERN ON THE BANNERS... THEY LOOK A LOT LIKE...
EL MORRITO
OH, YOU'VE GOT TO BE YANKING MY CHAIN.
EL MORRITO
I DON'T UNDERSTAND...
OVER THERE, REED... CAN'T YOU SEE...?

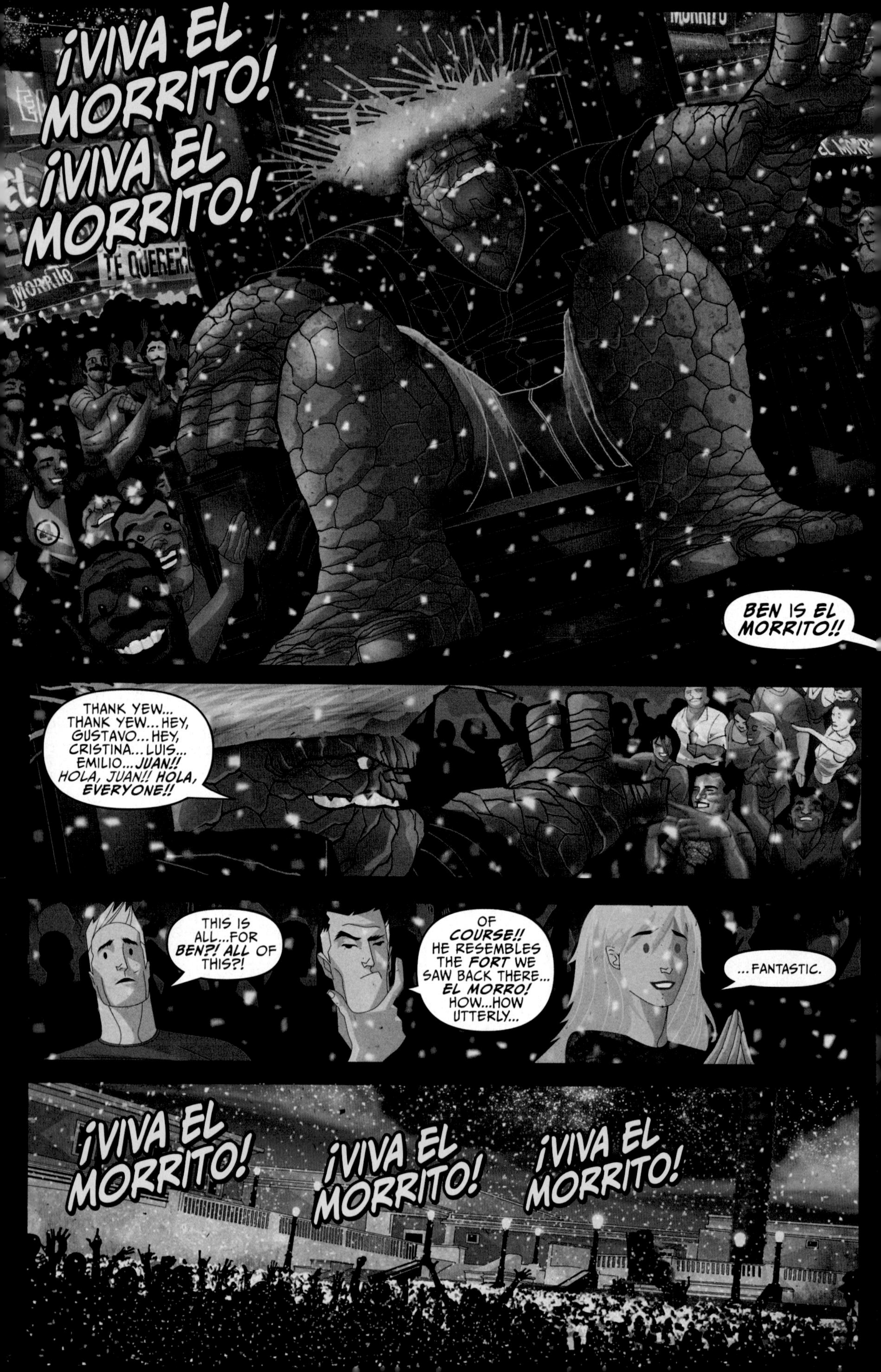
¡VIVA EL MORRITO! ¡VIVA EL MORRITO!
BEN IS EL MORRITO!!
THANK YEW... THANK YEW... HEY, GUSTAVO... HEY, CRISTINA... LUIS... EMILIO... JUAN!! HOLA, JUAN!! HOLA, EVERYONE!!
THIS IS ALL...FOR BEN?! ALL OF THIS?!
OF COURSE!! HE RESEMBLES THE FORT WE SAW BACK THERE... EL MORRO! HOW...HOW UTTERLY...
...FANTASTIC.
¡VIVA EL MORRITO!
¡VIVA EL MORRITO!
¡VIVA EL MORRITO!

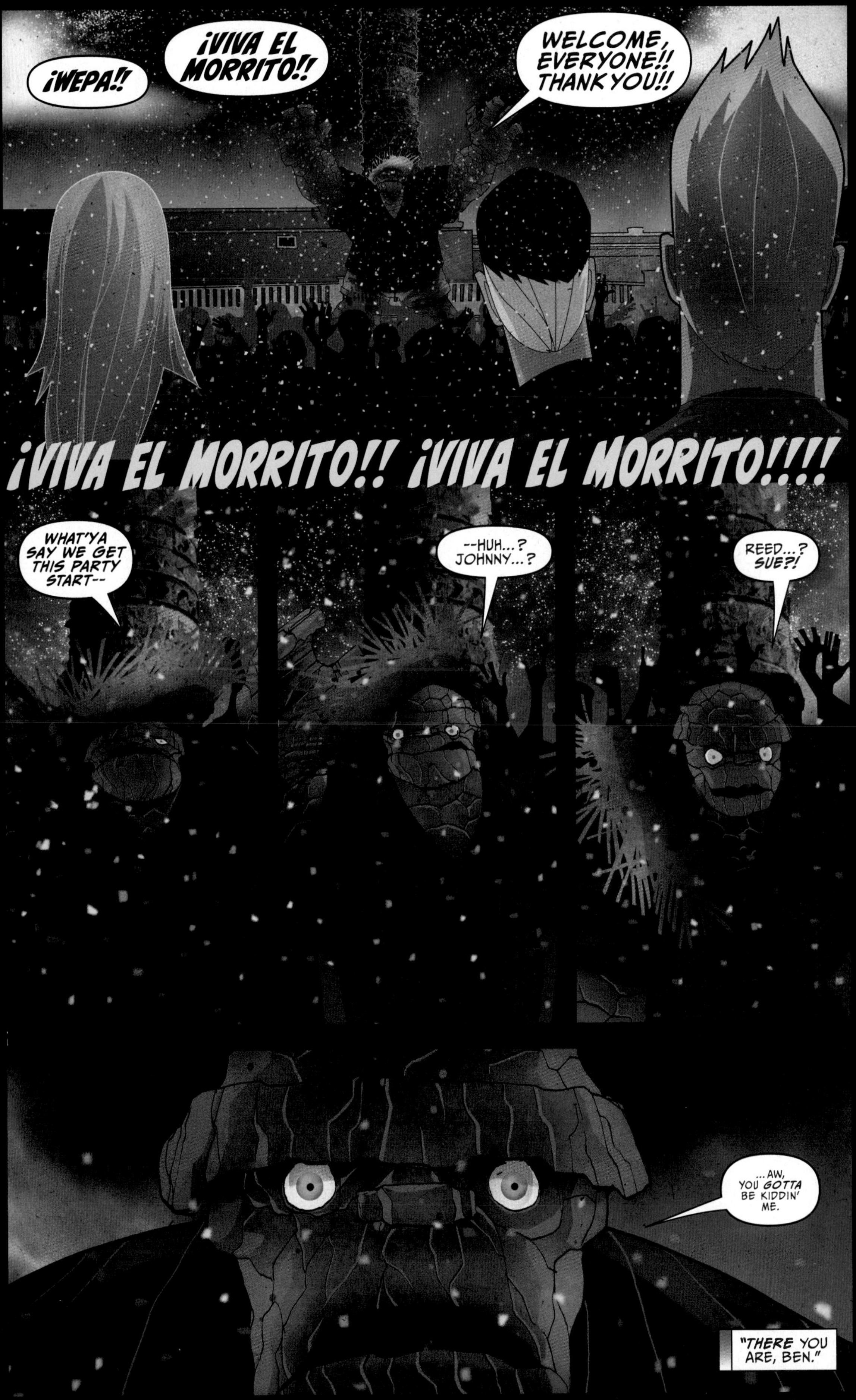

¡WEPA!!
¡VIVA EL MORRITO!!
WELCOME, EVERYONE!! THANK YOU!!
¡VIVA EL MORRITO!! ¡VIVA EL MORRITO!!!!
WHAT'YA SAY WE GET THIS PARTY START--
--HUH...? JOHNNY...?
REED...? SUE?!
...AW, YOU GOTTA BE KIDDIN' ME.
"THERE YOU ARE, BEN."

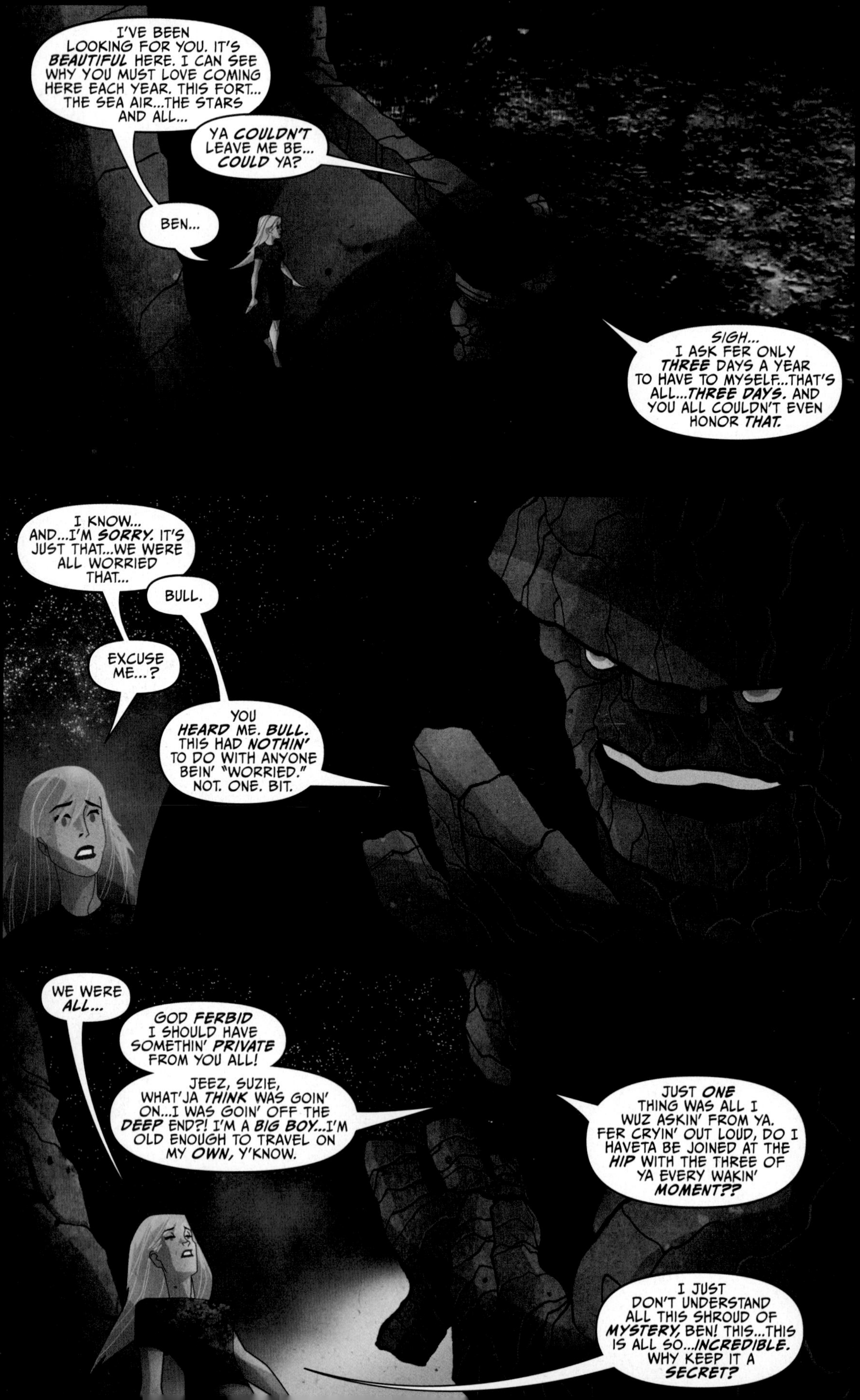
I'VE BEEN LOOKING FOR YOU. IT'S BEAUTIFUL HERE. I CAN SEE WHY YOU MUST LOVE COMING HERE EACH YEAR. THIS FORT... THE SEA AIR...THE STARS AND ALL...
YA COULDN'T LEAVE ME BE... COULD YA?
BEN...
SIGH... I ASK FER ONLY THREE DAYS A YEAR TO HAVE TO MYSELF...THAT'S ALL...THREE DAYS. AND YOU ALL COULDN'T EVEN HONOR THAT.
I KNOW... AND...I'M SORRY. IT'S JUST THAT...WE WERE ALL WORRIED THAT...
BULL.
EXCUSE ME...?
YOU HEARD ME. BULL. THIS HAD NOTHIN' TO DO WITH ANYONE BEIN' "WORRIED." NOT. ONE. BIT.
WE WERE ALL...
GOD FERBID I SHOULD HAVE SOMETHIN' PRIVATE FROM YOU ALL!
JEEZ, SUZIE, WHAT'JA THINK WAS GOIN' ON...I WAS GOIN' OFF THE DEEP END?! I'M A BIG BOY...I'M OLD ENOUGH TO TRAVEL ON MY OWN, Y'KNOW.
JUST ONE THING WAS ALL I WUZ ASKIN' FROM YA. FER CRYIN' OUT LOUD, DO I HAVETA BE JOINED AT THE HIP WITH THE THREE OF YA EVERY WAKIN' MOMENT??
I JUST DON'T UNDERSTAND ALL THIS SHROUD OF MYSTERY, BEN! THIS...THIS IS ALL SO...INCREDIBLE. WHY KEEP IT A SECRET?

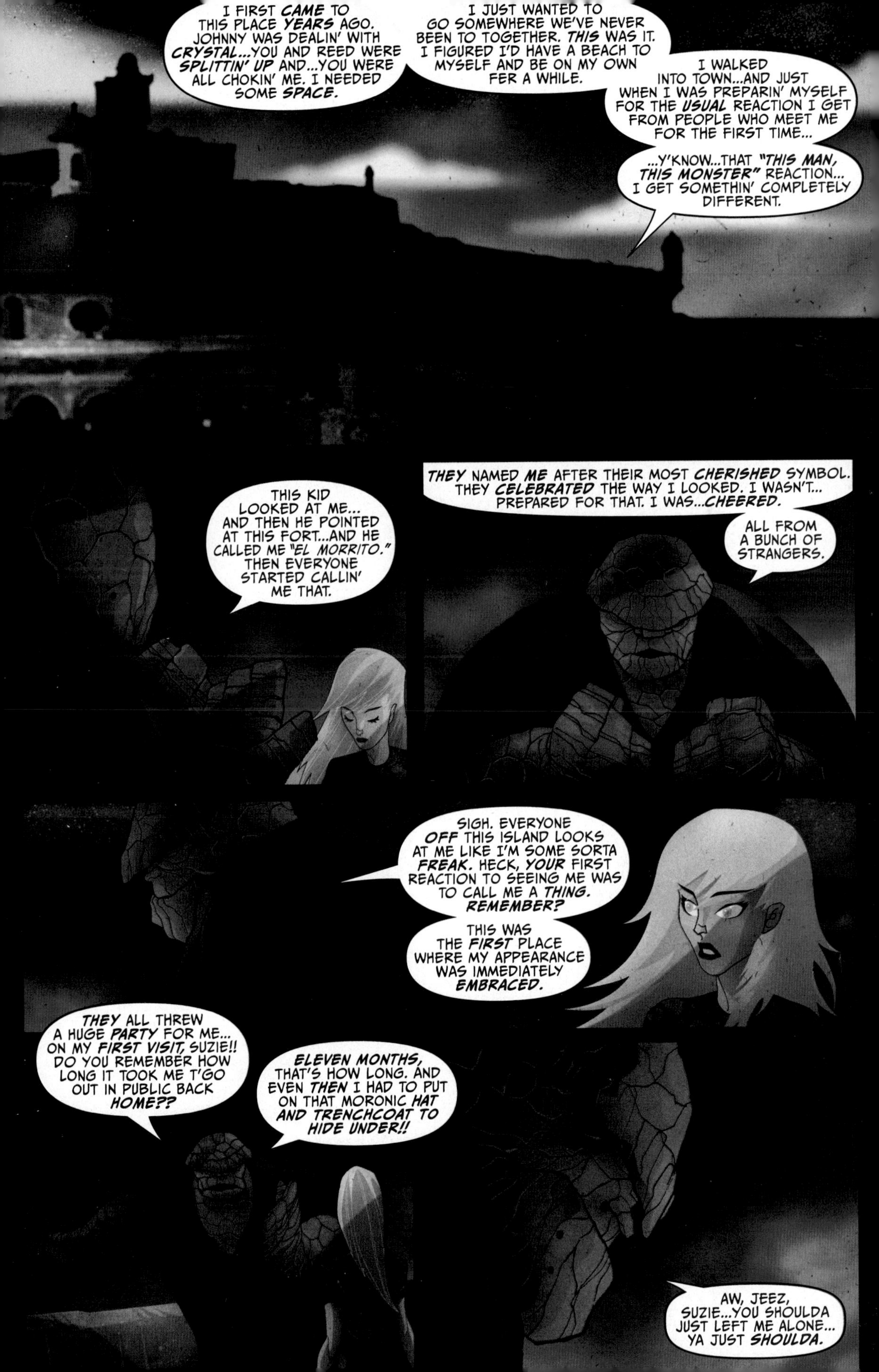
I FIRST CAME TO THIS PLACE YEARS AGO. JOHNNY WAS DEALIN' WITH CRYSTAL...YOU AND REED WERE SPLITTIN' UP AND...YOU WERE ALL CHOKIN' ME. I NEEDED SOME SPACE.
I JUST WANTED TO GO SOMEWHERE WE'VE NEVER BEEN TO TOGETHER. THIS WAS IT. I FIGURED I'D HAVE A BEACH TO MYSELF AND BE ON MY OWN FER A WHILE.
I WALKED INTO TOWN...AND JUST WHEN I WAS PREPARIN' MYSELF FOR THE USUAL REACTION I GET FROM PEOPLE WHO MEET ME FOR THE FIRST TIME...
...Y'KNOW...THAT "THIS MAN, THIS MONSTER" REACTION... I GET SOMETHIN' COMPLETELY DIFFERENT.
THIS KID LOOKED AT ME... AND THEN HE POINTED AT THIS FORT...AND HE CALLED ME "EL MORRITO." THEN EVERYONE STARTED CALLIN' ME THAT.
THEY NAMED ME AFTER THEIR MOST CHERISHED SYMBOL. THEY CELEBRATED THE WAY I LOOKED. I WASN'T... PREPARED FOR THAT. I WAS...CHEERED.
ALL FROM A BUNCH OF STRANGERS.
SIGH. EVERYONE OFF THIS ISLAND LOOKS AT ME LIKE I'M SOME SORTA FREAK. HECK, YOUR FIRST REACTION TO SEEING ME WAS TO CALL ME A THING. REMEMBER?
THIS WAS THE FIRST PLACE WHERE MY APPEARANCE WAS IMMEDIATELY EMBRACED.
THEY ALL THREW A HUGE PARTY FOR ME... ON MY FIRST VISIT, SUZIE!! DO YOU REMEMBER HOW LONG IT TOOK ME T'GO OUT IN PUBLIC BACK HOME??
ELEVEN MONTHS, THAT'S HOW LONG. AND EVEN THEN I HAD TO PUT ON THAT MORONIC HAT AND TRENCHCOAT TO HIDE UNDER!!
AW, JEEZ, SUZIE...YOU SHOULDA JUST LEFT ME ALONE... YA JUST SHOULDA.

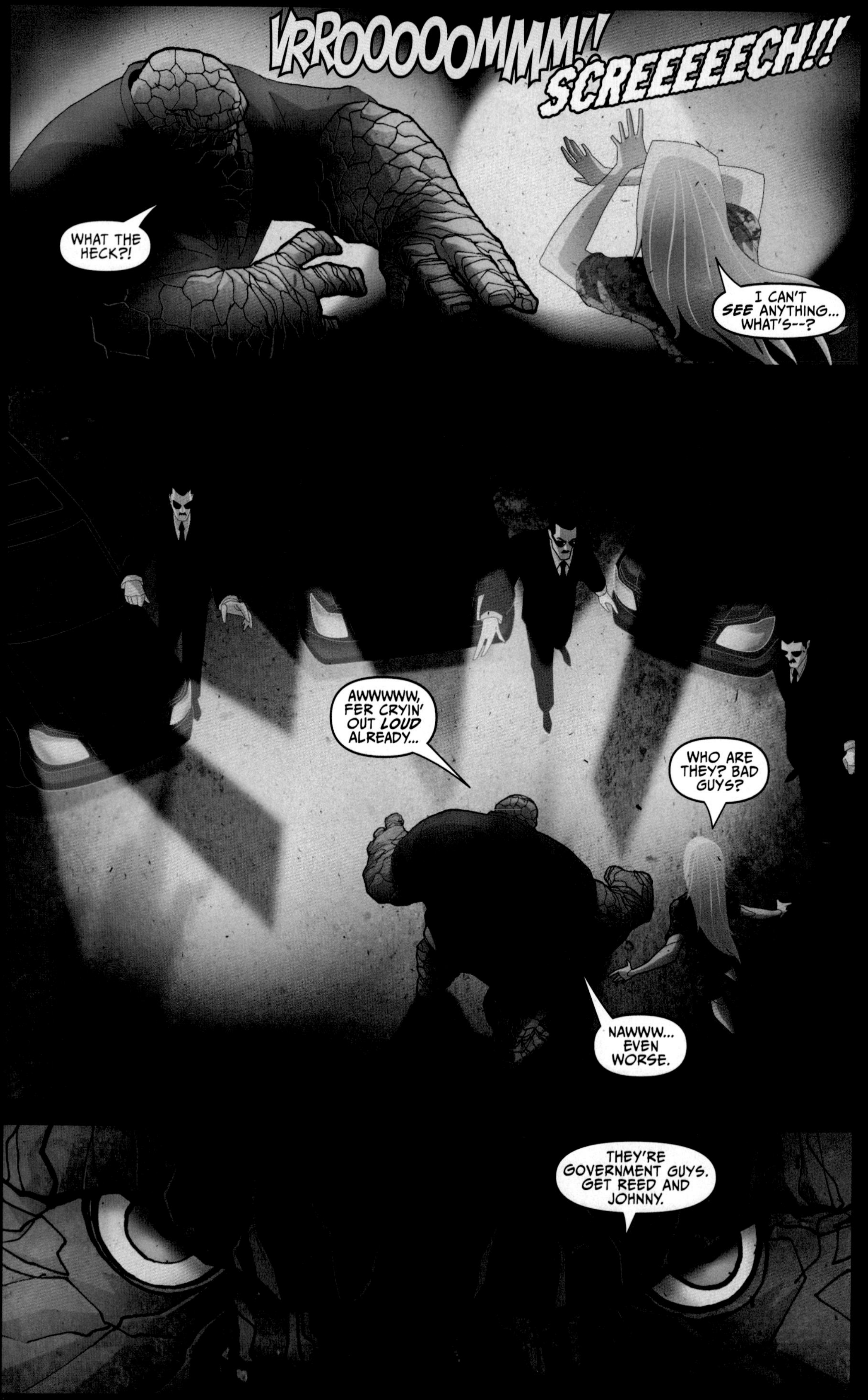
VRROOOOOMMM!!
SCREEEEEECH!!
WHAT THE HECK?!
I CAN'T SEE ANYTHING... WHAT'S--?
AWWWWW, FER CRYIN' OUT LOUD ALREADY...
WHO ARE THEY? BAD GUYS?
NAWWW... EVEN WORSE.
THEY'RE GOVERNMENT GUYS. GET REED AND JOHNNY.

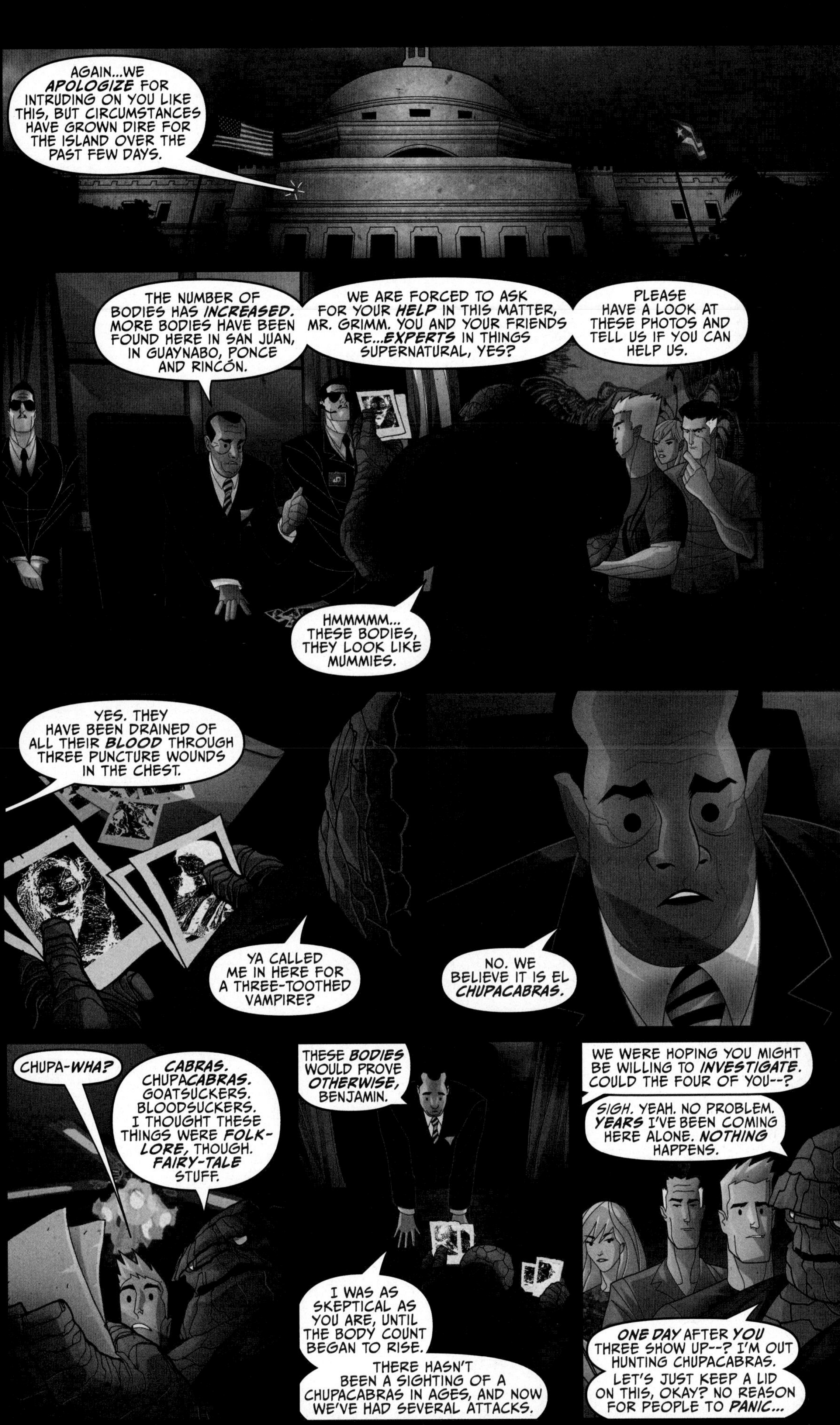
AGAIN...WE APOLOGIZE FOR INTRUDING ON YOU LIKE THIS, BUT CIRCUMSTANCES HAVE GROWN DIRE FOR THE ISLAND OVER THE PAST FEW DAYS.
THE NUMBER OF BODIES HAS INCREASED. MORE BODIES HAVE BEEN FOUND HERE IN SAN JUAN, IN GUAYNABO, PONCE AND RINCÓN.
WE ARE FORCED TO ASK FOR YOUR HELP IN THIS MATTER, MR. GRIMM. YOU AND YOUR FRIENDS ARE...EXPERTS IN THINGS SUPERNATURAL, YES?
PLEASE HAVE A LOOK AT THESE PHOTOS AND TELL US IF YOU CAN HELP US.
HMMMMM... THESE BODIES, THEY LOOK LIKE MUMMIES.
YES. THEY HAVE BEEN DRAINED OF ALL THEIR BLOOD THROUGH THREE PUNCTURE WOUNDS IN THE CHEST.
YA CALLED ME IN HERE FOR A THREE-TOOTHED VAMPIRE?
NO. WE BELIEVE IT IS EL CHUPACABRAS.
CHUPA-WHA?
CABRAS. CHUPACABRAS. GOATSUCKERS. BLOODSUCKERS. I THOUGHT THESE THINGS WERE FOLK-LORE, THOUGH. FAIRY-TALE STUFF.
THESE BODIES WOULD PROVE OTHERWISE, BENJAMIN.
I WAS AS SKEPTICAL AS YOU ARE, UNTIL THE BODY COUNT BEGAN TO RISE.
THERE HASN'T BEEN A SIGHTING OF A CHUPACABRAS IN AGES, AND NOW WE'VE HAD SEVERAL ATTACKS.
WE WERE HOPING YOU MIGHT BE WILLING TO INVESTIGATE. COULD THE FOUR OF YOU--?
SIGH. YEAH. NO PROBLEM. YEARS I'VE BEEN COMING HERE ALONE. NOTHING HAPPENS.
ONE DAY AFTER YOU THREE SHOW UP--? I'M OUT HUNTING CHUPACABRAS.
LET'S JUST KEEP A LID ON THIS, OKAY? NO REASON FOR PEOPLE TO PANIC...

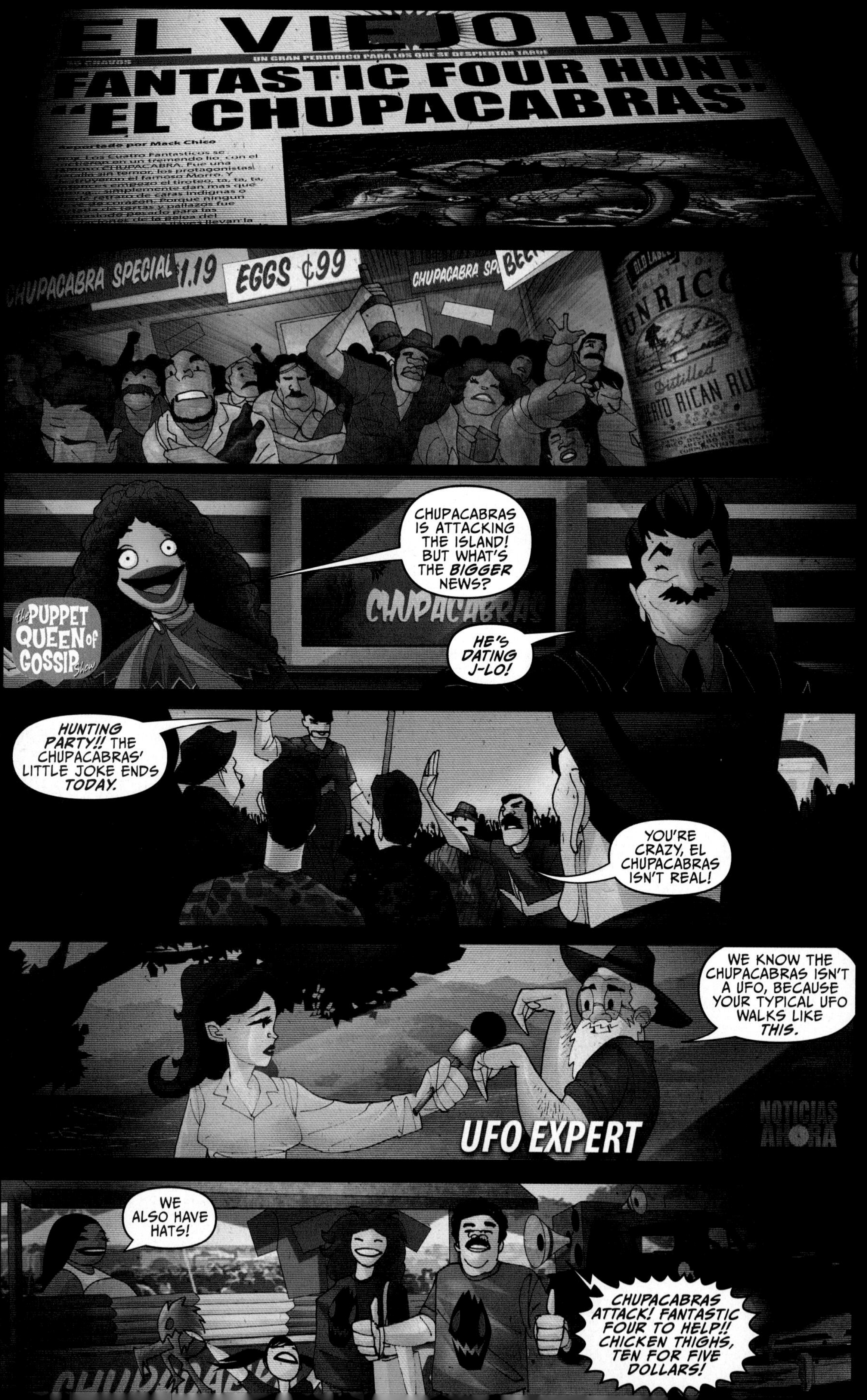

EL VIEJO DIA
UN GRAN PERIODICO PARA LOS QUE SE DESPIERTAN TARDE
FANTASTIC FOUR HUN
"EL CHUPACABRAS"
Reportado por Mack Chico
CHUPACABRA SPECIAL
1.19
EGGS ¢99
CHUPACABRA SP
Distilled
RICAN RU
CHUPACABRAS IS ATTACKING THE ISLAND! BUT WHAT'S THE BIGGER NEWS?
CHUPACABRAS
the PUPPET QUEEN of GOSSIP Show
HE'S DATING J-LO!
HUNTING PARTY!! THE CHUPACABRAS' LITTLE JOKE ENDS TODAY.
YOU'RE CRAZY, EL CHUPACABRAS ISN'T REAL!
WE KNOW THE CHUPACABRAS ISN'T A UFO, BECAUSE YOUR TYPICAL UFO WALKS LIKE THIS.
UFO EXPERT
NOTICIAS AHORA
WE ALSO HAVE HATS!
CHUPACABRAS ATTACK! FANTASTIC FOUR TO HELP!! CHICKEN THIGHS, TEN FOR FIVE DOLLARS!

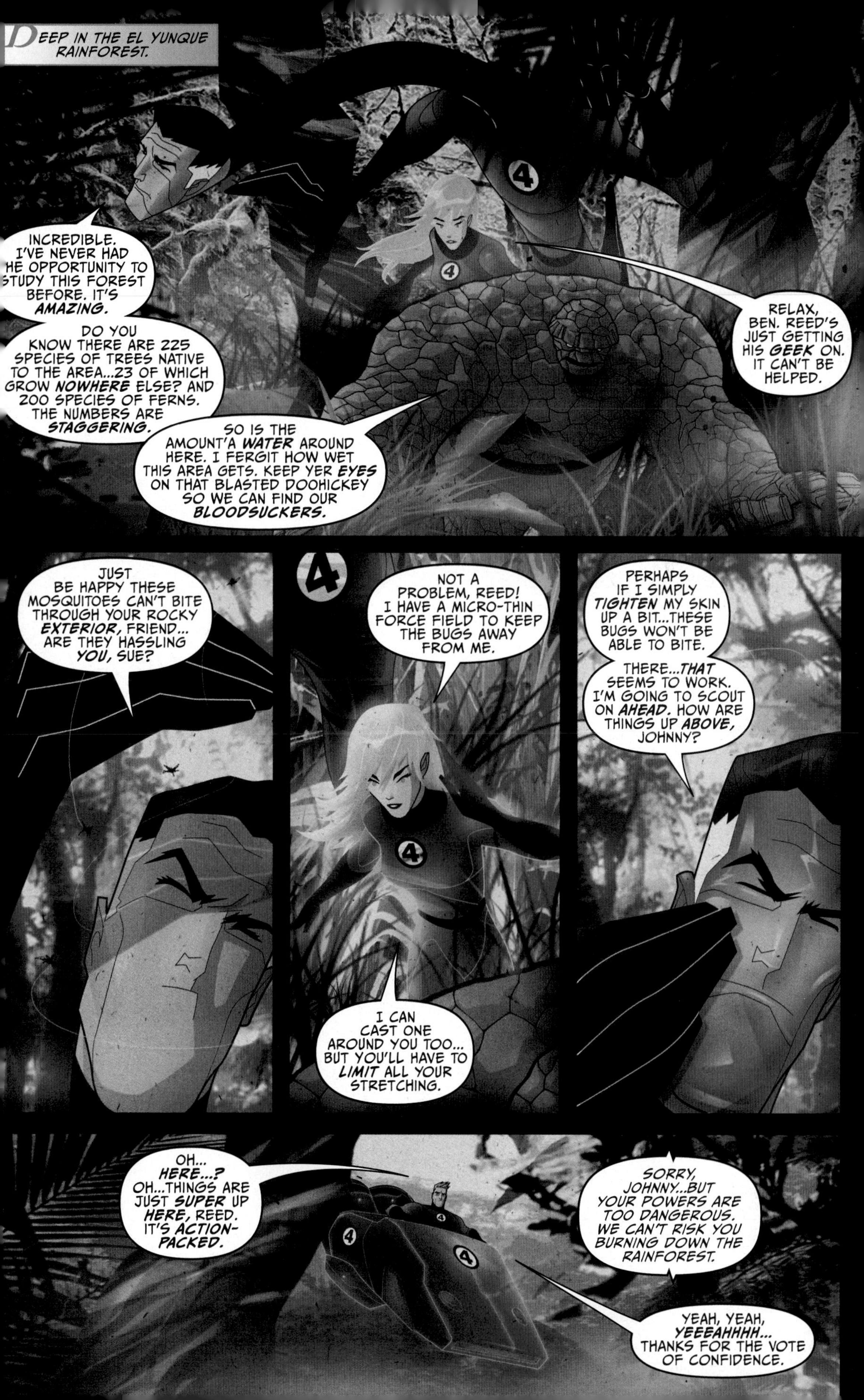
DEEP IN THE EL YUNQUE RAINFOREST.
INCREDIBLE. I'VE NEVER HAD HE OPPORTUNITY TO STUDY THIS FOREST BEFORE. IT'S AMAZING.
DO YOU KNOW THERE ARE 225 SPECIES OF TREES NATIVE TO THE AREA...23 OF WHICH GROW NOWHERE ELSE? AND 200 SPECIES OF FERNS. THE NUMBERS ARE STAGGERING.
SO IS THE AMOUNT'A WATER AROUND HERE. I FERGIT HOW WET THIS AREA GETS. KEEP YER EYES ON THAT BLASTED DOOHICKEY SO WE CAN FIND OUR BLOODSUCKERS.
RELAX, BEN. REED'S JUST GETTING HIS GEEK ON. IT CAN'T BE HELPED.
JUST BE HAPPY THESE MOSQUITOES CAN'T BITE THROUGH YOUR ROCKY EXTERIOR, FRIEND... ARE THEY HASSLING YOU, SUE?
NOT A PROBLEM, REED! I HAVE A MICRO-THIN FORCE FIELD TO KEEP THE BUGS AWAY FROM ME.
I CAN CAST ONE AROUND YOU TOO... BUT YOU'LL HAVE TO LIMIT ALL YOUR STRETCHING.
PERHAPS IF I SIMPLY TIGHTEN MY SKIN UP A BIT...THESE BUGS WON'T BE ABLE TO BITE.
THERE...THAT SEEMS TO WORK. I'M GOING TO SCOUT ON AHEAD. HOW ARE THINGS UP ABOVE, JOHNNY?
OH... HERE...? OH...THINGS ARE JUST SUPER UP HERE, REED. IT'S ACTION-PACKED.
SORRY, JOHNNY...BUT YOUR POWERS ARE TOO DANGEROUS. WE CAN'T RISK YOU BURNING DOWN THE RAINFOREST.
YEAH, YEAH, YEEEAHHHH... THANKS FOR THE VOTE OF CONFIDENCE.

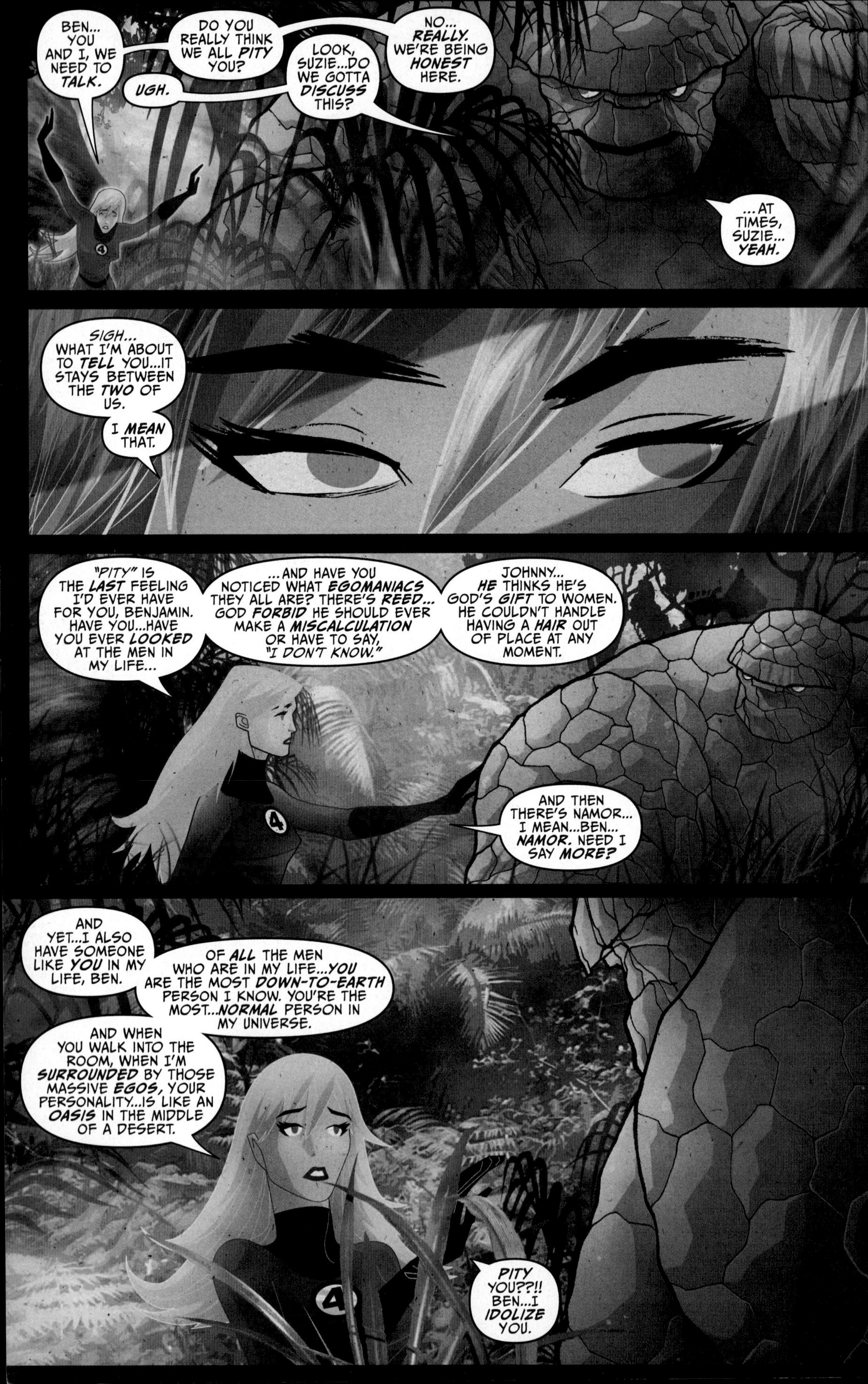
BEN... YOU AND I, WE NEED TO TALK.
DO YOU REALLY THINK WE ALL PITY YOU?
UGH.
LOOK, SUZIE...DO WE GOTTA DISCUSS THIS?
NO... REALLY. WE'RE BEING HONEST HERE.
...AT TIMES, SUZIE... YEAH.
SIGH... WHAT I'M ABOUT TO TELL YOU...IT STAYS BETWEEN THE TWO OF US.
I MEAN THAT.
"PITY" IS THE LAST FEELING I'D EVER HAVE FOR YOU, BENJAMIN. HAVE YOU...HAVE YOU EVER LOOKED AT THE MEN IN MY LIFE...
...AND HAVE YOU NOTICED WHAT EGOMANIACS THEY ALL ARE? THERE'S REED... GOD FORBID HE SHOULD EVER MAKE A MISCALCULATION OR HAVE TO SAY, "I DON'T KNOW."
JOHNNY... HE THINKS HE'S GOD'S GIFT TO WOMEN. HE COULDN'T HANDLE HAVING A HAIR OUT OF PLACE AT ANY MOMENT.
AND THEN THERE'S NAMOR... I MEAN...BEN... NAMOR. NEED I SAY MORE?
AND YET...I ALSO HAVE SOMEONE LIKE YOU IN MY LIFE, BEN.
OF ALL THE MEN WHO ARE IN MY LIFE...YOU ARE THE MOST DOWN-TO-EARTH PERSON I KNOW. YOU'RE THE MOST...NORMAL PERSON IN MY UNIVERSE.
AND WHEN YOU WALK INTO THE ROOM, WHEN I'M SURROUNDED BY THOSE MASSIVE EGOS, YOUR PERSONALITY...IS LIKE AN OASIS IN THE MIDDLE OF A DESERT.
PITY YOU??!! BEN...I IDOLIZE YOU.

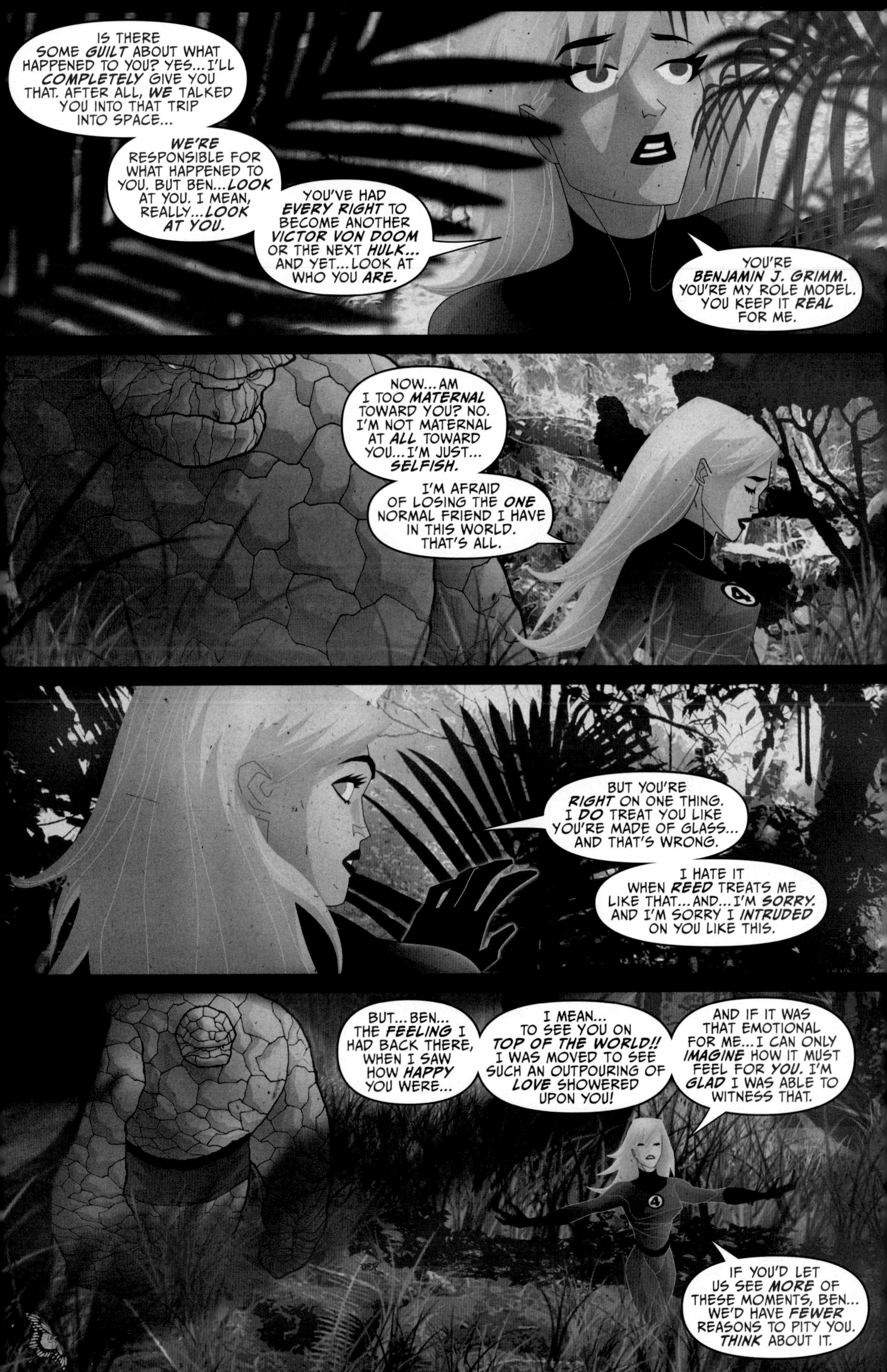
IS THERE SOME GUILT ABOUT WHAT HAPPENED TO YOU? YES...I'LL COMPLETELY GIVE YOU THAT. AFTER ALL, WE TALKED YOU INTO THAT TRIP INTO SPACE...
WE'RE RESPONSIBLE FOR WHAT HAPPENED TO YOU. BUT BEN...LOOK AT YOU. I MEAN, REALLY...LOOK AT YOU.
YOU'VE HAD EVERY RIGHT TO BECOME ANOTHER VICTOR VON DOOM OR THE NEXT HULK... AND YET...LOOK AT WHO YOU ARE.
YOU'RE BENJAMIN J. GRIMM. YOU'RE MY ROLE MODEL. YOU KEEP IT REAL FOR ME.
NOW...AM I TOO MATERNAL TOWARD YOU? NO. I'M NOT MATERNAL AT ALL TOWARD YOU...I'M JUST... SELFISH.
I'M AFRAID OF LOSING THE ONE NORMAL FRIEND I HAVE IN THIS WORLD. THAT'S ALL.
BUT YOU'RE RIGHT ON ONE THING. I DO TREAT YOU LIKE YOU'RE MADE OF GLASS... AND THAT'S WRONG.
I HATE IT WHEN REED TREATS ME LIKE THAT...AND...I'M SORRY. AND I'M SORRY I INTRUDED ON YOU LIKE THIS.
BUT...BEN... THE FEELING I HAD BACK THERE, WHEN I SAW HOW HAPPY YOU WERE...
I MEAN... TO SEE YOU ON TOP OF THE WORLD!! I WAS MOVED TO SEE SUCH AN OUTPOURING OF LOVE SHOWERED UPON YOU!
AND IF IT WAS THAT EMOTIONAL FOR ME...I CAN ONLY IMAGINE HOW IT MUST FEEL FOR YOU. I'M GLAD I WAS ABLE TO WITNESS THAT.
IF YOU'D LET US SEE MORE OF THESE MOMENTS, BEN... WE'D HAVE FEWER REASONS TO PITY YOU. THINK ABOUT IT.

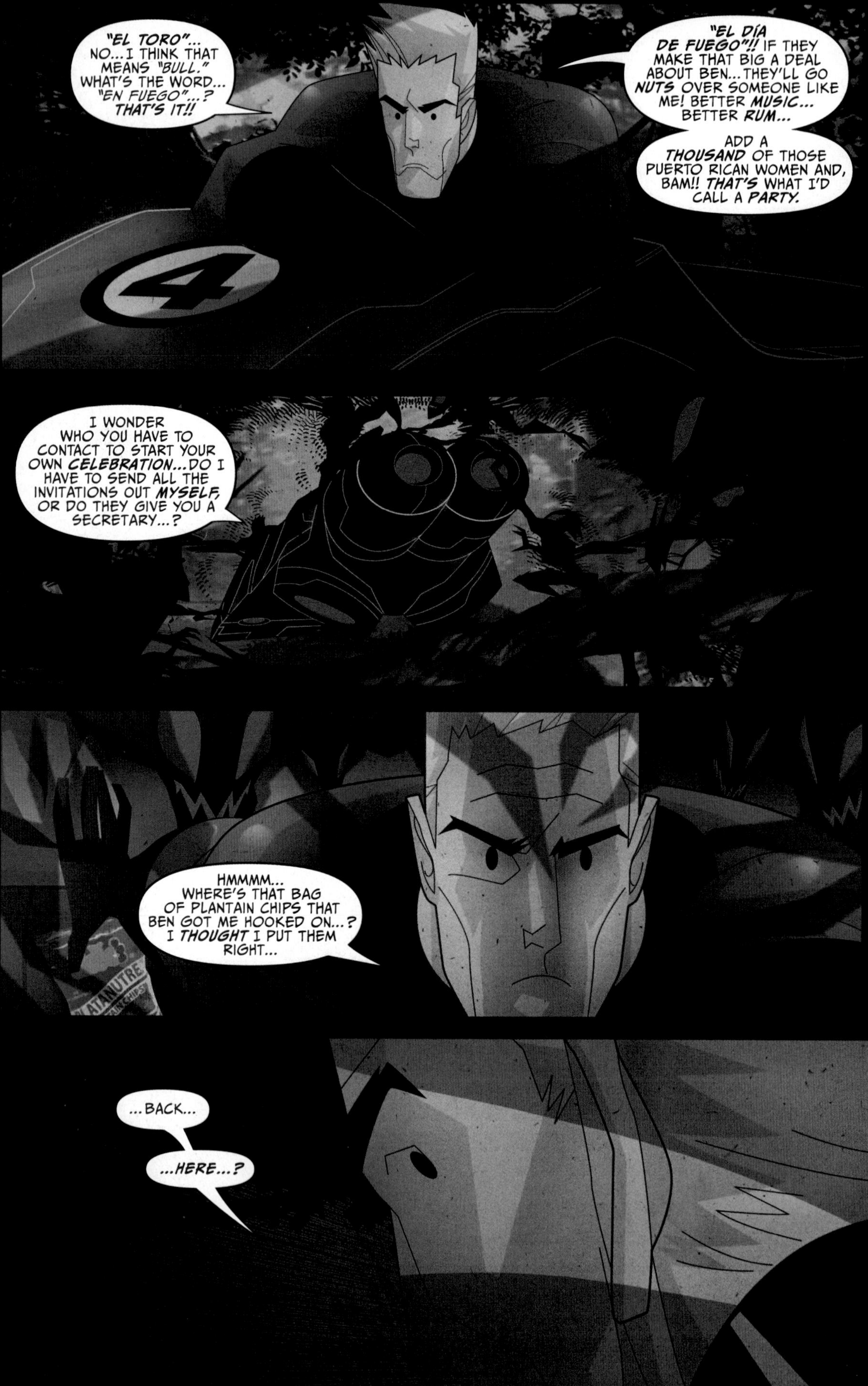
"EL TORO"... NO... I THINK THAT MEANS "BULL." WHAT'S THE WORD... "EN FUEGO"...? THAT'S IT!!
"EL DÍA DE FUEGO"!! IF THEY MAKE THAT BIG A DEAL ABOUT BEN... THEY'LL GO NUTS OVER SOMEONE LIKE ME! BETTER MUSIC... BETTER RUM...
ADD A THOUSAND OF THOSE PUERTO RICAN WOMEN AND, BAM!! THAT'S WHAT I'D CALL A PARTY.
I WONDER WHO YOU HAVE TO CONTACT TO START YOUR OWN CELEBRATION... DO I HAVE TO SEND ALL THE INVITATIONS OUT MYSELF, OR DO THEY GIVE YOU A SECRETARY...?
HMMMM... WHERE'S THAT BAG OF PLANTAIN CHIPS THAT BEN GOT ME HOOKED ON...? I THOUGHT I PUT THEM RIGHT...
...BACK...
...HERE...?

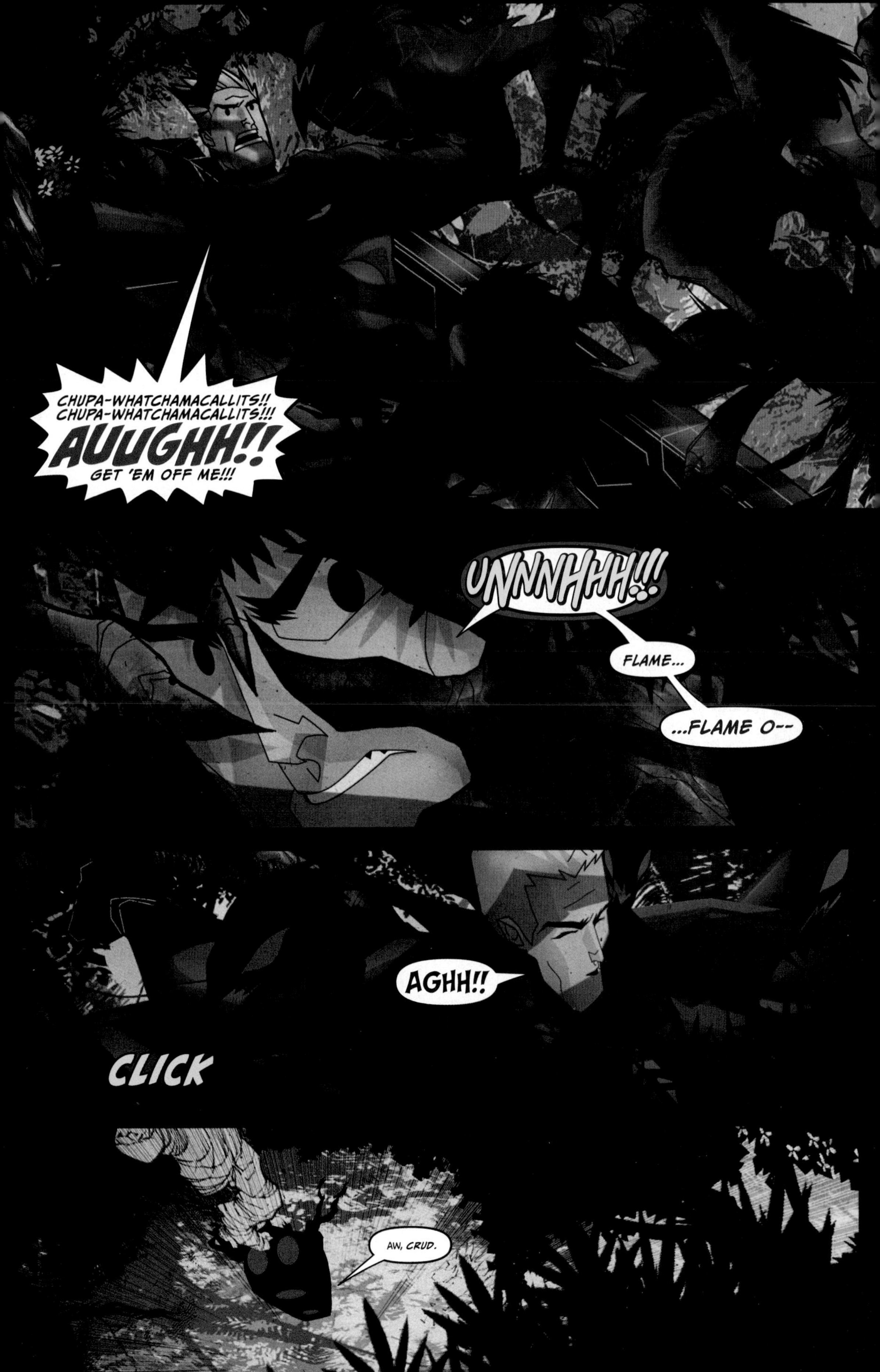
CHUPA-WHATCHAMACALLITS!! CHUPA-WHATCHAMACALLITS!!! AUUGHH!! GET 'EM OFF ME!!!
UNNNHHH!!!
FLAME...
...FLAME O--
AGHH!!
CLICK
AW, CRUD.

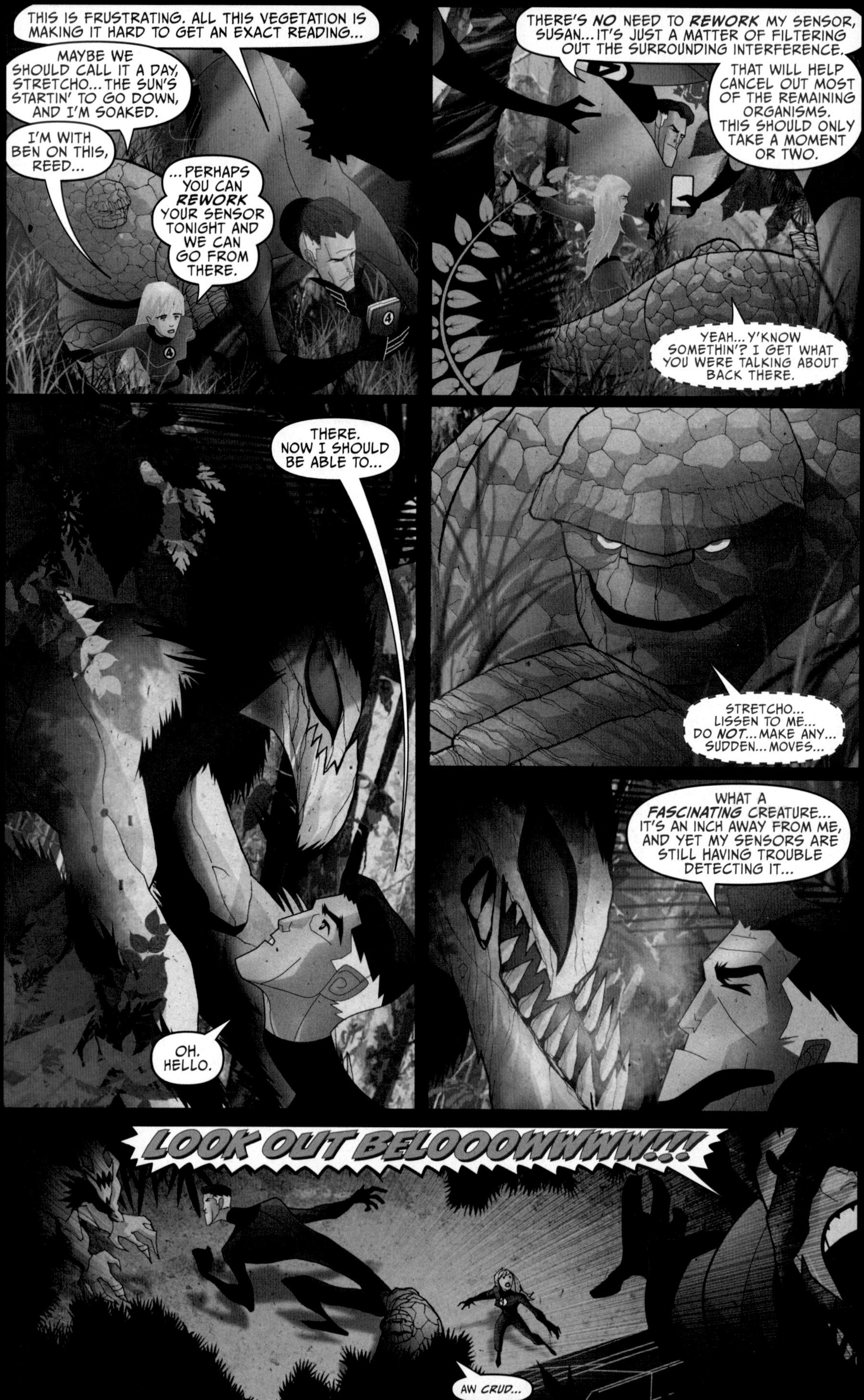
THIS IS FRUSTRATING. ALL THIS VEGETATION IS MAKING IT HARD TO GET AN EXACT READING...
MAYBE WE SHOULD CALL IT A DAY, STRETCHO... THE SUN'S STARTIN' TO GO DOWN, AND I'M SOAKED.
I'M WITH BEN ON THIS, REED...
...PERHAPS YOU CAN REWORK YOUR SENSOR TONIGHT AND WE CAN GO FROM THERE.
THERE'S NO NEED TO REWORK MY SENSOR, SUSAN... IT'S JUST A MATTER OF FILTERING OUT THE SURROUNDING INTERFERENCE.
THAT WILL HELP CANCEL OUT MOST OF THE REMAINING ORGANISMS. THIS SHOULD ONLY TAKE A MOMENT OR TWO.
YEAH... Y'KNOW SOMETHIN'? I GET WHAT YOU WERE TALKING ABOUT BACK THERE.
THERE. NOW I SHOULD BE ABLE TO...
OH. HELLO.
STRETCHO... LISSEN TO ME... DO NOT... MAKE ANY... SUDDEN... MOVES...
WHAT A FASCINATING CREATURE... IT'S AN INCH AWAY FROM ME, AND YET MY SENSORS ARE STILL HAVING TROUBLE DETECTING IT...
LOOK OUT BELOOOWWWW!!!
AW CRUD...

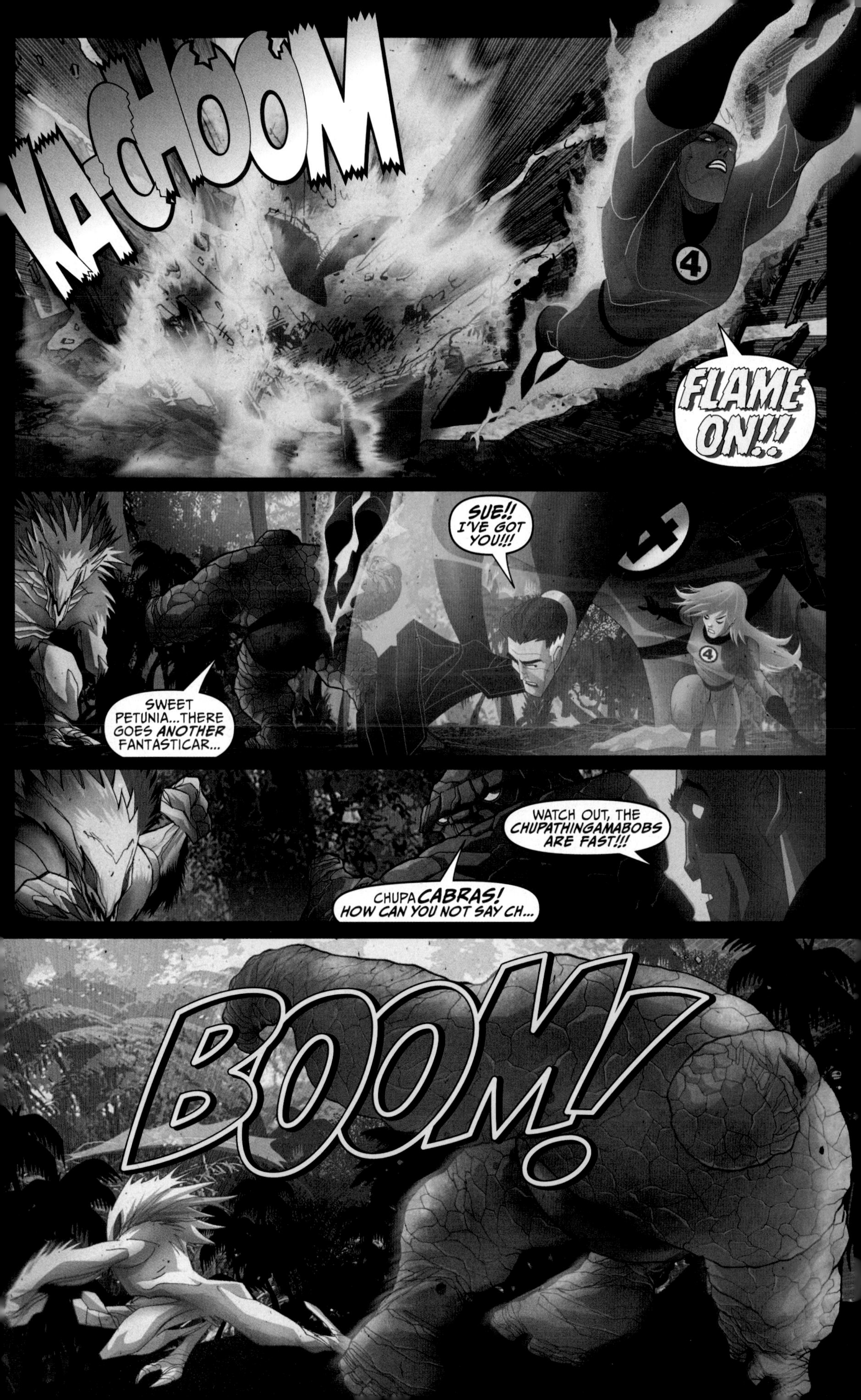
KA-CHOOM
FLAME ON!!!
SUE!! I'VE GOT YOU!!!
SWEET PETUNIA...THERE GOES ANOTHER FANTASTICAR...
WATCH OUT, THE CHUPATHINGAMABOBS ARE FAST!!!
CHUPACABRAS! HOW CAN YOU NOT SAY CH...
BOOM!

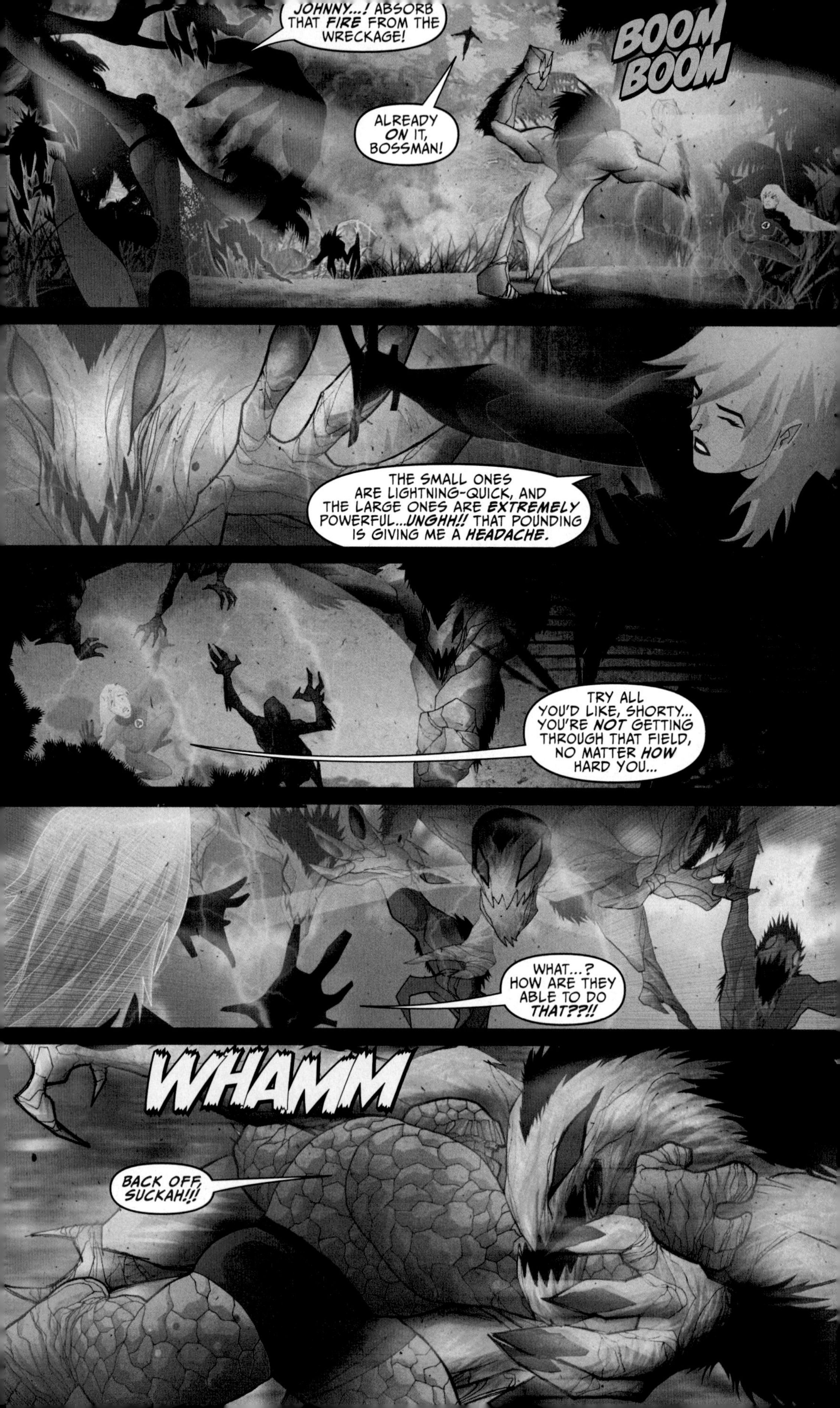

JOHNNY...! ABSORB THAT FIRE FROM THE WRECKAGE!
ALREADY ON IT, BOSSMAN!
BOOM BOOM
THE SMALL ONES ARE LIGHTNING-QUICK, AND THE LARGE ONES ARE EXTREMELY POWERFUL...UNGHH!! THAT POUNDING IS GIVING ME A HEADACHE.
TRY ALL YOU'D LIKE, SHORTY... YOU'RE NOT GETTING THROUGH THAT FIELD, NO MATTER HOW HARD YOU...
WHAT...? HOW ARE THEY ABLE TO DO THAT??!!
WHAMM
BACK OFF, SUCKAH!!!

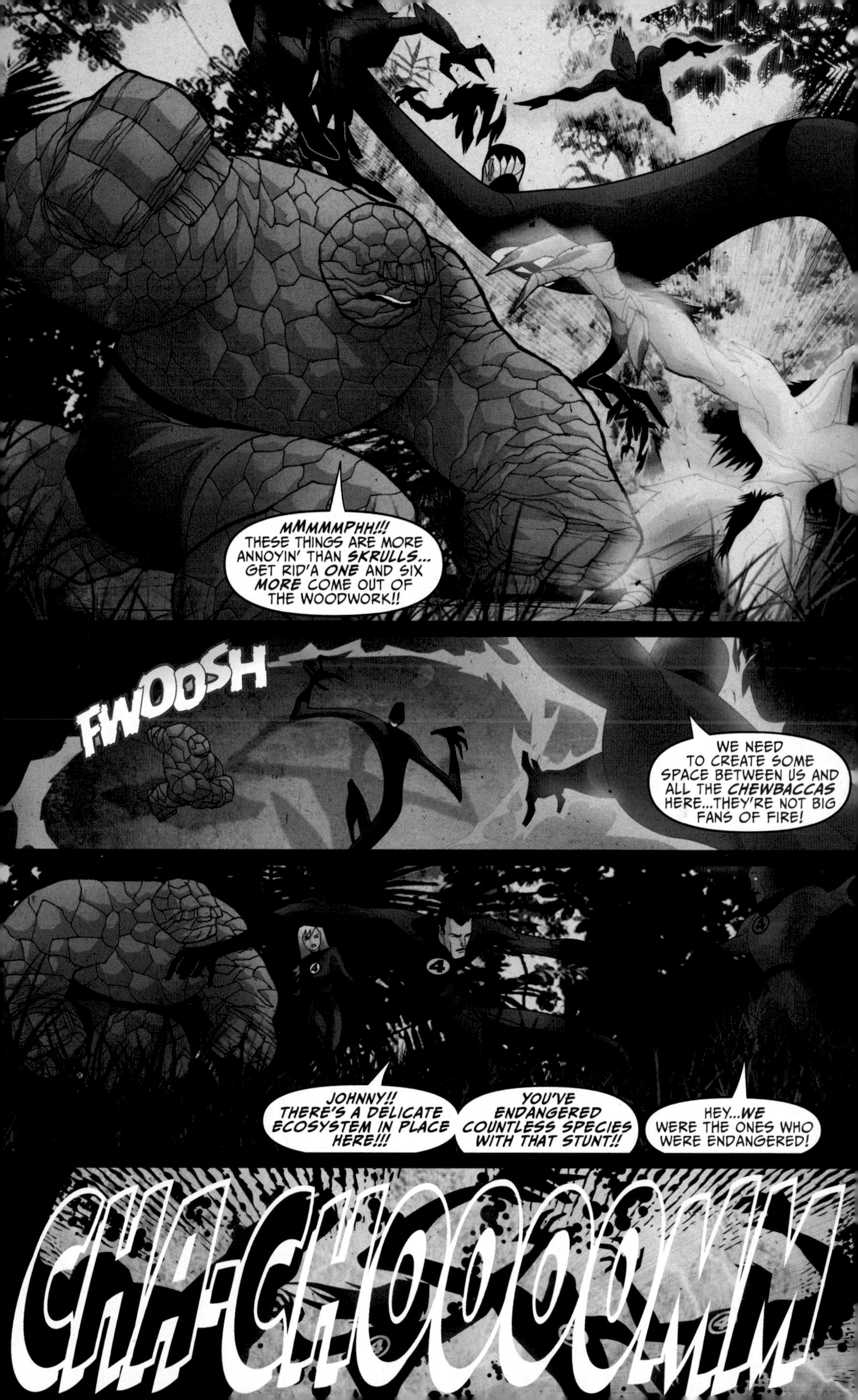
MMMMMPHH!!! THESE THINGS ARE MORE ANNOYIN' THAN SKRULLS... GET RID'A ONE AND SIX MORE COME OUT OF THE WOODWORK!!
FWOOSH
WE NEED TO CREATE SOME SPACE BETWEEN US AND ALL THE CHEWBACCAS HERE...THEY'RE NOT BIG FANS OF FIRE!
JOHNNY!! THERE'S A DELICATE ECOSYSTEM IN PLACE HERE!!!
YOU'VE ENDANGERED COUNTLESS SPECIES WITH THAT STUNT!!
HEY...WE WERE THE ONES WHO WERE ENDANGERED!
CHA-CHOOOOOM

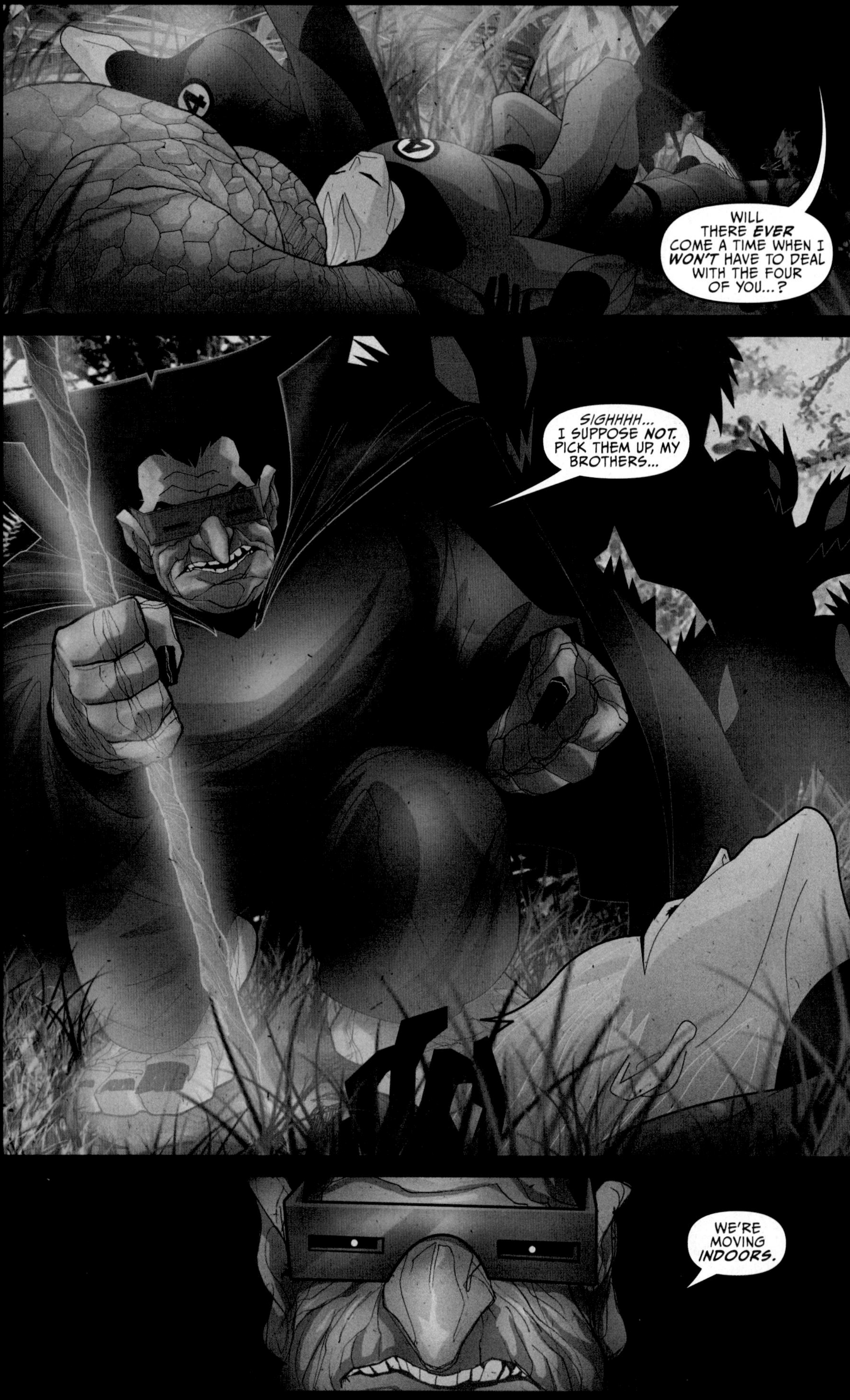
WILL THERE EVER COME A TIME WHEN I WON'T HAVE TO DEAL WITH THE FOUR OF YOU...?
SIGHHHH... I SUPPOSE NOT. PICK THEM UP, MY BROTHERS...
WE'RE MOVING INDOORS.

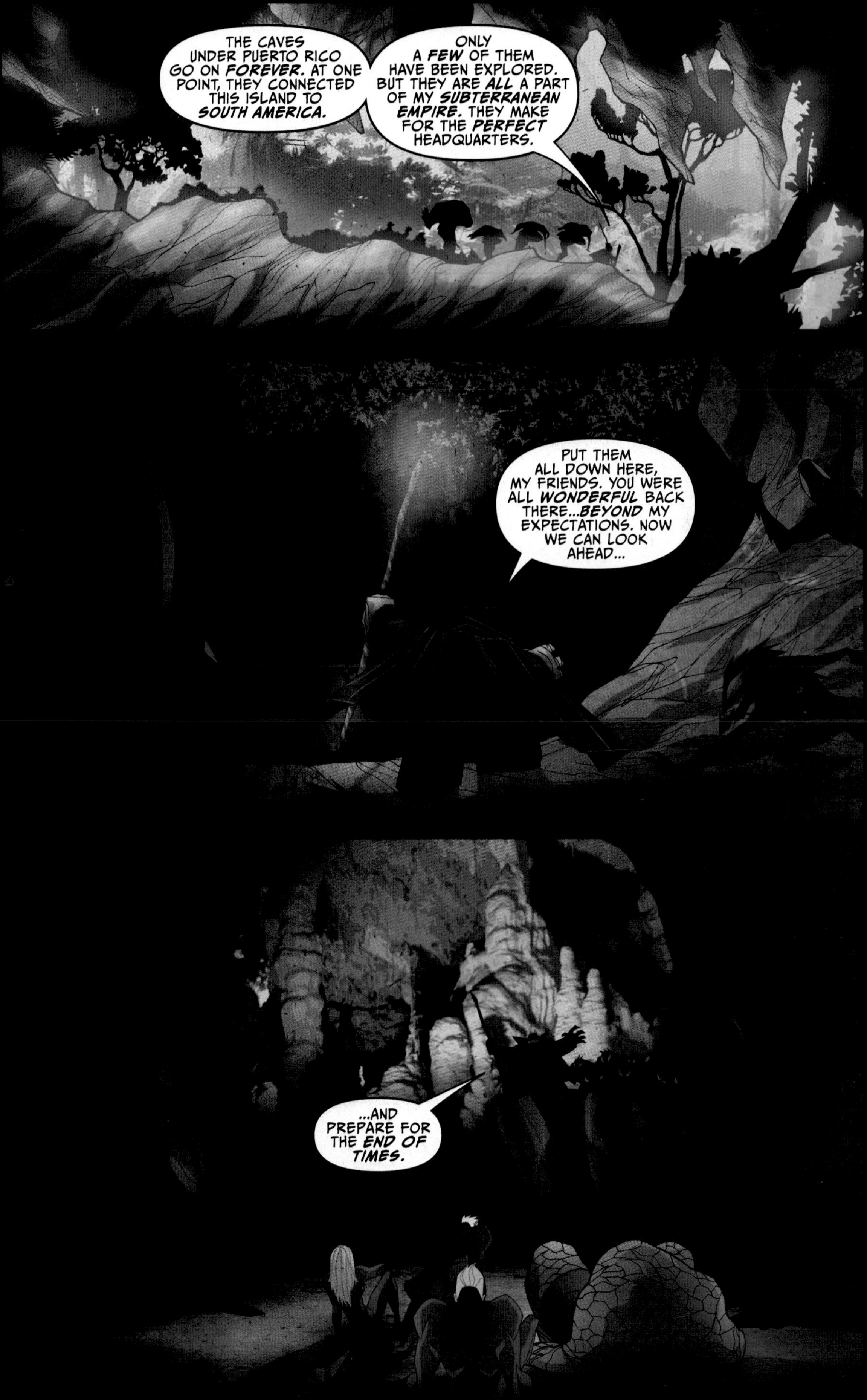
THE CAVES UNDER PUERTO RICO GO ON FOREVER. AT ONE POINT, THEY CONNECTED THIS ISLAND TO SOUTH AMERICA.
ONLY A FEW OF THEM HAVE BEEN EXPLORED. BUT THEY ARE ALL A PART OF MY SUBTERRANEAN EMPIRE. THEY MAKE FOR THE PERFECT HEADQUARTERS.
PUT THEM ALL DOWN HERE, MY FRIENDS. YOU WERE ALL WONDERFUL BACK THERE...BEYOND MY EXPECTATIONS. NOW WE CAN LOOK AHEAD...
...AND PREPARE FOR THE END OF TIMES.

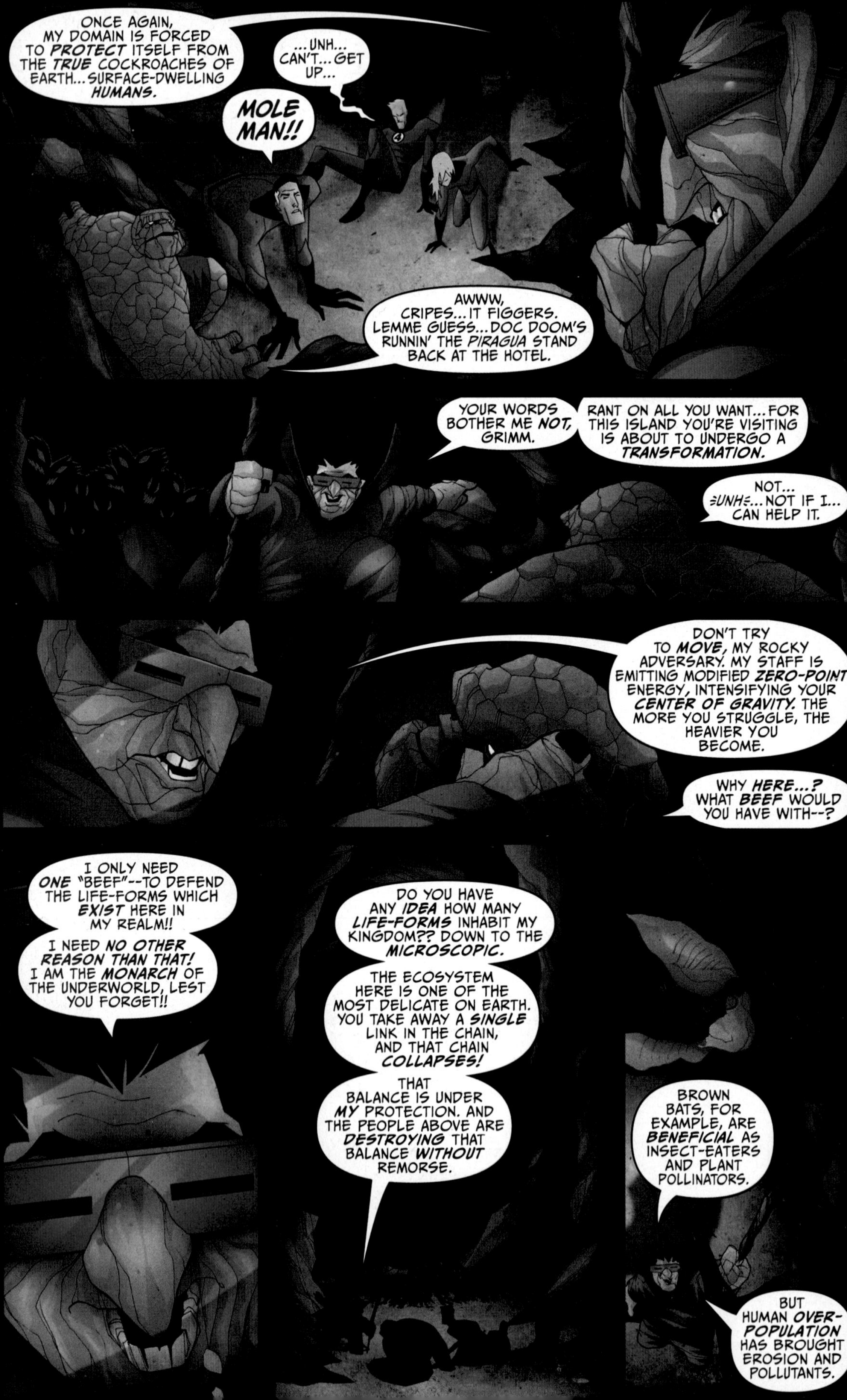
ONCE AGAIN, MY DOMAIN IS FORCED TO PROTECT ITSELF FROM THE TRUE COCKROACHES OF EARTH... SURFACE-DWELLING HUMANS.
...UNH... CAN'T... GET UP...
MOLE MAN!!
AWWW, CRIPES... IT FIGGERS. LEMME GUESS... DOC DOOM'S RUNNIN' THE PIRAGUA STAND BACK AT THE HOTEL.
YOUR WORDS BOTHER ME NOT, GRIMM.
RANT ON ALL YOU WANT... FOR THIS ISLAND YOU'RE VISITING IS ABOUT TO UNDERGO A TRANSFORMATION.
NOT... UNH... NOT IF I... CAN HELP IT.
DON'T TRY TO MOVE, MY ROCKY ADVERSARY. MY STAFF IS EMITTING MODIFIED ZERO-POINT ENERGY, INTENSIFYING YOUR CENTER OF GRAVITY. THE MORE YOU STRUGGLE, THE HEAVIER YOU BECOME.
WHY HERE...? WHAT BEEF WOULD YOU HAVE WITH--?
I ONLY NEED ONE "BEEF"--TO DEFEND THE LIFE-FORMS WHICH EXIST HERE IN MY REALM!!
I NEED NO OTHER REASON THAN THAT! I AM THE MONARCH OF THE UNDERWORLD, LEST YOU FORGET!!
DO YOU HAVE ANY IDEA HOW MANY LIFE-FORMS INHABIT MY KINGDOM?? DOWN TO THE MICROSCOPIC.
THE ECOSYSTEM HERE IS ONE OF THE MOST DELICATE ON EARTH. YOU TAKE AWAY A SINGLE LINK IN THE CHAIN, AND THAT CHAIN COLLAPSES!
THAT BALANCE IS UNDER MY PROTECTION. AND THE PEOPLE ABOVE ARE DESTROYING THAT BALANCE WITHOUT REMORSE.
BROWN BATS, FOR EXAMPLE, ARE BENEFICIAL AS INSECT-EATERS AND PLANT POLLINATORS.
BUT HUMAN OVER-POPULATION HAS BROUGHT EROSION AND POLLUTANTS.

HUMANS ARE CREATURES OF *CORPORATE GREED.* THEY DO ANYTHING FOR FINANCIAL GAIN...NO MATTER WHICH INNOCENT CREATURE PAYS THE PRICE.

MY CITIZENS...FROM THE BATS ABOVE...TO THE MICROSCOPIC LIFE-FORMS LIVING IN THESE POOLS OF WATER...CARE *LITTLE* ABOUT A STOCK PORTFOLIO. THEY CARE ONLY ABOUT *EXISTENCE.*

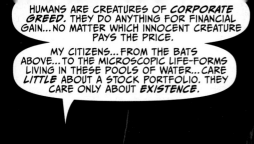

WITNESS "EL COMECOGOLLOS"...

...AND "THE MOCA VAMPIRE."

ONCE *MIGHTY* EVOLUTIONARY FOREBEARS OF EL CHUPACABRAS--NOW *EXTINCT!*

NATURE BLESSED THE ASTONISHING CHUPACABRAS WITH FLIGHT, STRENGTH AND OTHER ABILITIES SCIENCE CANNOT *BEGIN* TO COMPREHEND!

SIGHTINGS HAVE BEEN REPORTED ALL OVER THE WORLD. BUT THEY'VE AVOIDED *ALL* INTERACTION WITH HUMANS. THEY FIND YOU... *UNINTERESTING* AT BEST.

THIS ISLAND, HOWEVER, THEY CALL *HOME.*

THIS IS WHERE THEY MIGRATE EVERY TEN YEARS TO *BREED.* BUT THOSE HABITATS HAVE BEEN *REPLACED* BY CONDOS AND HIGHWAYS.

MAN HAD NEARLY WIPED THEM *OUT* OF EXISTENCE...

...UNTIL *I* STEPPED IN. I TOOK THEM UNDER MY CARE, AND NOW...NOW THEY *THRIVE* AGAIN!

THE TIME HAS COME FOR THE CHUPACABRAS TO *RECLAIM* THEIR HOMELAND. SINCE *HUMAN OVER-POPULATION* DEPLETED THEIR FOOD SUPPLY...WE SHALL *RECTIFY* THAT SITUATION.

MY SOLDIERS WILL SET FORTH TO ELIMINATE *ONE-THIRD* OF THE ISLAND'S POPULATION--OVER *ONE MILLION PEOPLE.* THE CHUPACABRAS HAVE A *RIGHT* TO THEIR BREEDING GROUNDS.

WHENEVER YOU'RE *READY,* DARLING.

THANK YOU, DEAR.

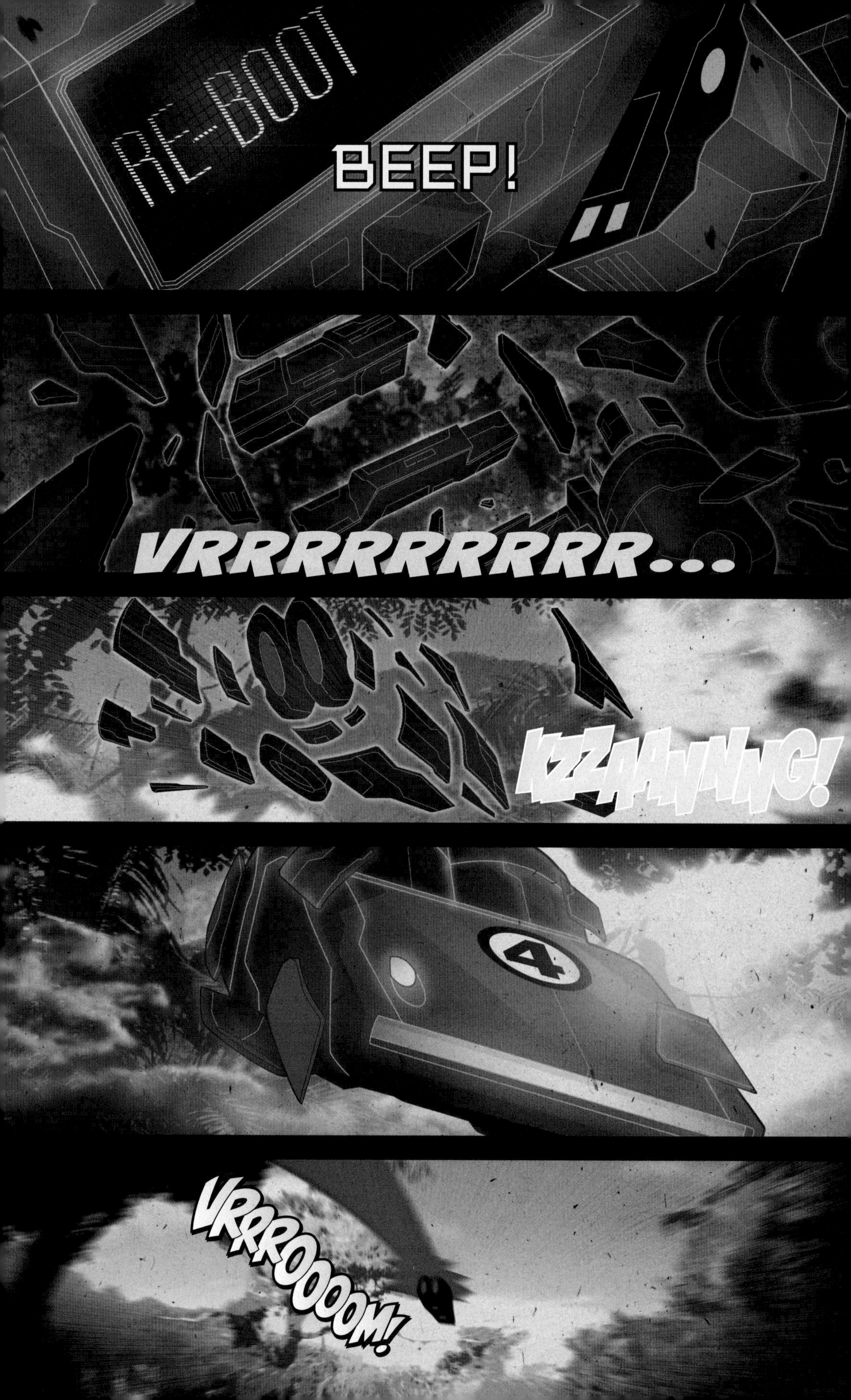
RE-BOOT
BEEP!
VRRRRRRRRRR...
KZZAANNNG!
VRRROOOOOM!

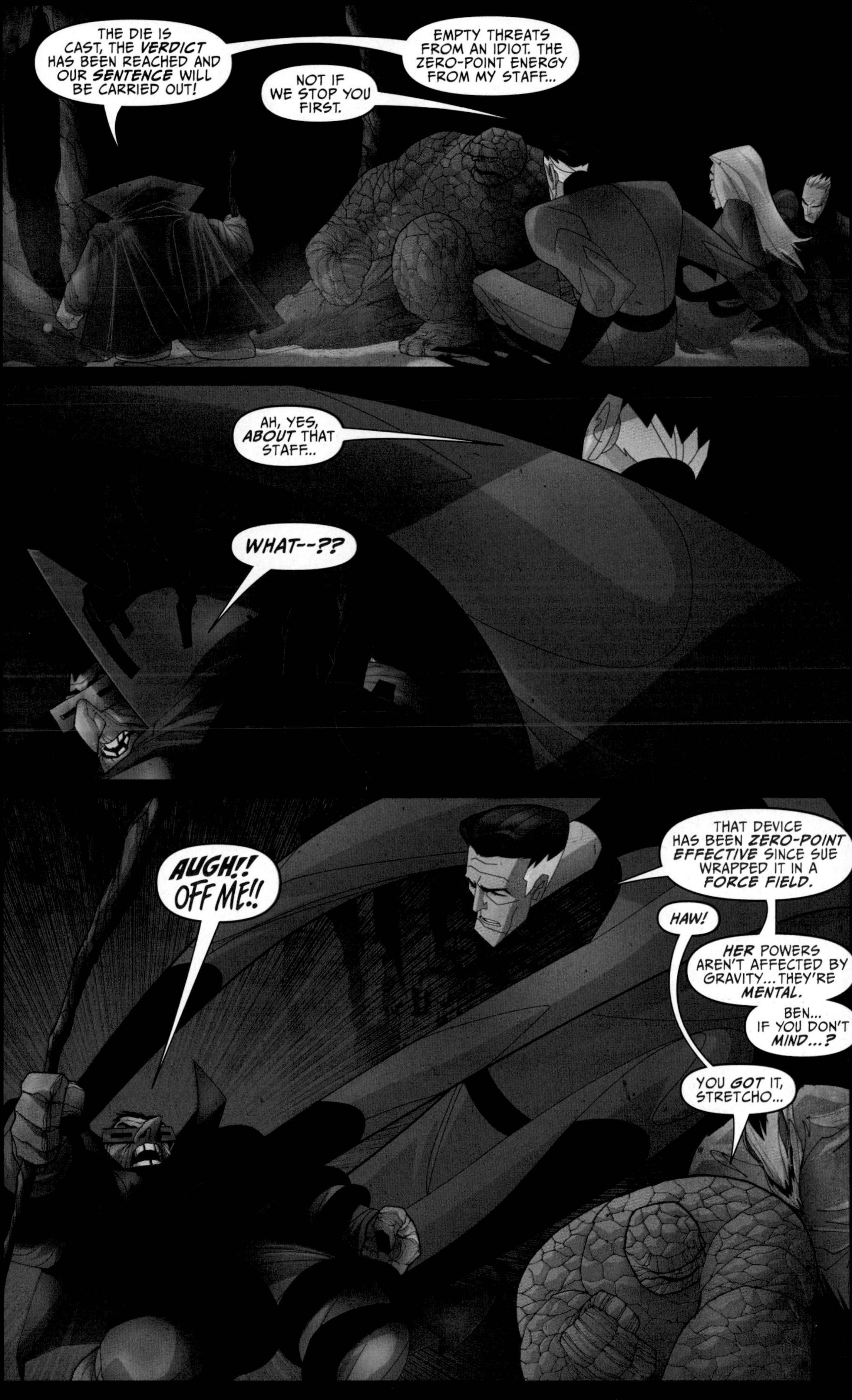
THE DIE IS CAST, THE VERDICT HAS BEEN REACHED AND OUR SENTENCE WILL BE CARRIED OUT!
EMPTY THREATS FROM AN IDIOT. THE ZERO-POINT ENERGY FROM MY STAFF...
NOT IF WE STOP YOU FIRST.
AH, YES, ABOUT THAT STAFF...
WHAT--??
AUGH!! OFF ME!!
THAT DEVICE HAS BEEN ZERO-POINT EFFECTIVE SINCE SUE WRAPPED IT IN A FORCE FIELD.
HAW!
HER POWERS AREN'T AFFECTED BY GRAVITY... THEY'RE MENTAL.
BEN... IF YOU DON'T MIND...?
YOU GOT IT, STRETCHO...

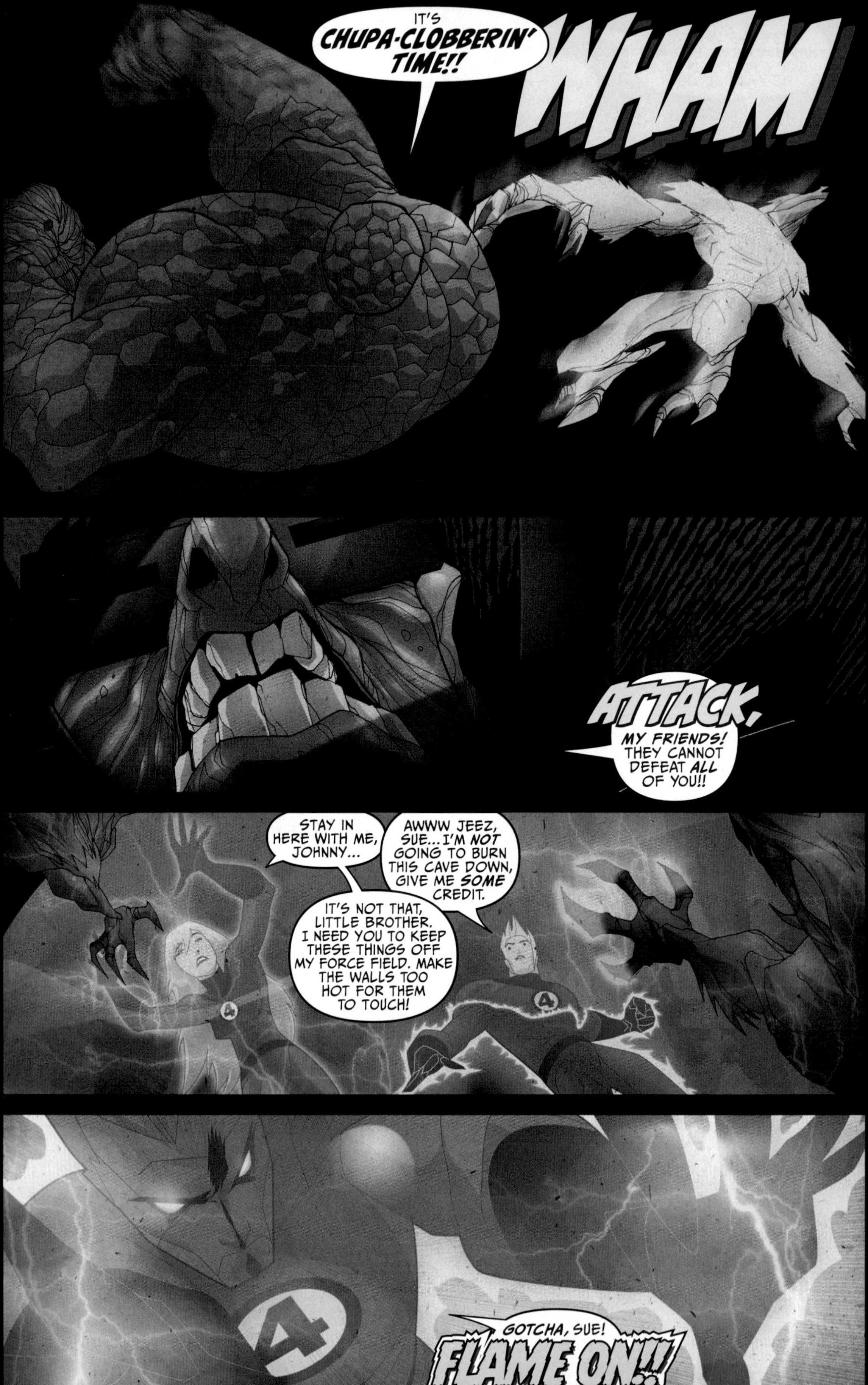
IT'S CHUPA-CLOBBERIN' TIME!!
WHAM
ATTACK, MY FRIENDS! THEY CANNOT DEFEAT ALL OF YOU!!
STAY IN HERE WITH ME, JOHNNY...
AWWW JEEZ, SUE... I'M NOT GOING TO BURN THIS CAVE DOWN, GIVE ME SOME CREDIT.
IT'S NOT THAT, LITTLE BROTHER. I NEED YOU TO KEEP THESE THINGS OFF MY FORCE FIELD. MAKE THE WALLS TOO HOT FOR THEM TO TOUCH!
GOTCHA, SUE!
FLAME ON!!

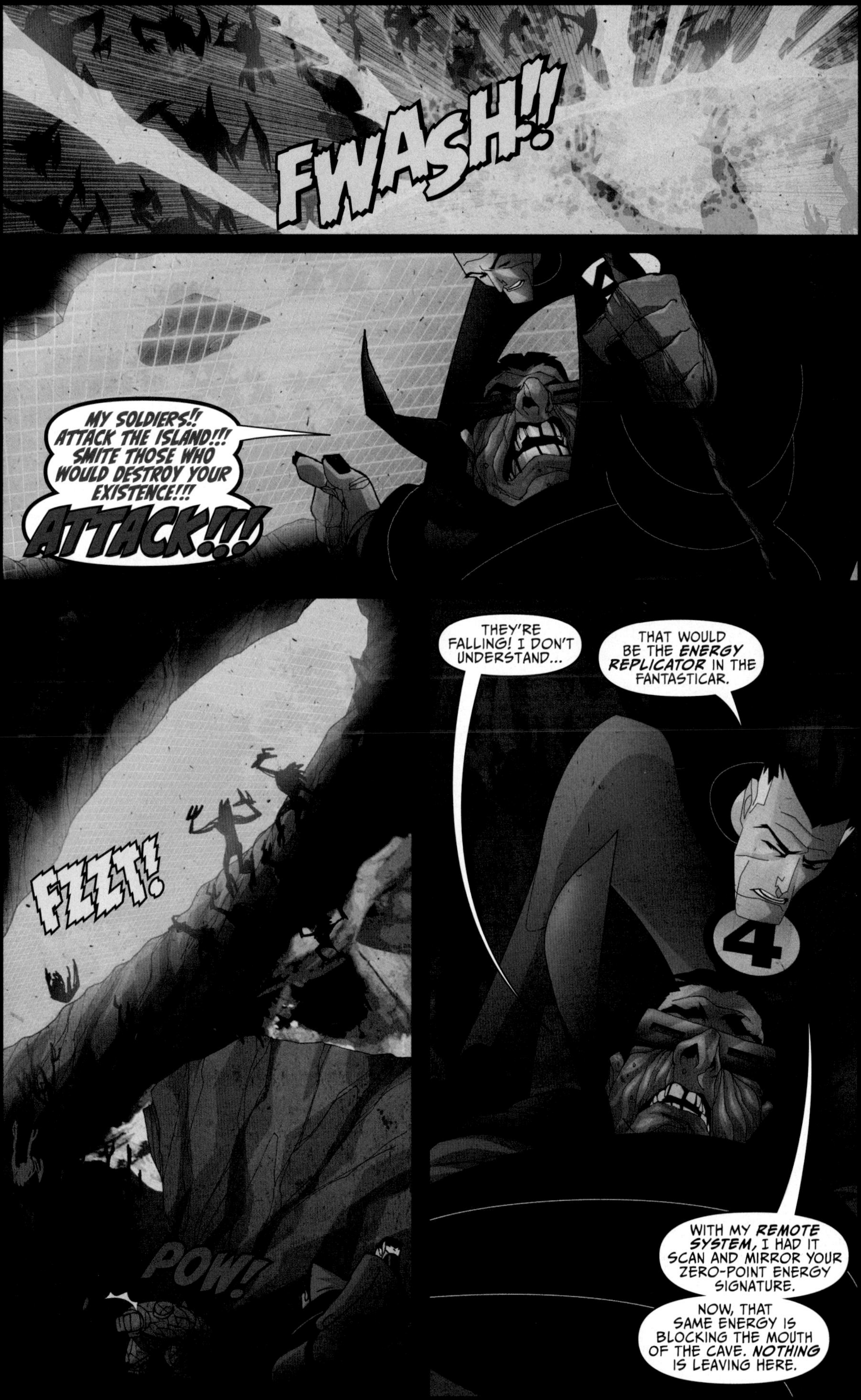
FWASH!!
MY SOLDIERS!! ATTACK THE ISLAND!!! SMITE THOSE WHO WOULD DESTROY YOUR EXISTENCE!!! ATTACK!!!
FZZT!
POW!
THEY'RE FALLING! I DON'T UNDERSTAND...
THAT WOULD BE THE ENERGY REPLICATOR IN THE FANTASTICAR.
WITH MY REMOTE SYSTEM, I HAD IT SCAN AND MIRROR YOUR ZERO-POINT ENERGY SIGNATURE.
NOW, THAT SAME ENERGY IS BLOCKING THE MOUTH OF THE CAVE. NOTHING IS LEAVING HERE.

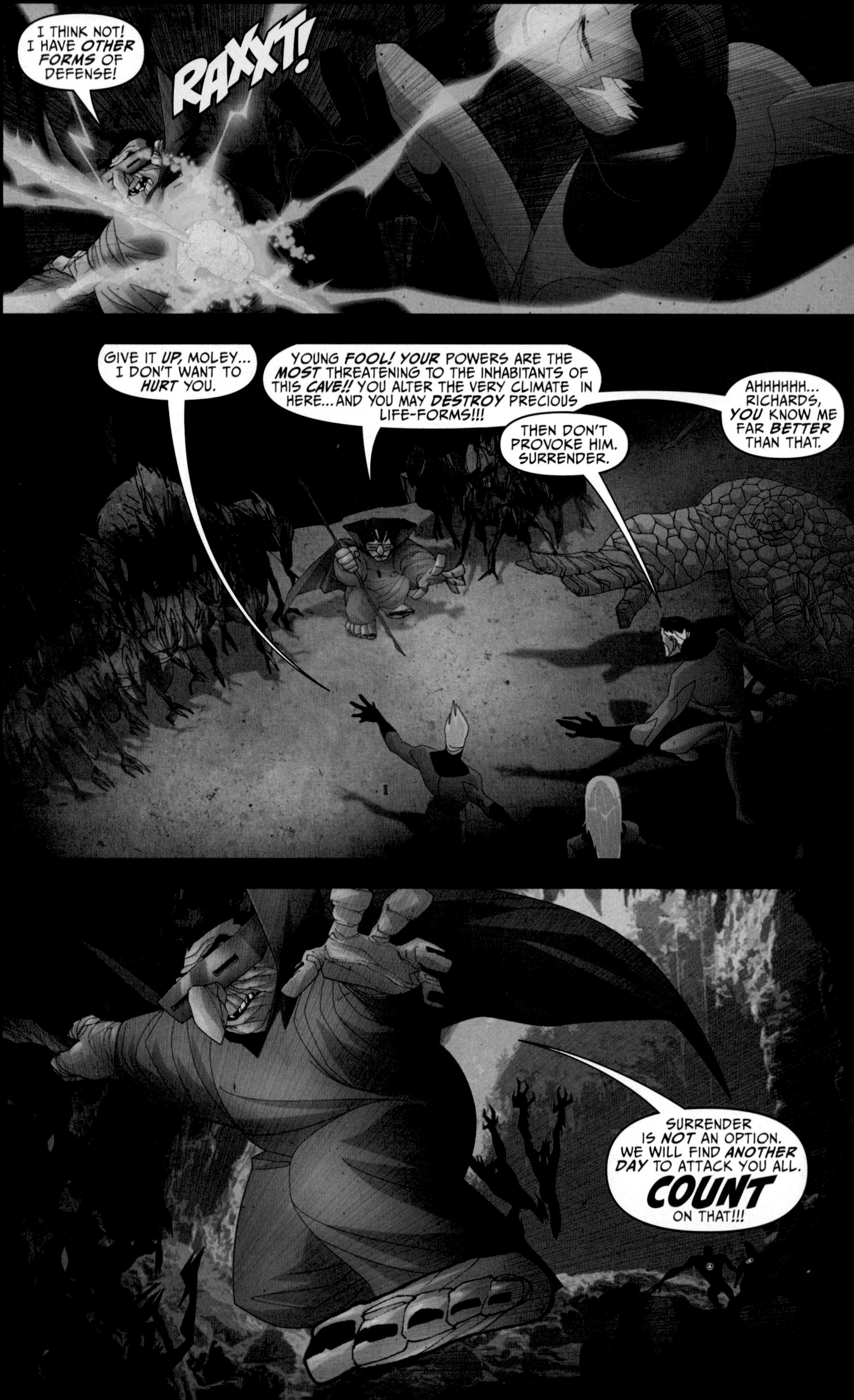

I THINK NOT! I HAVE OTHER FORMS OF DEFENSE!
RAXXT!
GIVE IT UP, MOLEY... I DON'T WANT TO HURT YOU.
YOUNG FOOL! YOUR POWERS ARE THE MOST THREATENING TO THE INHABITANTS OF THIS CAVE!! YOU ALTER THE VERY CLIMATE IN HERE...AND YOU MAY DESTROY PRECIOUS LIFE-FORMS!!!
THEN DON'T PROVOKE HIM. SURRENDER.
AHHHHHH... RICHARDS, YOU KNOW ME FAR BETTER THAN THAT.
SURRENDER IS NOT AN OPTION. WE WILL FIND ANOTHER DAY TO ATTACK YOU ALL. COUNT ON THAT!!!

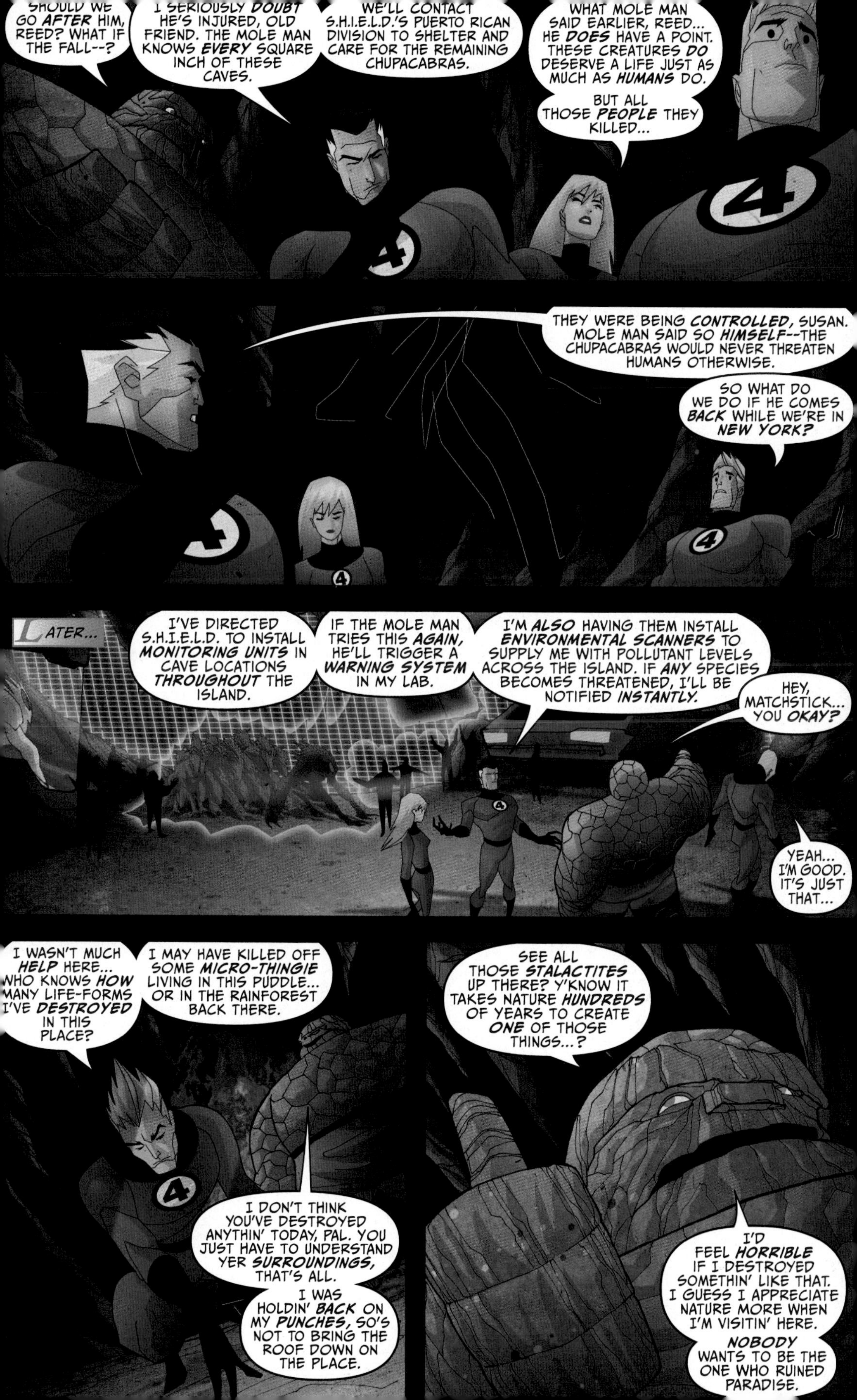
SHOULD WE GO AFTER HIM, REED? WHAT IF THE FALL--?
I SERIOUSLY DOUBT HE'S INJURED, OLD FRIEND. THE MOLE MAN KNOWS EVERY SQUARE INCH OF THESE CAVES.
WE'LL CONTACT S.H.I.E.L.D.'S PUERTO RICAN DIVISION TO SHELTER AND CARE FOR THE REMAINING CHUPACABRAS.
WHAT MOLE MAN SAID EARLIER, REED... HE DOES HAVE A POINT. THESE CREATURES DO DESERVE A LIFE JUST AS MUCH AS HUMANS DO.
BUT ALL THOSE PEOPLE THEY KILLED...
THEY WERE BEING CONTROLLED, SUSAN. MOLE MAN SAID SO HIMSELF--THE CHUPACABRAS WOULD NEVER THREATEN HUMANS OTHERWISE.
SO WHAT DO WE DO IF HE COMES BACK WHILE WE'RE IN NEW YORK?
LATER...
I'VE DIRECTED S.H.I.E.L.D. TO INSTALL MONITORING UNITS IN CAVE LOCATIONS THROUGHOUT THE ISLAND.
IF THE MOLE MAN TRIES THIS AGAIN, HE'LL TRIGGER A WARNING SYSTEM IN MY LAB.
I'M ALSO HAVING THEM INSTALL ENVIRONMENTAL SCANNERS TO SUPPLY ME WITH POLLUTANT LEVELS ACROSS THE ISLAND. IF ANY SPECIES BECOMES THREATENED, I'LL BE NOTIFIED INSTANTLY.
HEY, MATCHSTICK... YOU OKAY?
YEAH... I'M GOOD. IT'S JUST THAT...
I WASN'T MUCH HELP HERE... WHO KNOWS HOW MANY LIFE-FORMS I'VE DESTROYED IN THIS PLACE?
I MAY HAVE KILLED OFF SOME MICRO-THINGIE LIVING IN THIS PUDDLE... OR IN THE RAINFOREST BACK THERE.
I DON'T THINK YOU'VE DESTROYED ANYTHIN' TODAY, PAL. YOU JUST HAVE TO UNDERSTAND YER SURROUNDINGS, THAT'S ALL.
I WAS HOLDIN' BACK ON MY PUNCHES, SO'S NOT TO BRING THE ROOF DOWN ON THE PLACE.
SEE ALL THOSE STALACTITES UP THERE? Y'KNOW IT TAKES NATURE HUNDREDS OF YEARS TO CREATE ONE OF THOSE THINGS...?
I'D FEEL HORRIBLE IF I DESTROYED SOMETHIN' LIKE THAT. I GUESS I APPRECIATE NATURE MORE WHEN I'M VISITIN' HERE.
NOBODY WANTS TO BE THE ONE WHO RUINED PARADISE.

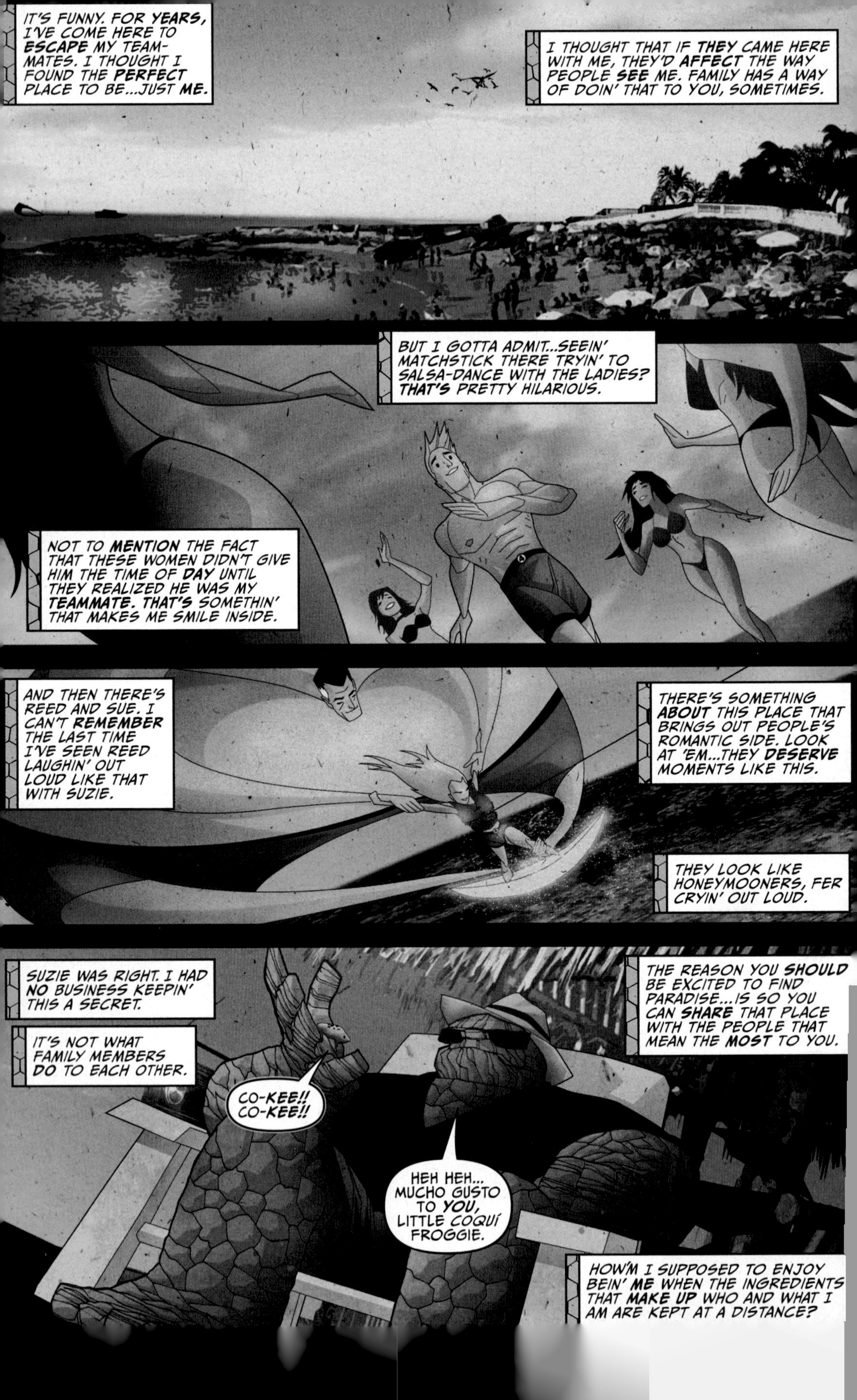
IT'S FUNNY. FOR YEARS, I'VE COME HERE TO ESCAPE MY TEAM-MATES. I THOUGHT I FOUND THE PERFECT PLACE TO BE...JUST ME.
I THOUGHT THAT IF THEY CAME HERE WITH ME, THEY'D AFFECT THE WAY PEOPLE SEE ME. FAMILY HAS A WAY OF DOIN' THAT TO YOU, SOMETIMES.
BUT I GOTTA ADMIT...SEEIN' MATCHSTICK THERE TRYIN' TO SALSA-DANCE WITH THE LADIES? THAT'S PRETTY HILARIOUS.
NOT TO MENTION THE FACT THAT THESE WOMEN DIDN'T GIVE HIM THE TIME OF DAY UNTIL THEY REALIZED HE WAS MY TEAMMATE. THAT'S SOMETHIN' THAT MAKES ME SMILE INSIDE.
AND THEN THERE'S REED AND SUE. I CAN'T REMEMBER THE LAST TIME I'VE SEEN REED LAUGHIN' OUT LOUD LIKE THAT WITH SUZIE.
THERE'S SOMETHING ABOUT THIS PLACE THAT BRINGS OUT PEOPLE'S ROMANTIC SIDE. LOOK AT 'EM...THEY DESERVE MOMENTS LIKE THIS.
THEY LOOK LIKE HONEYMOONERS, FER CRYIN' OUT LOUD.
SUZIE WAS RIGHT. I HAD NO BUSINESS KEEPIN' THIS A SECRET.
IT'S NOT WHAT FAMILY MEMBERS DO TO EACH OTHER.
THE REASON YOU SHOULD BE EXCITED TO FIND PARADISE...IS SO YOU CAN SHARE THAT PLACE WITH THE PEOPLE THAT MEAN THE MOST TO YOU.
CO-KEE!! CO-KEE!!
HEH HEH... MUCHO GUSTO TO YOU, LITTLE COQUÍ FROGGIE.
HOW'M I SUPPOSED TO ENJOY BEIN' ME WHEN THE INGREDIENTS THAT MAKE UP WHO AND WHAT I AM ARE KEPT AT A DISTANCE?

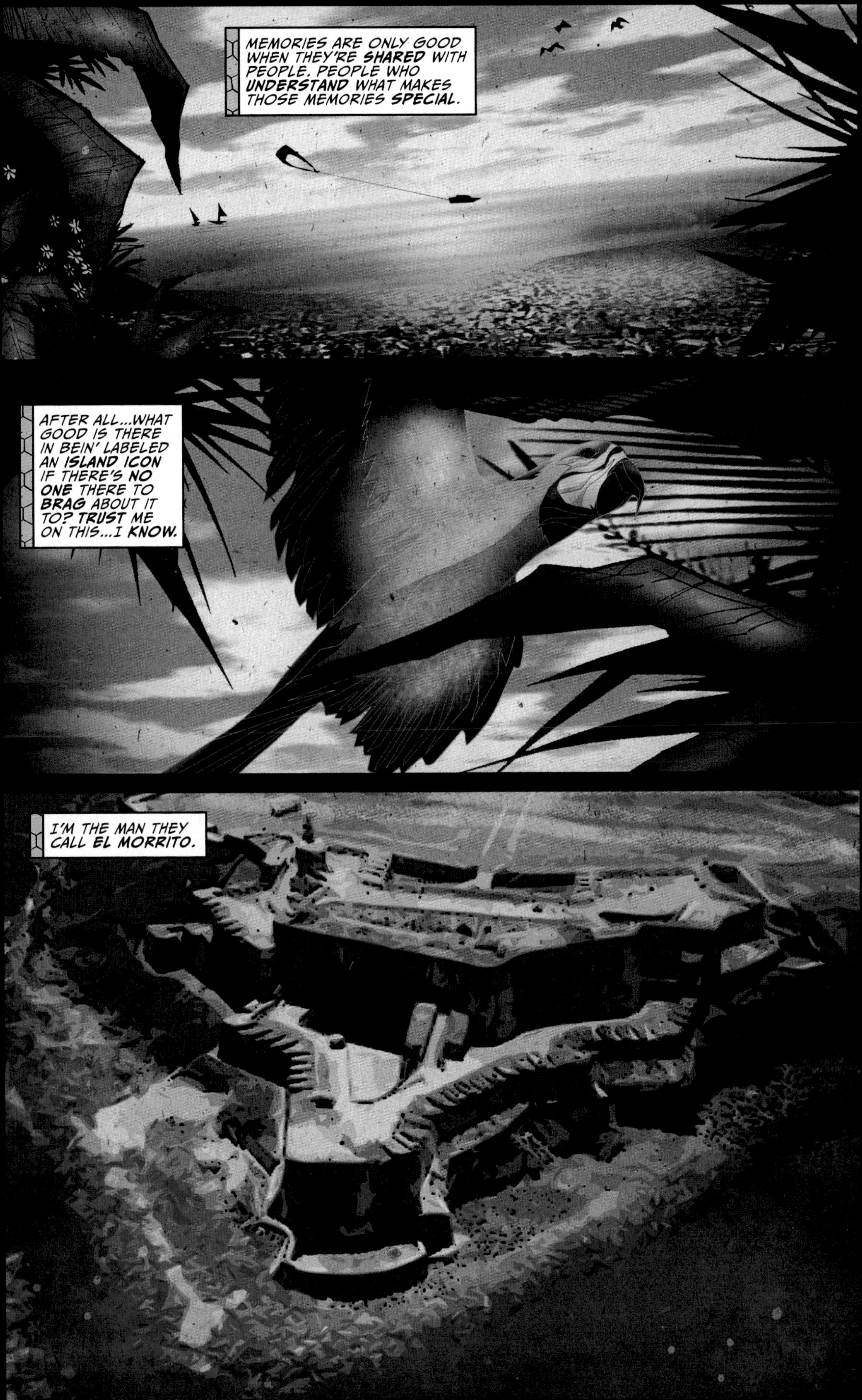
MEMORIES ARE ONLY GOOD WHEN THEY'RE SHARED WITH PEOPLE. PEOPLE WHO UNDERSTAND WHAT MAKES THOSE MEMORIES SPECIAL.
AFTER ALL...WHAT GOOD IS THERE IN BEIN' LABELED AN ISLAND ICON IF THERE'S NO ONE THERE TO BRAG ABOUT IT TO? TRUST ME ON THIS...I KNOW.
I'M THE MAN THEY CALL EL MORRITO.

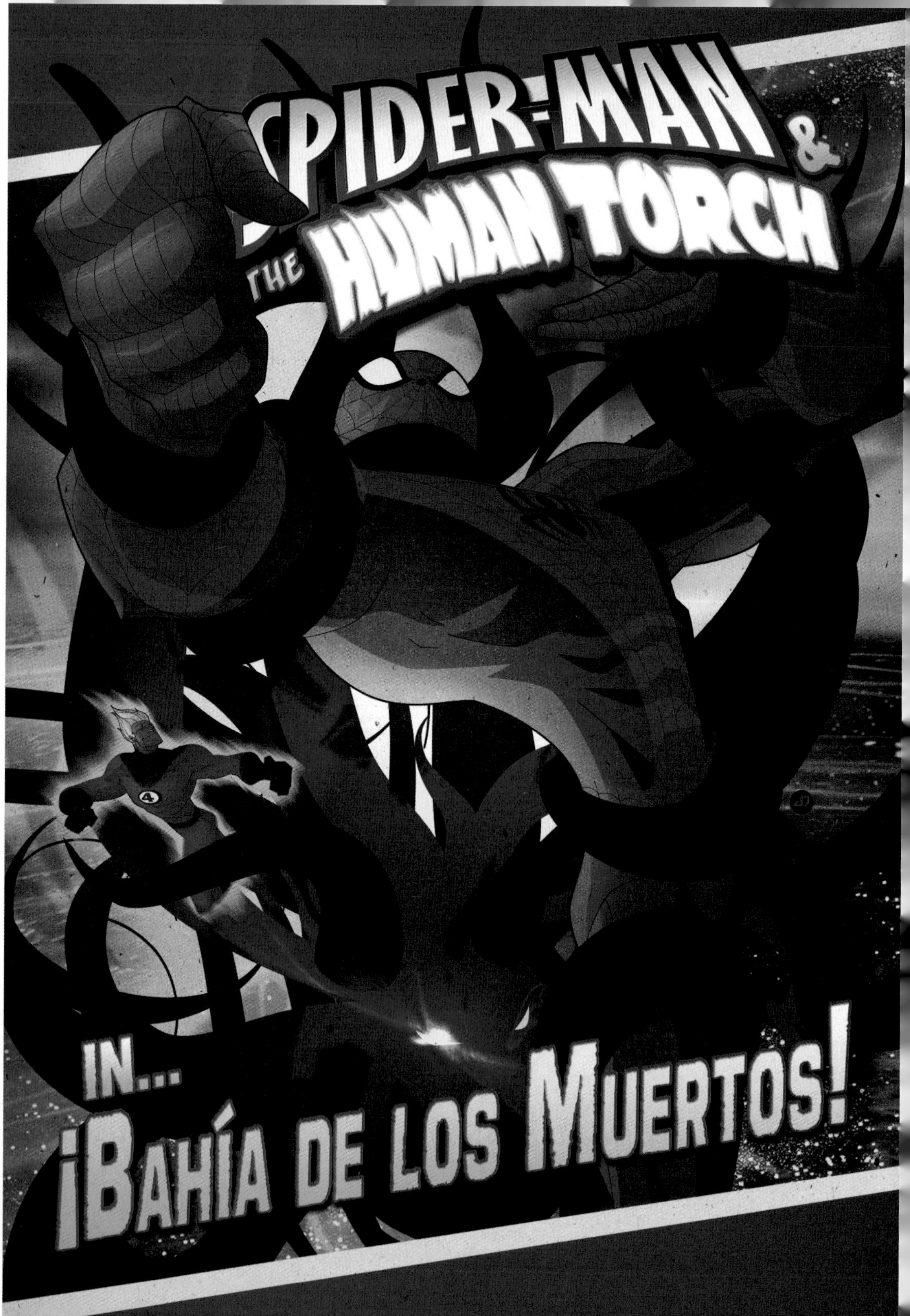
SPIDER-MAN & THE HUMAN TORCH
IN...
¡BAHÍA DE LOS MUERTOS!

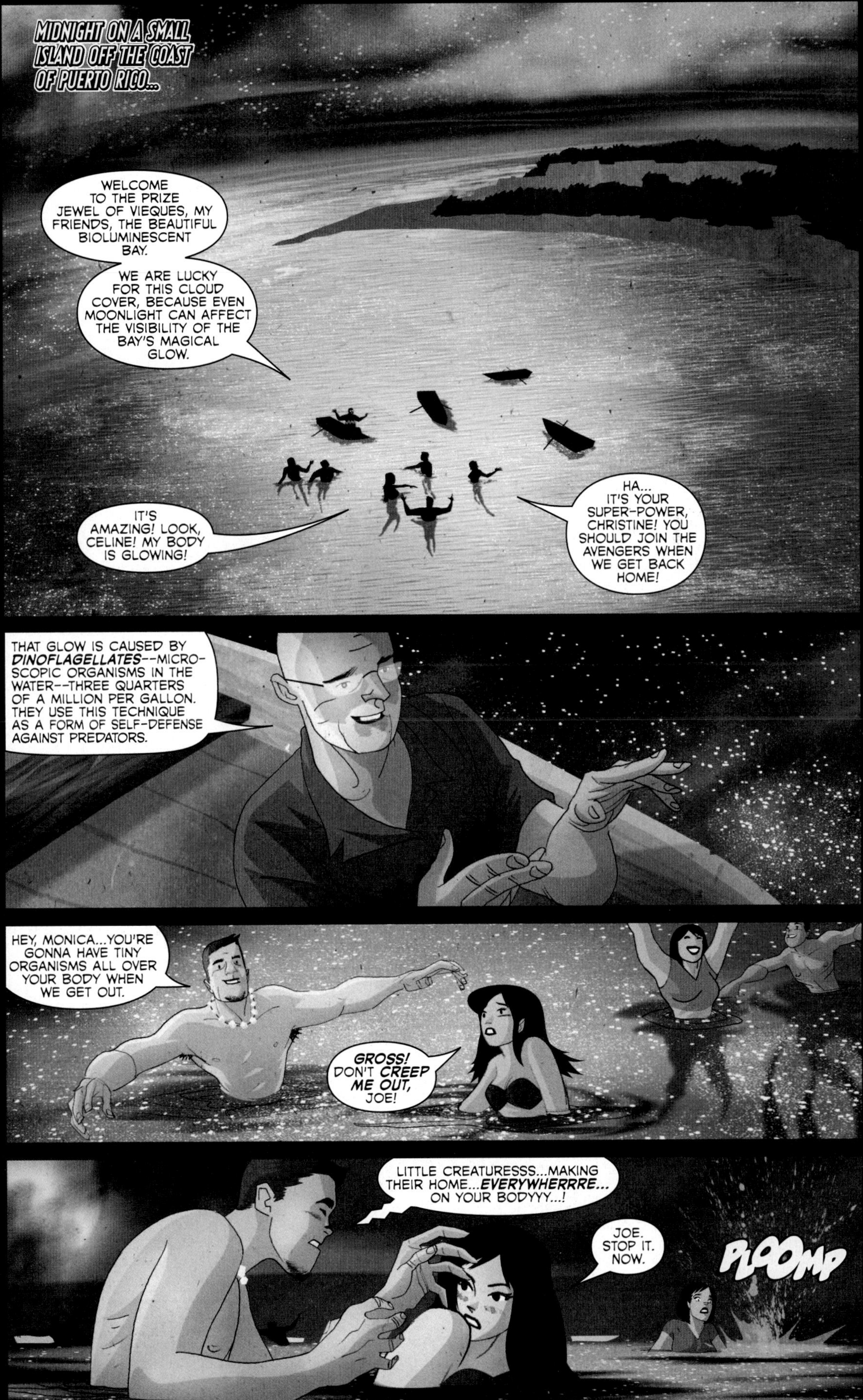
MIDNIGHT ON A SMALL ISLAND OFF THE COAST OF PUERTO RICO...
WELCOME TO THE PRIZE JEWEL OF VIEQUES, MY FRIENDS, THE BEAUTIFUL BIOLUMINESCENT BAY.
WE ARE LUCKY FOR THIS CLOUD COVER, BECAUSE EVEN MOONLIGHT CAN AFFECT THE VISIBILITY OF THE BAY'S MAGICAL GLOW.
IT'S AMAZING! LOOK, CELINE! MY BODY IS GLOWING!
HA... IT'S YOUR SUPER-POWER, CHRISTINE! YOU SHOULD JOIN THE AVENGERS WHEN WE GET BACK HOME!
THAT GLOW IS CAUSED BY *DINOFLAGELLATES*--MICROSCOPIC ORGANISMS IN THE WATER--THREE QUARTERS OF A MILLION PER GALLON. THEY USE THIS TECHNIQUE AS A FORM OF SELF-DEFENSE AGAINST PREDATORS.
HEY, MONICA...YOU'RE GONNA HAVE TINY ORGANISMS ALL OVER YOUR BODY WHEN WE GET OUT.
GROSS! DON'T *CREEP ME OUT,* JOE!
LITTLE CREATURESSS...MAKING THEIR HOME...*EVERYWHERRRE...* ON YOUR BODYYY...!
JOE. STOP IT. NOW.
PLOOMP

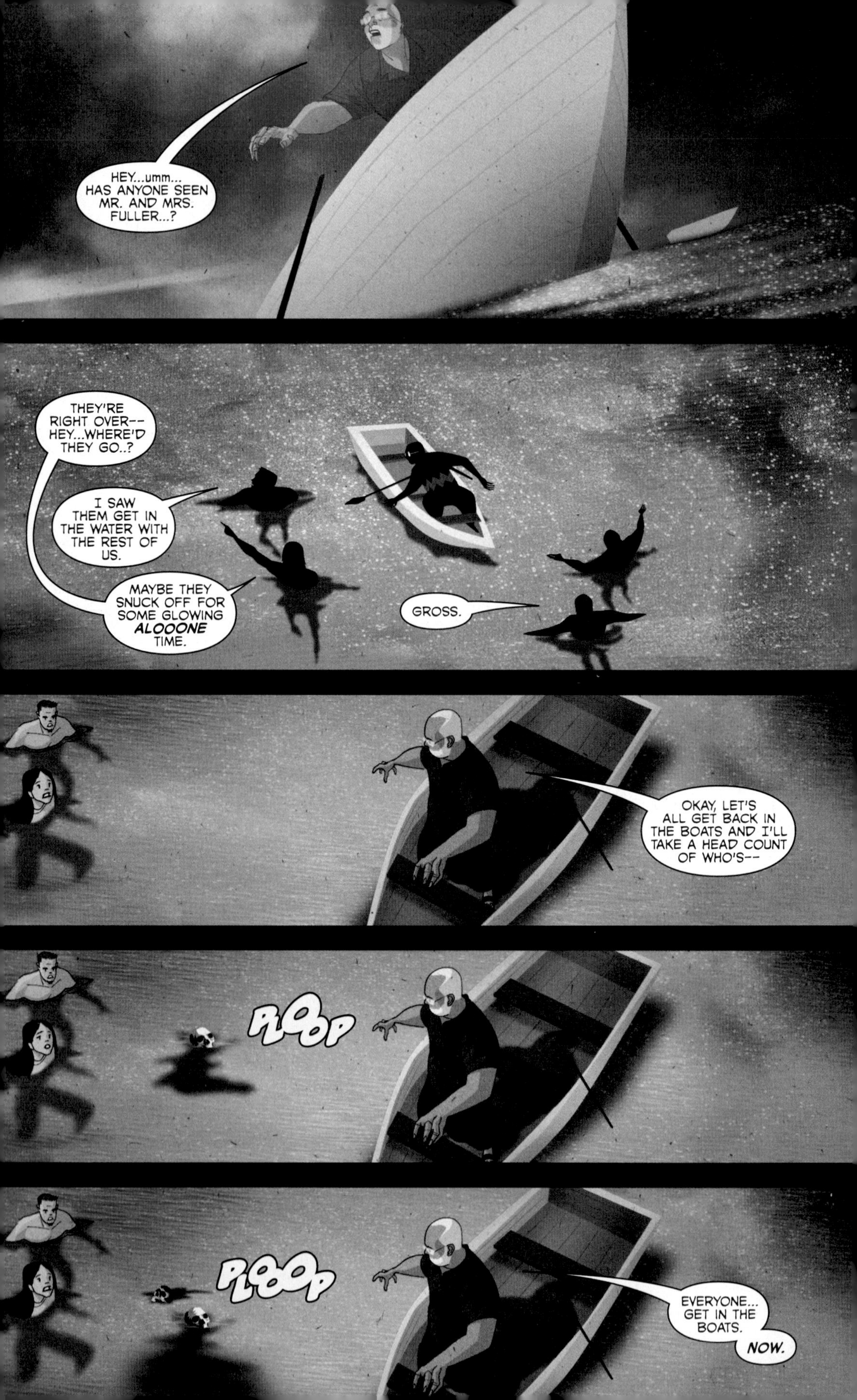
HEY...umm... HAS ANYONE SEEN MR. AND MRS. FULLER...?
THEY'RE RIGHT OVER-- HEY...WHERE'D THEY GO..?
I SAW THEM GET IN THE WATER WITH THE REST OF US.
MAYBE THEY SNUCK OFF FOR SOME GLOWING **ALOOONE** TIME.
GROSS.
OKAY, LET'S ALL GET BACK IN THE BOATS AND I'LL TAKE A HEAD COUNT OF WHO'S--
PLOOP
PLOOOP
EVERYONE... GET IN THE BOATS.
NOW.

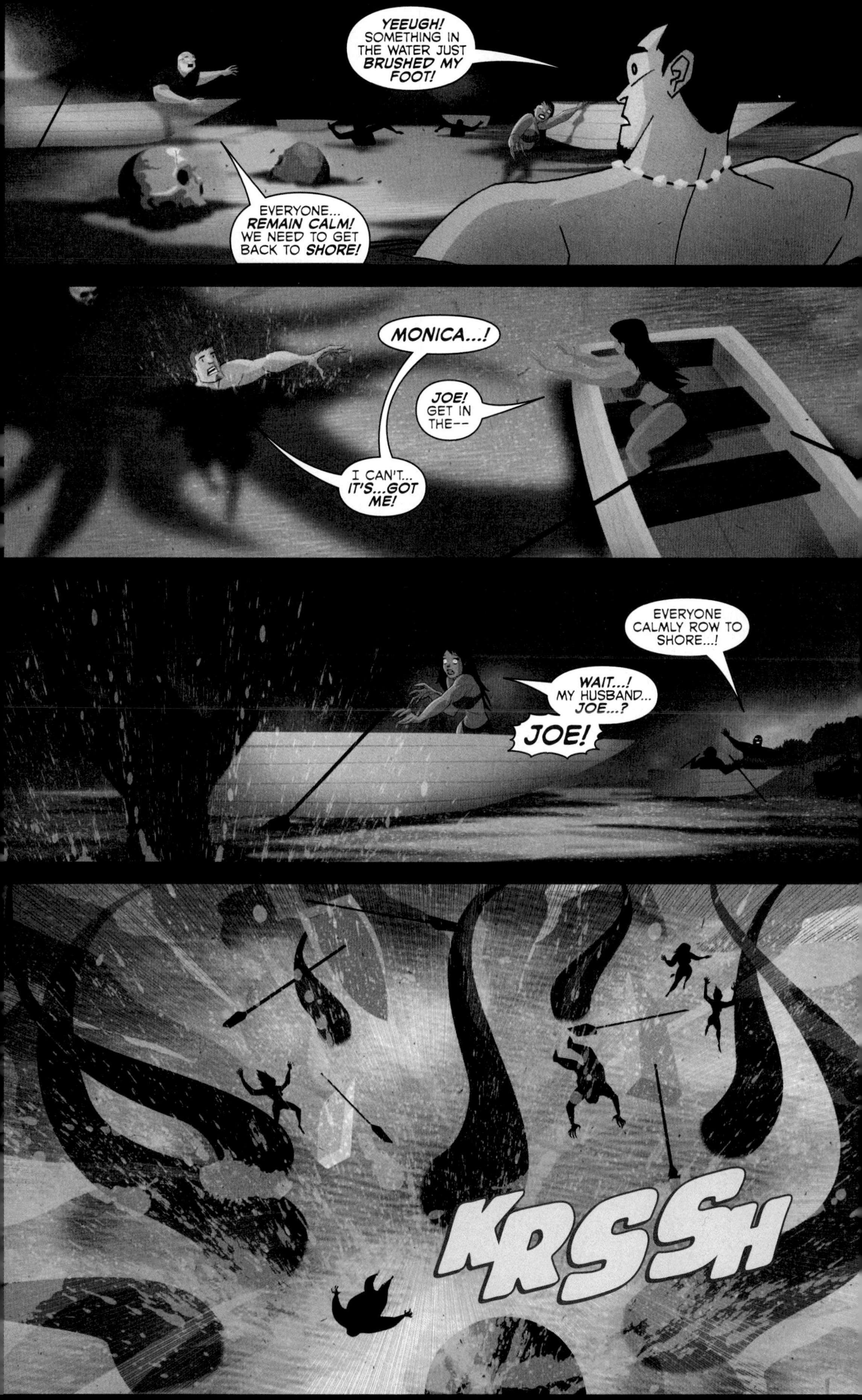

YEEUGH! SOMETHING IN THE WATER JUST BRUSHED MY FOOT!
EVERYONE... REMAIN CALM! WE NEED TO GET BACK TO SHORE!
MONICA...!
JOE! GET IN THE--
I CAN'T... IT'S...GOT ME!
EVERYONE CALMLY ROW TO SHORE...!
WAIT...! MY HUSBAND... JOE...?
JOE!
KRSSH

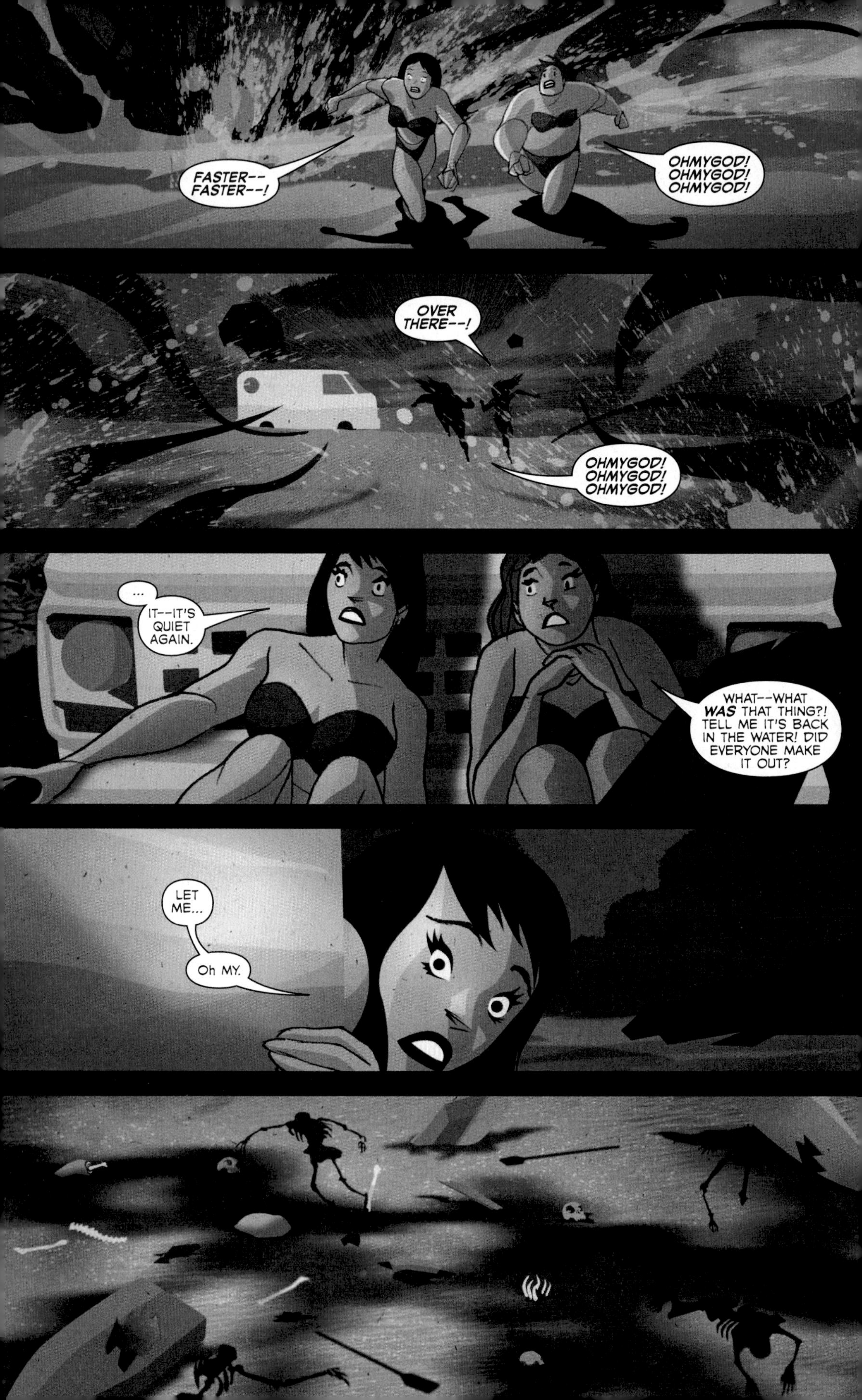
FASTER--
FASTER--!
OHMYGOD!
OHMYGOD!
OHMYGOD!
OVER THERE--!
OHMYGOD!
OHMYGOD!
OHMYGOD!
...
IT--IT'S QUIET AGAIN.
WHAT--WHAT **WAS** THAT THING?! TELL ME IT'S BACK IN THE WATER! DID EVERYONE MAKE IT OUT?
LET ME...
Oh MY.

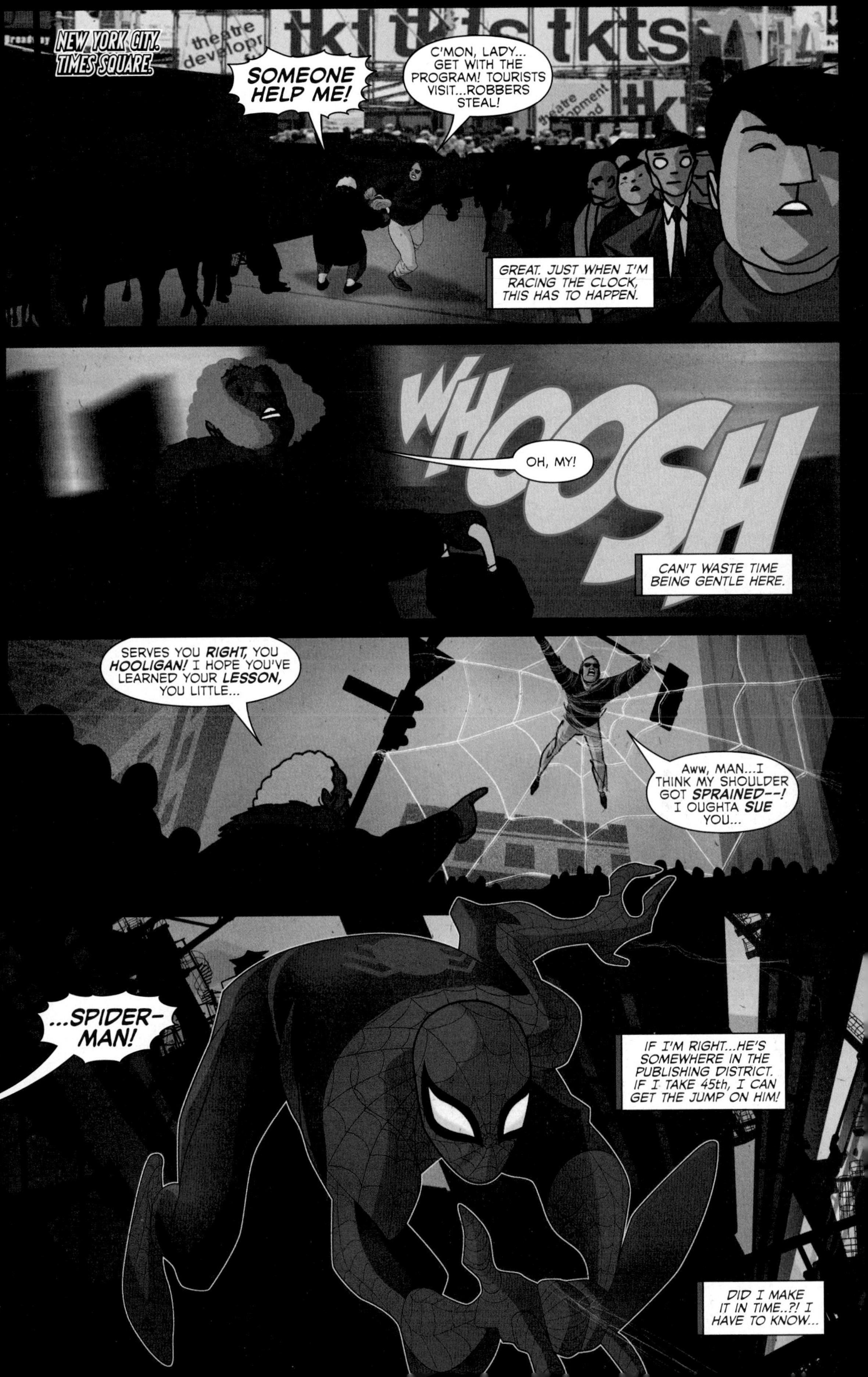
NEW YORK CITY. TIMES SQUARE.
SOMEONE HELP ME!
C'MON, LADY... GET WITH THE PROGRAM! TOURISTS VISIT...ROBBERS STEAL!
GREAT. JUST WHEN I'M RACING THE CLOCK, THIS HAS TO HAPPEN.
WHOOSH
OH, MY!
CAN'T WASTE TIME BEING GENTLE HERE.
SERVES YOU RIGHT, YOU HOOLIGAN! I HOPE YOU'VE LEARNED YOUR LESSON, YOU LITTLE...
AWW, MAN...I THINK MY SHOULDER GOT SPRAINED--! I OUGHTA SUE YOU...
...SPIDER-MAN!
IF I'M RIGHT...HE'S SOMEWHERE IN THE PUBLISHING DISTRICT. IF I TAKE 45th, I CAN GET THE JUMP ON HIM!
DID I MAKE IT IN TIME..?! I HAVE TO KNOW...

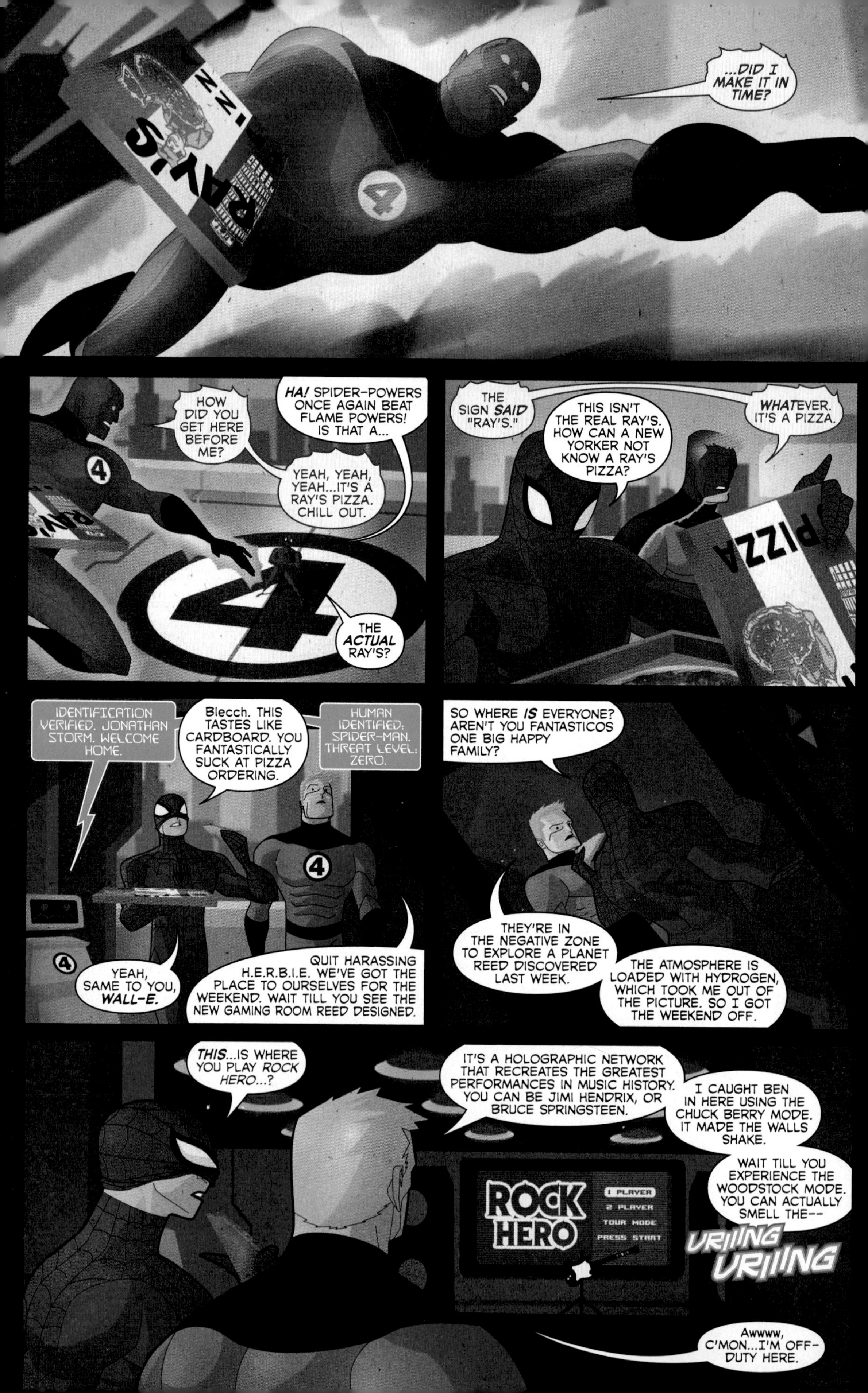
...DID I MAKE IT IN TIME?
HOW DID YOU GET HERE BEFORE ME?
HA! SPIDER-POWERS ONCE AGAIN BEAT FLAME POWERS! IS THAT A...
YEAH, YEAH, YEAH...IT'S A RAY'S PIZZA. CHILL OUT.
THE ACTUAL RAY'S?
THE SIGN SAID "RAY'S."
THIS ISN'T THE REAL RAY'S. HOW CAN A NEW YORKER NOT KNOW A RAY'S PIZZA?
WHATEVER. IT'S A PIZZA.
IDENTIFICATION VERIFIED. JONATHAN STORM. WELCOME HOME.
Blecch. THIS TASTES LIKE CARDBOARD. YOU FANTASTICALLY SUCK AT PIZZA ORDERING.
HUMAN IDENTIFIED: SPIDER-MAN. THREAT LEVEL: ZERO.
YEAH, SAME TO YOU, WALL-E.
QUIT HARASSING H.E.R.B.I.E. WE'VE GOT THE PLACE TO OURSELVES FOR THE WEEKEND. WAIT TILL YOU SEE THE NEW GAMING ROOM REED DESIGNED.
SO WHERE IS EVERYONE? AREN'T YOU FANTASTICOS ONE BIG HAPPY FAMILY?
THEY'RE IN THE NEGATIVE ZONE TO EXPLORE A PLANET REED DISCOVERED LAST WEEK.
THE ATMOSPHERE IS LOADED WITH HYDROGEN, WHICH TOOK ME OUT OF THE PICTURE. SO I GOT THE WEEKEND OFF.
THIS...IS WHERE YOU PLAY ROCK HERO...?
IT'S A HOLOGRAPHIC NETWORK THAT RECREATES THE GREATEST PERFORMANCES IN MUSIC HISTORY. YOU CAN BE JIMI HENDRIX, OR BRUCE SPRINGSTEEN.
I CAUGHT BEN IN HERE USING THE CHUCK BERRY MODE. IT MADE THE WALLS SHAKE.
WAIT TILL YOU EXPERIENCE THE WOODSTOCK MODE. YOU CAN ACTUALLY SMELL THE--
ROCK HERO
1 PLAYER
2 PLAYER
TOUR MODE
PRESS START
URIIING URIIING
Awwww, C'MON...I'M OFF-DUTY HERE.

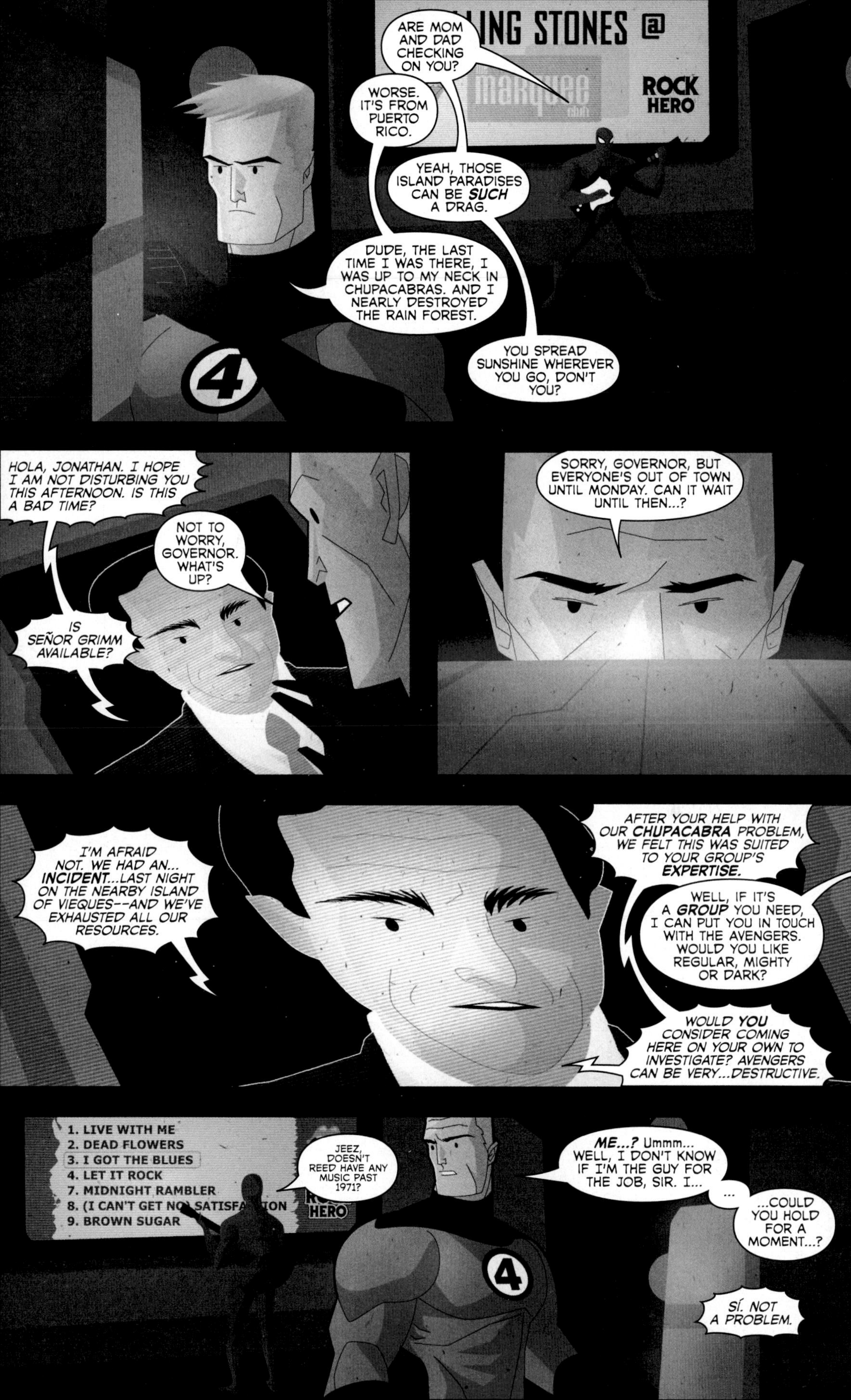
LING STONES @
marquee club
ROCK HERO
ARE MOM AND DAD CHECKING ON YOU?
WORSE. IT'S FROM PUERTO RICO.
YEAH, THOSE ISLAND PARADISES CAN BE SUCH A DRAG.
DUDE, THE LAST TIME I WAS THERE, I WAS UP TO MY NECK IN CHUPACABRAS. AND I NEARLY DESTROYED THE RAIN FOREST.
YOU SPREAD SUNSHINE WHEREVER YOU GO, DON'T YOU?
HOLA, JONATHAN. I HOPE I AM NOT DISTURBING YOU THIS AFTERNOON. IS THIS A BAD TIME?
NOT TO WORRY, GOVERNOR. WHAT'S UP?
IS SEÑOR GRIMM AVAILABLE?
SORRY, GOVERNOR, BUT EVERYONE'S OUT OF TOWN UNTIL MONDAY. CAN IT WAIT UNTIL THEN...?
I'M AFRAID NOT. WE HAD AN... INCIDENT...LAST NIGHT ON THE NEARBY ISLAND OF VIEQUES--AND WE'VE EXHAUSTED ALL OUR RESOURCES.
AFTER YOUR HELP WITH OUR CHUPACABRA PROBLEM, WE FELT THIS WAS SUITED TO YOUR GROUP'S EXPERTISE.
WELL, IF IT'S A GROUP YOU NEED, I CAN PUT YOU IN TOUCH WITH THE AVENGERS. WOULD YOU LIKE REGULAR, MIGHTY OR DARK?
WOULD YOU CONSIDER COMING HERE ON YOUR OWN TO INVESTIGATE? AVENGERS CAN BE VERY...DESTRUCTIVE.
1. LIVE WITH ME
2. DEAD FLOWERS
3. I GOT THE BLUES
4. LET IT ROCK
7. MIDNIGHT RAMBLER
8. (I CAN'T GET NO) SATISFA ION
9. BROWN SUGAR
JEEZ, DOESN'T REED HAVE ANY MUSIC PAST 1971?
ME...? Ummm... WELL, I DON'T KNOW IF I'M THE GUY FOR THE JOB, SIR. I...
...
...COULD YOU HOLD FOR A MOMENT...?
SÍ. NOT A PROBLEM.

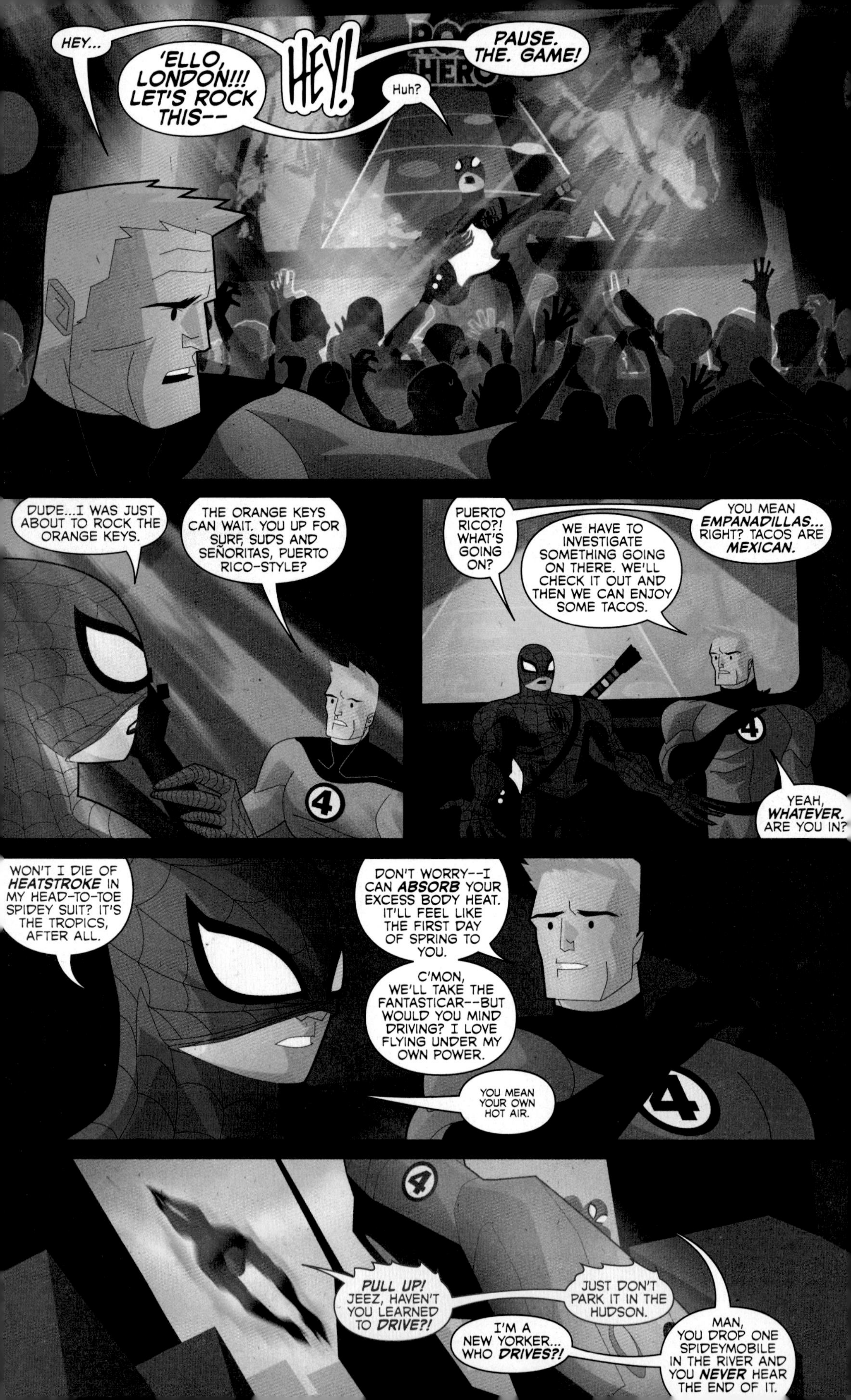
HEY...
'ELLO, LONDON!!! LET'S ROCK THIS--
HEY!
PAUSE. THE. GAME!
Huh?
DUDE...I WAS JUST ABOUT TO ROCK THE ORANGE KEYS.
THE ORANGE KEYS CAN WAIT. YOU UP FOR SURF, SUDS AND SEÑORITAS, PUERTO RICO-STYLE?
PUERTO RICO?! WHAT'S GOING ON?
WE HAVE TO INVESTIGATE SOMETHING GOING ON THERE. WE'LL CHECK IT OUT AND THEN WE CAN ENJOY SOME TACOS.
YOU MEAN EMPANADILLAS... RIGHT? TACOS ARE MEXICAN.
YEAH, WHATEVER. ARE YOU IN?
WON'T I DIE OF HEATSTROKE IN MY HEAD-TO-TOE SPIDEY SUIT? IT'S THE TROPICS, AFTER ALL.
DON'T WORRY--I CAN ABSORB YOUR EXCESS BODY HEAT. IT'LL FEEL LIKE THE FIRST DAY OF SPRING TO YOU.
C'MON, WE'LL TAKE THE FANTASTICAR--BUT WOULD YOU MIND DRIVING? I LOVE FLYING UNDER MY OWN POWER.
YOU MEAN YOUR OWN HOT AIR.
PULL UP! JEEZ, HAVEN'T YOU LEARNED TO DRIVE?!
JUST DON'T PARK IT IN THE HUDSON.
I'M A NEW YORKER... WHO DRIVES?!
MAN, YOU DROP ONE SPIDEYMOBILE IN THE RIVER AND YOU NEVER HEAR THE END OF IT.

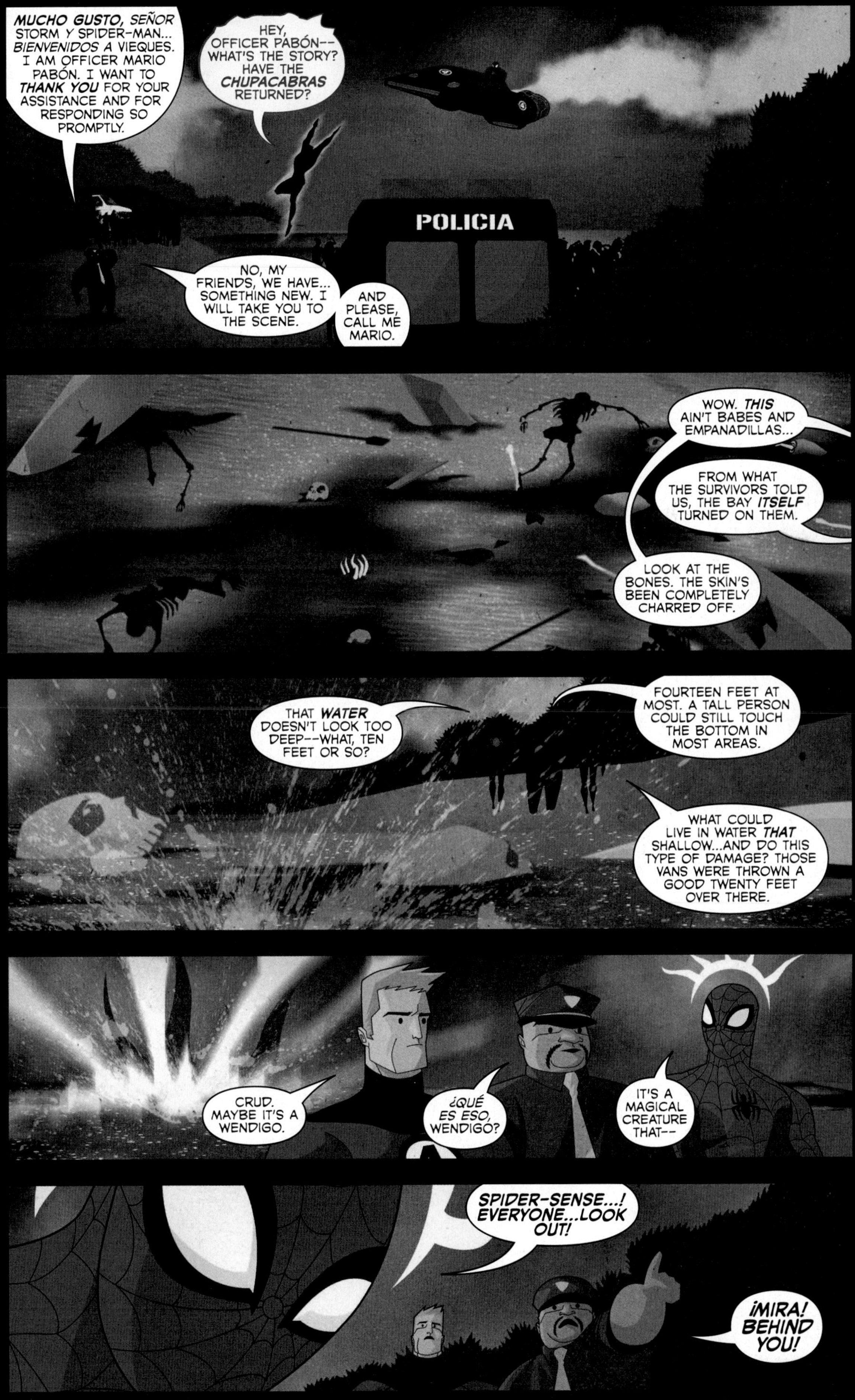

MUCHO GUSTO, SEÑOR STORM Y SPIDER-MAN... BIENVENIDOS A VIEQUES. I AM OFFICER MARIO PABÓN. I WANT TO THANK YOU FOR YOUR ASSISTANCE AND FOR RESPONDING SO PROMPTLY.
HEY, OFFICER PABÓN-- WHAT'S THE STORY? HAVE THE CHUPACABRAS RETURNED?
POLICIA
NO, MY FRIENDS, WE HAVE... SOMETHING NEW. I WILL TAKE YOU TO THE SCENE.
AND PLEASE, CALL ME MARIO.
WOW. THIS AIN'T BABES AND EMPANADILLAS...
FROM WHAT THE SURVIVORS TOLD US, THE BAY ITSELF TURNED ON THEM.
LOOK AT THE BONES. THE SKIN'S BEEN COMPLETELY CHARRED OFF.
THAT WATER DOESN'T LOOK TOO DEEP--WHAT, TEN FEET OR SO?
FOURTEEN FEET AT MOST. A TALL PERSON COULD STILL TOUCH THE BOTTOM IN MOST AREAS.
WHAT COULD LIVE IN WATER THAT SHALLOW...AND DO THIS TYPE OF DAMAGE? THOSE VANS WERE THROWN A GOOD TWENTY FEET OVER THERE.
CRUD. MAYBE IT'S A WENDIGO.
¿QUÉ ES ESO, WENDIGO?
IT'S A MAGICAL CREATURE THAT--
SPIDER-SENSE...! EVERYONE...LOOK OUT!
¡MIRA! BEHIND YOU!

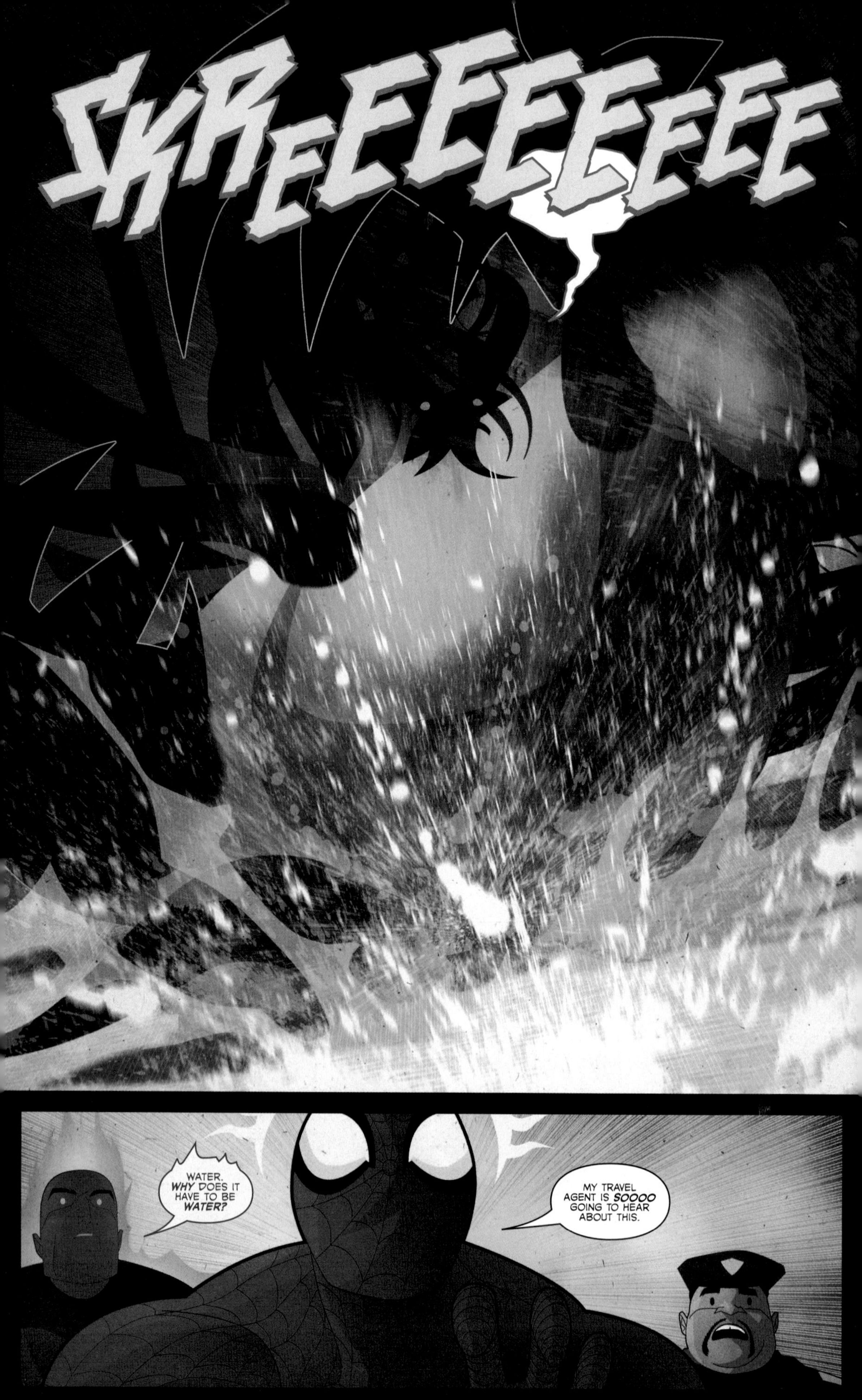
SKREEEEEEEE
WATER. WHY DOES IT HAVE TO BE WATER?
MY TRAVEL AGENT IS SOOOO GOING TO HEAR ABOUT THIS.

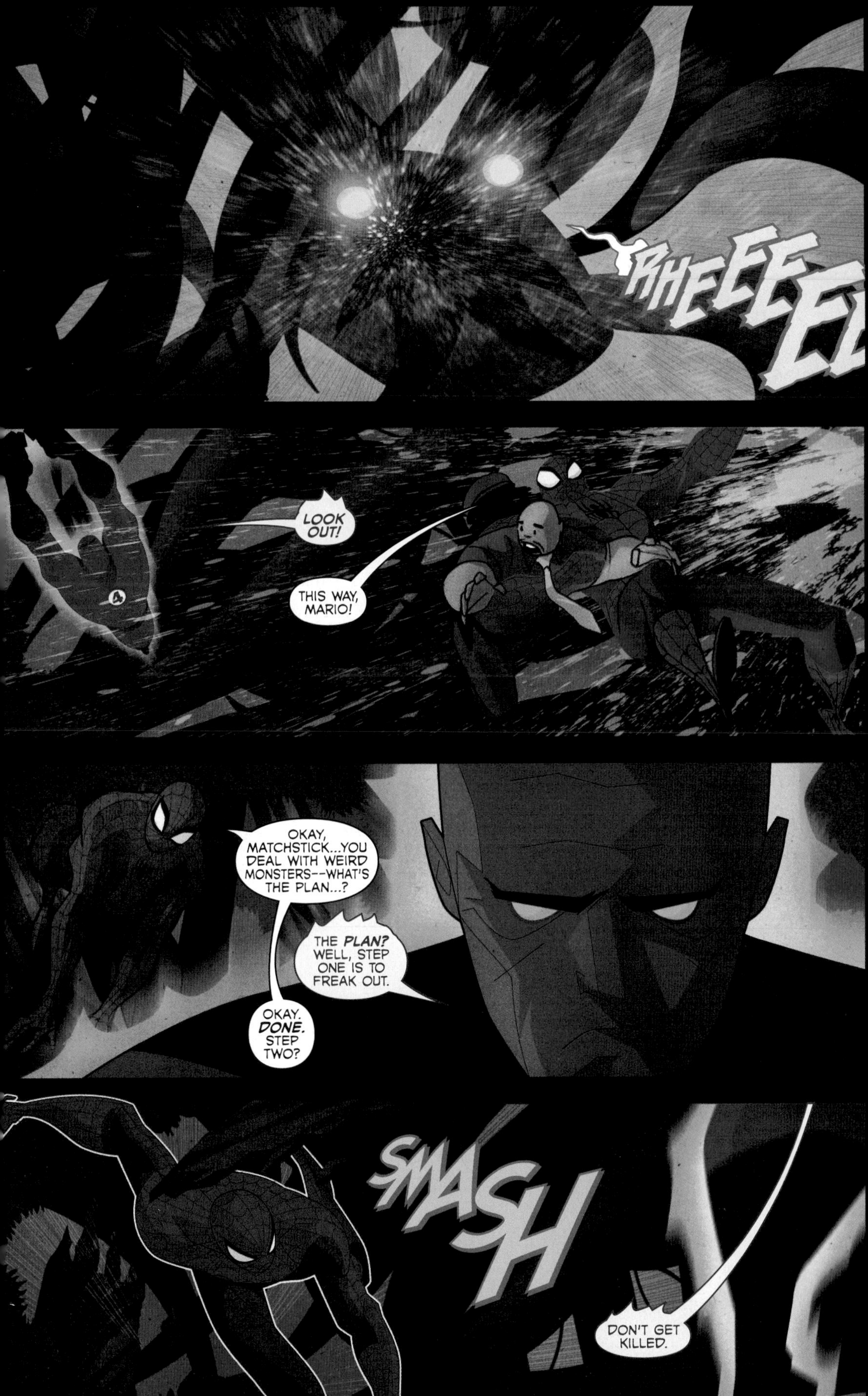
RHEEEEE
LOOK OUT!
THIS WAY, MARIO!
OKAY, MATCHSTICK...YOU DEAL WITH WEIRD MONSTERS--WHAT'S THE PLAN...?
THE *PLAN?* WELL, STEP ONE IS TO FREAK OUT.
OKAY. *DONE.* STEP TWO?
SMASH
DON'T GET KILLED.

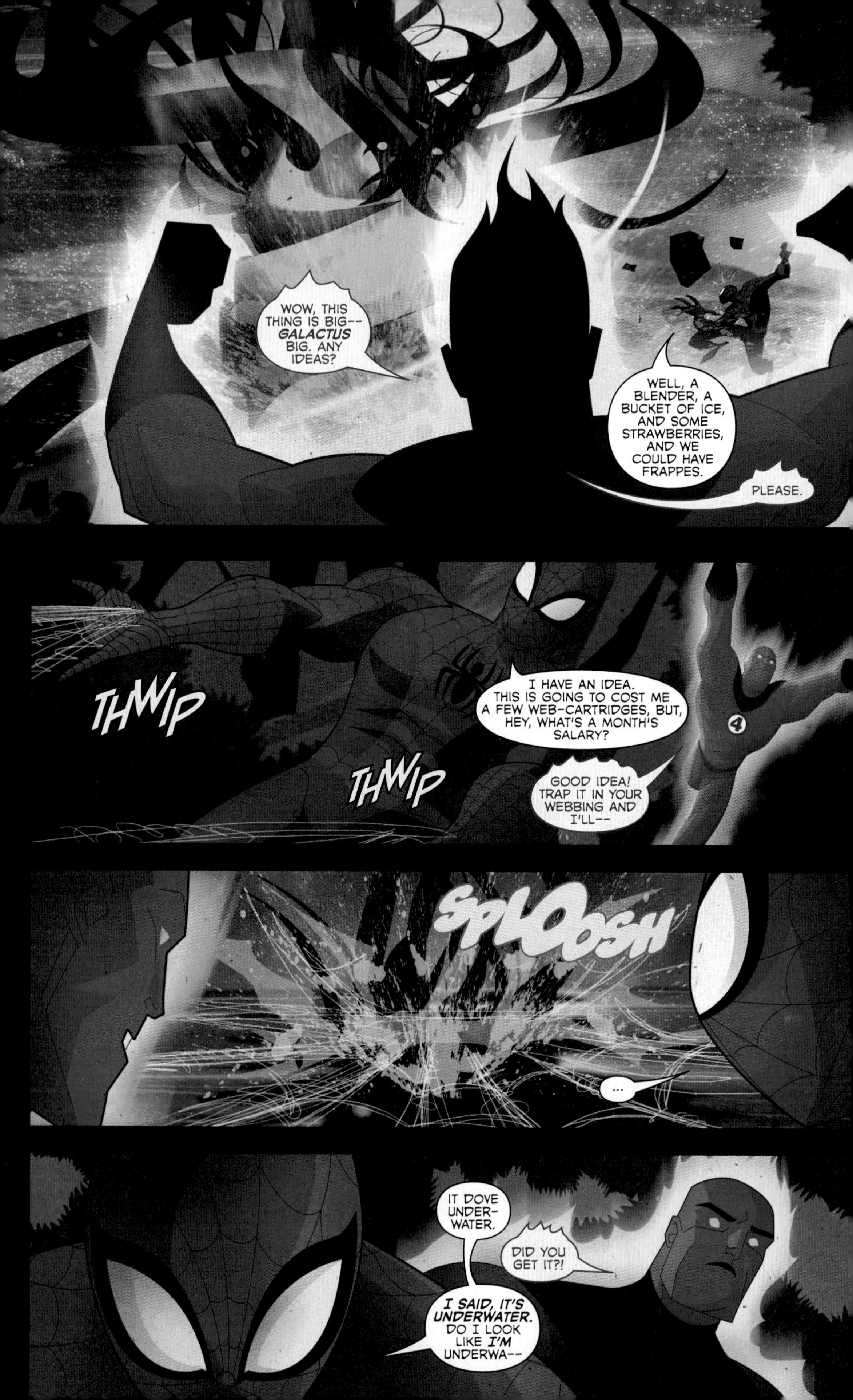
WOW, THIS THING IS BIG-- GALACTUS BIG. ANY IDEAS?
WELL, A BLENDER, A BUCKET OF ICE, AND SOME STRAWBERRIES, AND WE COULD HAVE FRAPPES.
PLEASE.
THWIP
I HAVE AN IDEA. THIS IS GOING TO COST ME A FEW WEB-CARTRIDGES, BUT, HEY, WHAT'S A MONTH'S SALARY?
THWIP
GOOD IDEA! TRAP IT IN YOUR WEBBING AND I'LL--
SPLOOSH
...
IT DOVE UNDER-WATER.
DID YOU GET IT?!
I SAID, IT'S UNDERWATER. DO I LOOK LIKE I'M UNDERWA--

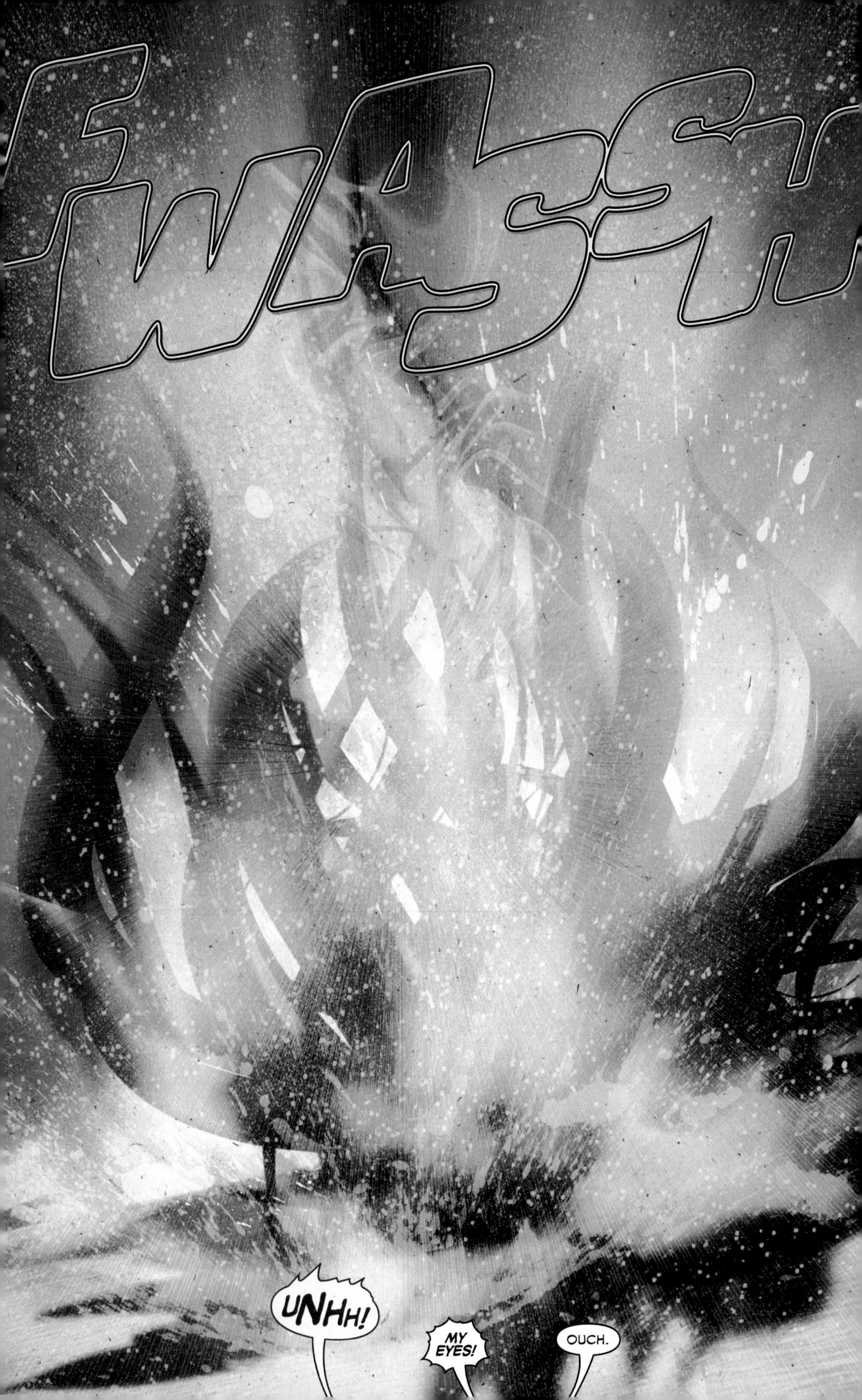
UNHH!
MY EYES!
OUCH.

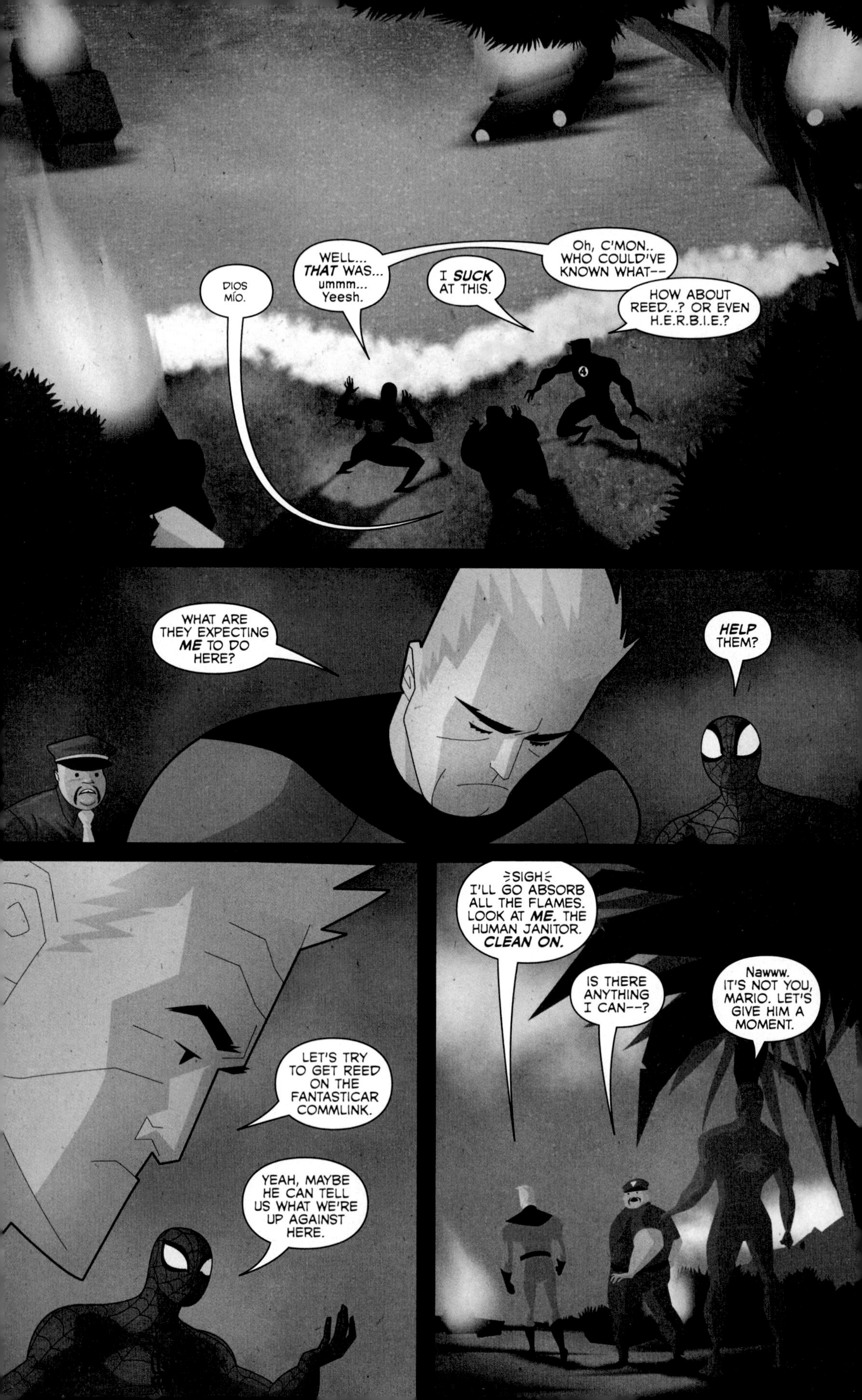
DIOS MÍO.
WELL... THAT WAS... ummm... Yeesh.
Oh, C'MON.. WHO COULD'VE KNOWN WHAT--
I SUCK AT THIS.
HOW ABOUT REED...? OR EVEN H.E.R.B.I.E.?
WHAT ARE THEY EXPECTING ME TO DO HERE?
HELP THEM?
LET'S TRY TO GET REED ON THE FANTASTICAR COMMLINK.
YEAH, MAYBE HE CAN TELL US WHAT WE'RE UP AGAINST HERE.
≥SIGH≤ I'LL GO ABSORB ALL THE FLAMES. LOOK AT ME. THE HUMAN JANITOR. CLEAN ON.
IS THERE ANYTHING I CAN--?
Nawww. IT'S NOT YOU, MARIO. LET'S GIVE HIM A MOMENT.

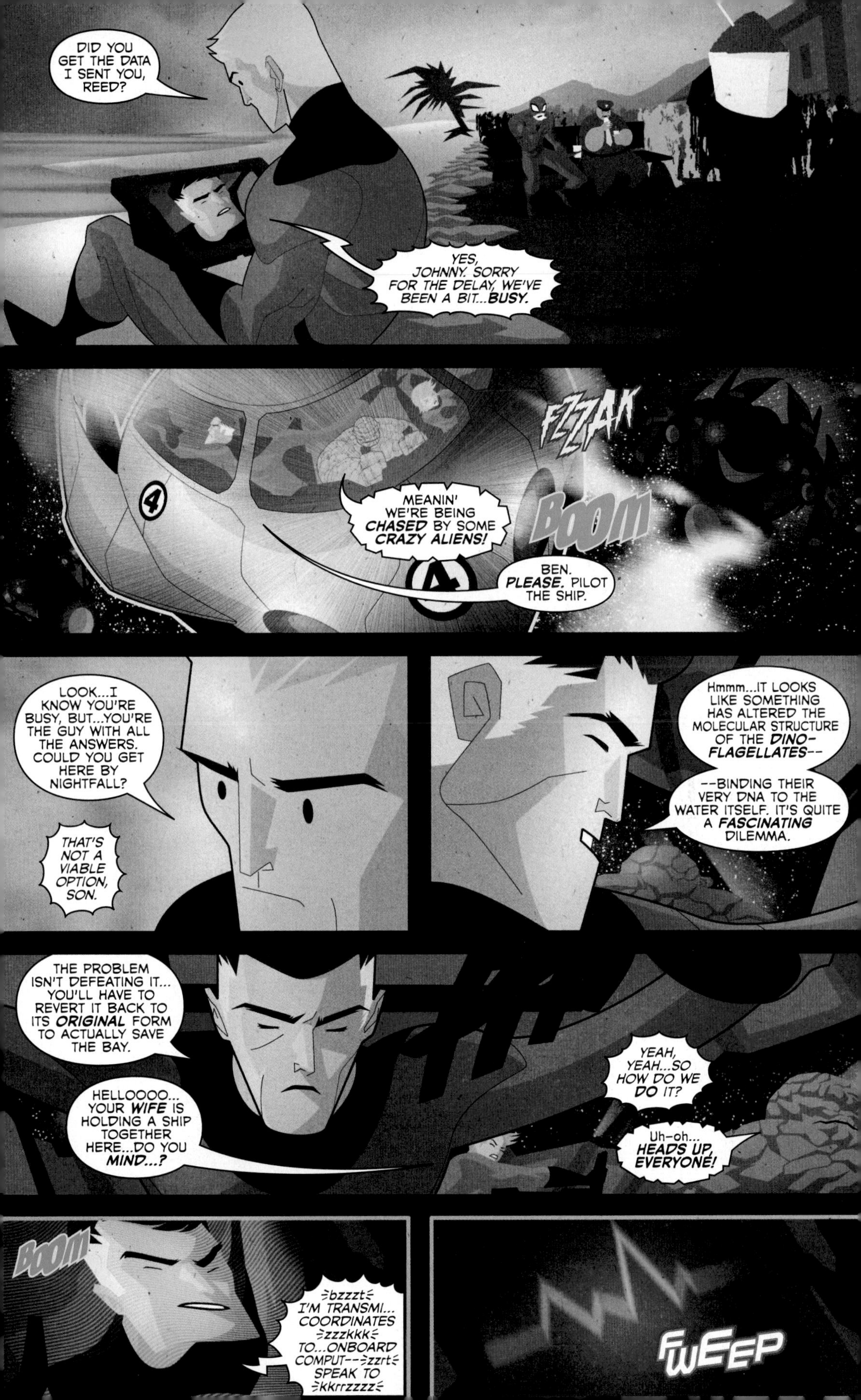
DID YOU GET THE DATA I SENT YOU, REED?
YES, JOHNNY. SORRY FOR THE DELAY, WE'VE BEEN A BIT...BUSY.
FZZAK
MEANIN' WE'RE BEING CHASED BY SOME CRAZY ALIENS!
BOOM
BEN. PLEASE. PILOT THE SHIP.
LOOK...I KNOW YOU'RE BUSY, BUT...YOU'RE THE GUY WITH ALL THE ANSWERS. COULD YOU GET HERE BY NIGHTFALL?
THAT'S NOT A VIABLE OPTION, SON.
Hmmm...IT LOOKS LIKE SOMETHING HAS ALTERED THE MOLECULAR STRUCTURE OF THE DINO-FLAGELLATES--
--BINDING THEIR VERY DNA TO THE WATER ITSELF. IT'S QUITE A FASCINATING DILEMMA.
THE PROBLEM ISN'T DEFEATING IT... YOU'LL HAVE TO REVERT IT BACK TO ITS ORIGINAL FORM TO ACTUALLY SAVE THE BAY.
HELLOOOO... YOUR WIFE IS HOLDING A SHIP TOGETHER HERE...DO YOU MIND...?
YEAH, YEAH...SO HOW DO WE DO IT?
Uh-oh... HEADS UP, EVERYONE!
BOOM
bzzzt I'M TRANSMI... COORDINATES zzzkkk TO...ONBOARD COMPUT-- zzrt SPEAK TO kkrrzzzz
FWEEP

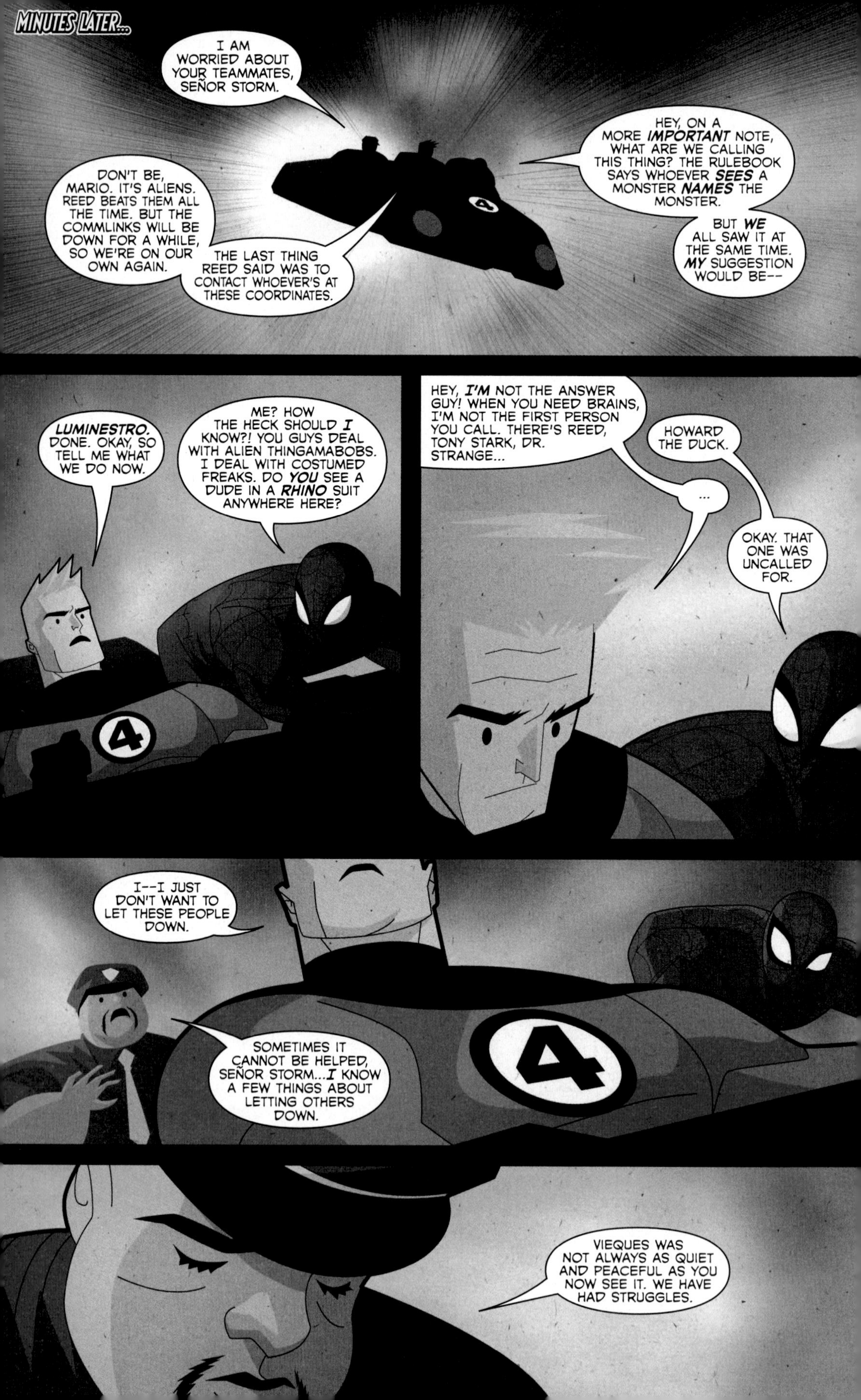
MINUTES LATER...
I AM WORRIED ABOUT YOUR TEAMMATES, SEÑOR STORM.
DON'T BE, MARIO. IT'S ALIENS. REED BEATS THEM ALL THE TIME. BUT THE COMMLINKS WILL BE DOWN FOR A WHILE, SO WE'RE ON OUR OWN AGAIN.
THE LAST THING REED SAID WAS TO CONTACT WHOEVER'S AT THESE COORDINATES.
HEY, ON A MORE IMPORTANT NOTE, WHAT ARE WE CALLING THIS THING? THE RULEBOOK SAYS WHOEVER SEES A MONSTER NAMES THE MONSTER.
BUT WE ALL SAW IT AT THE SAME TIME. MY SUGGESTION WOULD BE--
LUMINESTRO. DONE. OKAY, SO TELL ME WHAT WE DO NOW.
ME? HOW THE HECK SHOULD I KNOW?! YOU GUYS DEAL WITH ALIEN THINGAMABOBS. I DEAL WITH COSTUMED FREAKS. DO YOU SEE A DUDE IN A RHINO SUIT ANYWHERE HERE?
HEY, I'M NOT THE ANSWER GUY! WHEN YOU NEED BRAINS, I'M NOT THE FIRST PERSON YOU CALL. THERE'S REED, TONY STARK, DR. STRANGE...
HOWARD THE DUCK.
...
OKAY. THAT ONE WAS UNCALLED FOR.
I--I JUST DON'T WANT TO LET THESE PEOPLE DOWN.
SOMETIMES IT CANNOT BE HELPED, SEÑOR STORM...I KNOW A FEW THINGS ABOUT LETTING OTHERS DOWN.
VIEQUES WAS NOT ALWAYS AS QUIET AND PEACEFUL AS YOU NOW SEE IT. WE HAVE HAD STRUGGLES.

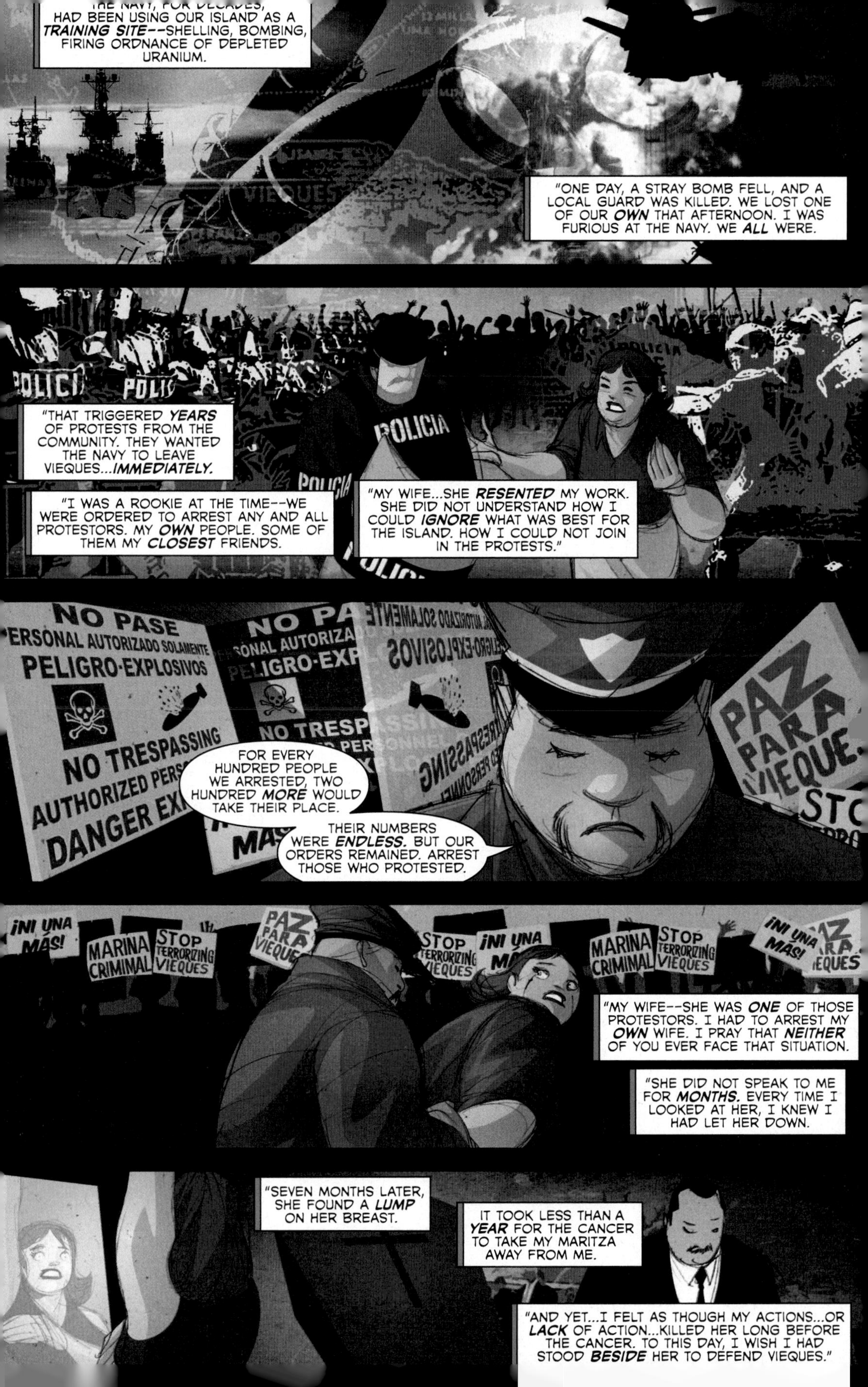
THE NAVY, FOR DECADES, HAD BEEN USING OUR ISLAND AS A TRAINING SITE--SHELLING, BOMBING, FIRING ORDNANCE OF DEPLETED URANIUM.
VIEQUES
"ONE DAY, A STRAY BOMB FELL, AND A LOCAL GUARD WAS KILLED. WE LOST ONE OF OUR OWN THAT AFTERNOON. I WAS FURIOUS AT THE NAVY. WE ALL WERE.
POLICIA
"THAT TRIGGERED YEARS OF PROTESTS FROM THE COMMUNITY. THEY WANTED THE NAVY TO LEAVE VIEQUES...IMMEDIATELY.
"I WAS A ROOKIE AT THE TIME--WE WERE ORDERED TO ARREST ANY AND ALL PROTESTORS. MY OWN PEOPLE. SOME OF THEM MY CLOSEST FRIENDS.
"MY WIFE...SHE RESENTED MY WORK. SHE DID NOT UNDERSTAND HOW I COULD IGNORE WHAT WAS BEST FOR THE ISLAND. HOW I COULD NOT JOIN IN THE PROTESTS."
NO PASE
PERSONAL AUTORIZADO SOLAMENTE
PELIGRO-EXPLOSIVOS
NO TRESPASSING
AUTHORIZED PERS
DANGER EX
PAZ PARA VIEQUE
FOR EVERY HUNDRED PEOPLE WE ARRESTED, TWO HUNDRED MORE WOULD TAKE THEIR PLACE.
THEIR NUMBERS WERE ENDLESS. BUT OUR ORDERS REMAINED. ARREST THOSE WHO PROTESTED.
¡NI UNA MÁS!
MARINA CRIMINAL
STOP TERRORIZING VIEQUES
"MY WIFE--SHE WAS ONE OF THOSE PROTESTORS. I HAD TO ARREST MY OWN WIFE. I PRAY THAT NEITHER OF YOU EVER FACE THAT SITUATION.
"SHE DID NOT SPEAK TO ME FOR MONTHS. EVERY TIME I LOOKED AT HER, I KNEW I HAD LET HER DOWN.
"SEVEN MONTHS LATER, SHE FOUND A LUMP ON HER BREAST.
IT TOOK LESS THAN A YEAR FOR THE CANCER TO TAKE MY MARITZA AWAY FROM ME.
"AND YET...I FELT AS THOUGH MY ACTIONS...OR LACK OF ACTION...KILLED HER LONG BEFORE THE CANCER. TO THIS DAY, I WISH I HAD STOOD BESIDE HER TO DEFEND VIEQUES."

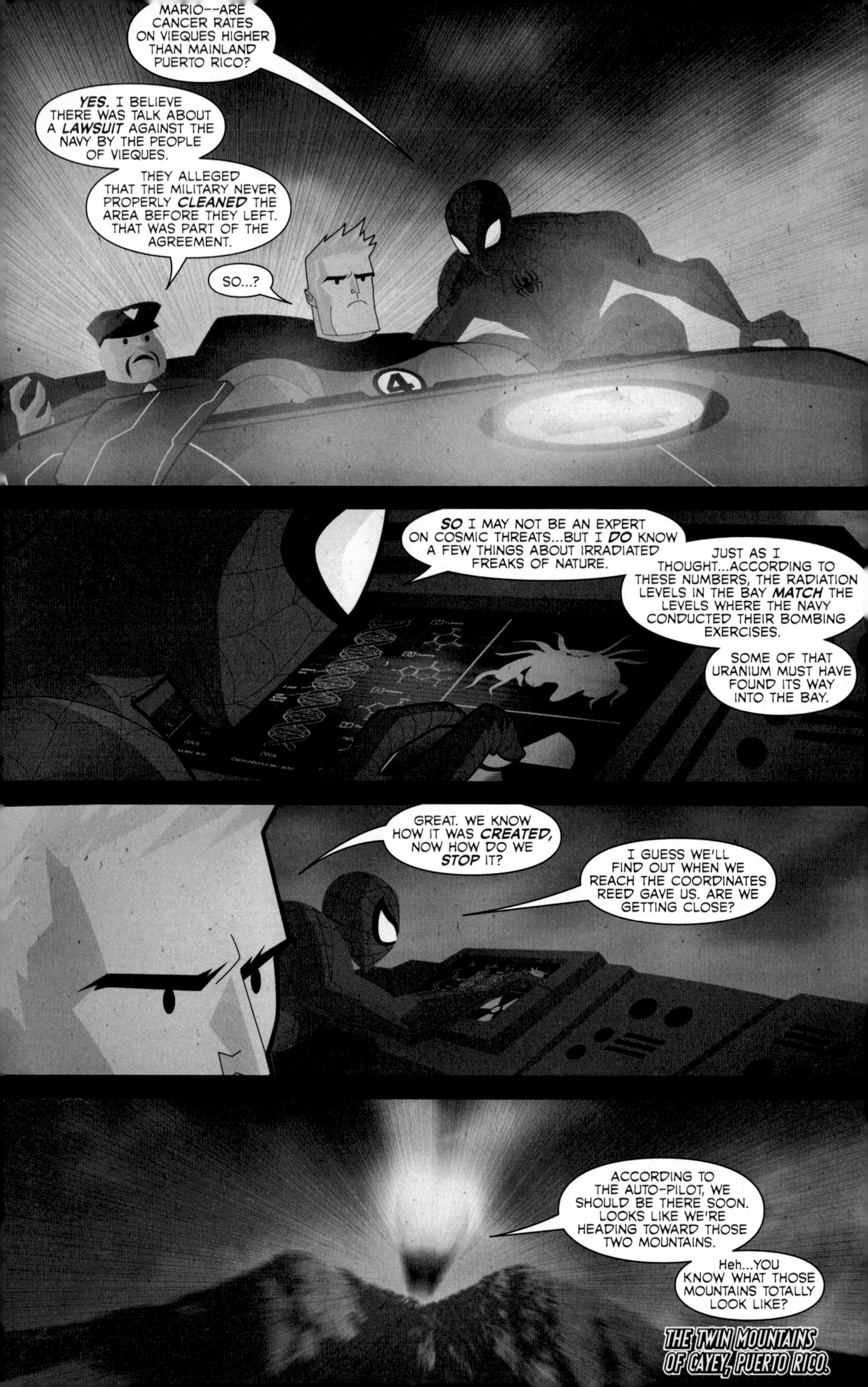
MARIO--ARE CANCER RATES ON VIEQUES HIGHER THAN MAINLAND PUERTO RICO?
YES. I BELIEVE THERE WAS TALK ABOUT A *LAWSUIT* AGAINST THE NAVY BY THE PEOPLE OF VIEQUES.
THEY ALLEGED THAT THE MILITARY NEVER PROPERLY *CLEANED* THE AREA BEFORE THEY LEFT. THAT WAS PART OF THE AGREEMENT.
SO...?
SO I MAY NOT BE AN EXPERT ON COSMIC THREATS...BUT I *DO* KNOW A FEW THINGS ABOUT IRRADIATED FREAKS OF NATURE.
JUST AS I THOUGHT...ACCORDING TO THESE NUMBERS, THE RADIATION LEVELS IN THE BAY *MATCH* THE LEVELS WHERE THE NAVY CONDUCTED THEIR BOMBING EXERCISES.
SOME OF THAT URANIUM MUST HAVE FOUND ITS WAY INTO THE BAY.
RNA
DNA
GREAT. WE KNOW HOW IT WAS *CREATED*, NOW HOW DO WE *STOP* IT?
I GUESS WE'LL FIND OUT WHEN WE REACH THE COORDINATES REED GAVE US. ARE WE GETTING CLOSE?
ACCORDING TO THE AUTO-PILOT, WE SHOULD BE THERE SOON. LOOKS LIKE WE'RE HEADING TOWARD THOSE TWO MOUNTAINS.
Heh...YOU KNOW WHAT THOSE MOUNTAINS TOTALLY LOOK LIKE?
THE TWIN MOUNTAINS OF CAYEY, PUERTO RICO.

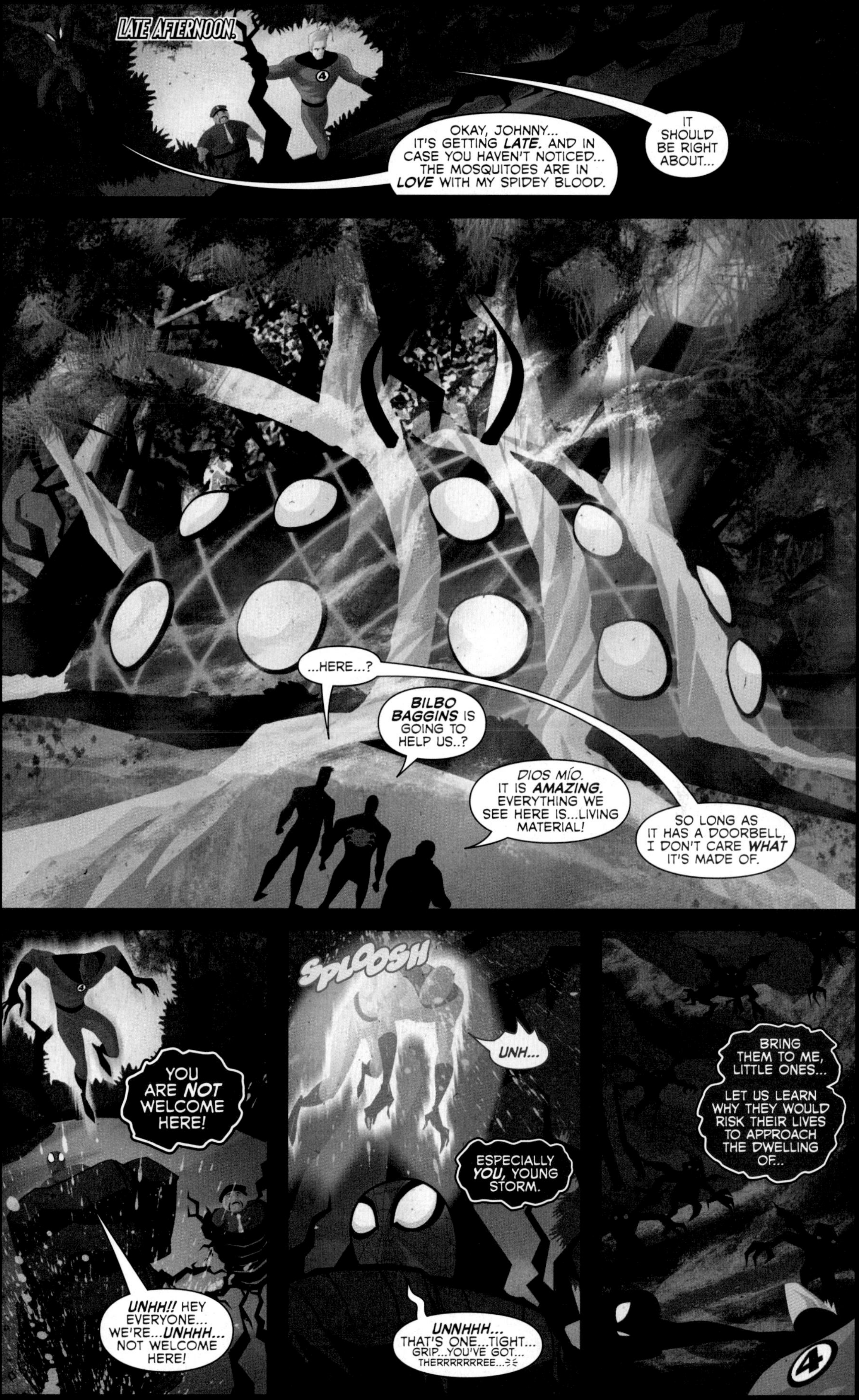
LATE AFTERNOON.
OKAY, JOHNNY... IT'S GETTING LATE. AND IN CASE YOU HAVEN'T NOTICED... THE MOSQUITOES ARE IN LOVE WITH MY SPIDEY BLOOD.
IT SHOULD BE RIGHT ABOUT...
...HERE...?
BILBO BAGGINS IS GOING TO HELP US..?
DIOS MÍO. IT IS AMAZING. EVERYTHING WE SEE HERE IS...LIVING MATERIAL!
SO LONG AS IT HAS A DOORBELL, I DON'T CARE WHAT IT'S MADE OF.
YOU ARE NOT WELCOME HERE!
UNHH!! HEY EVERYONE... WE'RE...UNHHH... NOT WELCOME HERE!
SPLOOSH
UNH...
ESPECIALLY YOU, YOUNG STORM.
UNNHHH... THAT'S ONE...TIGHT... GRIP...YOU'VE GOT... THERRRRRRREE...
BRING THEM TO ME, LITTLE ONES...
LET US LEARN WHY THEY WOULD RISK THEIR LIVES TO APPROACH THE DWELLING OF...

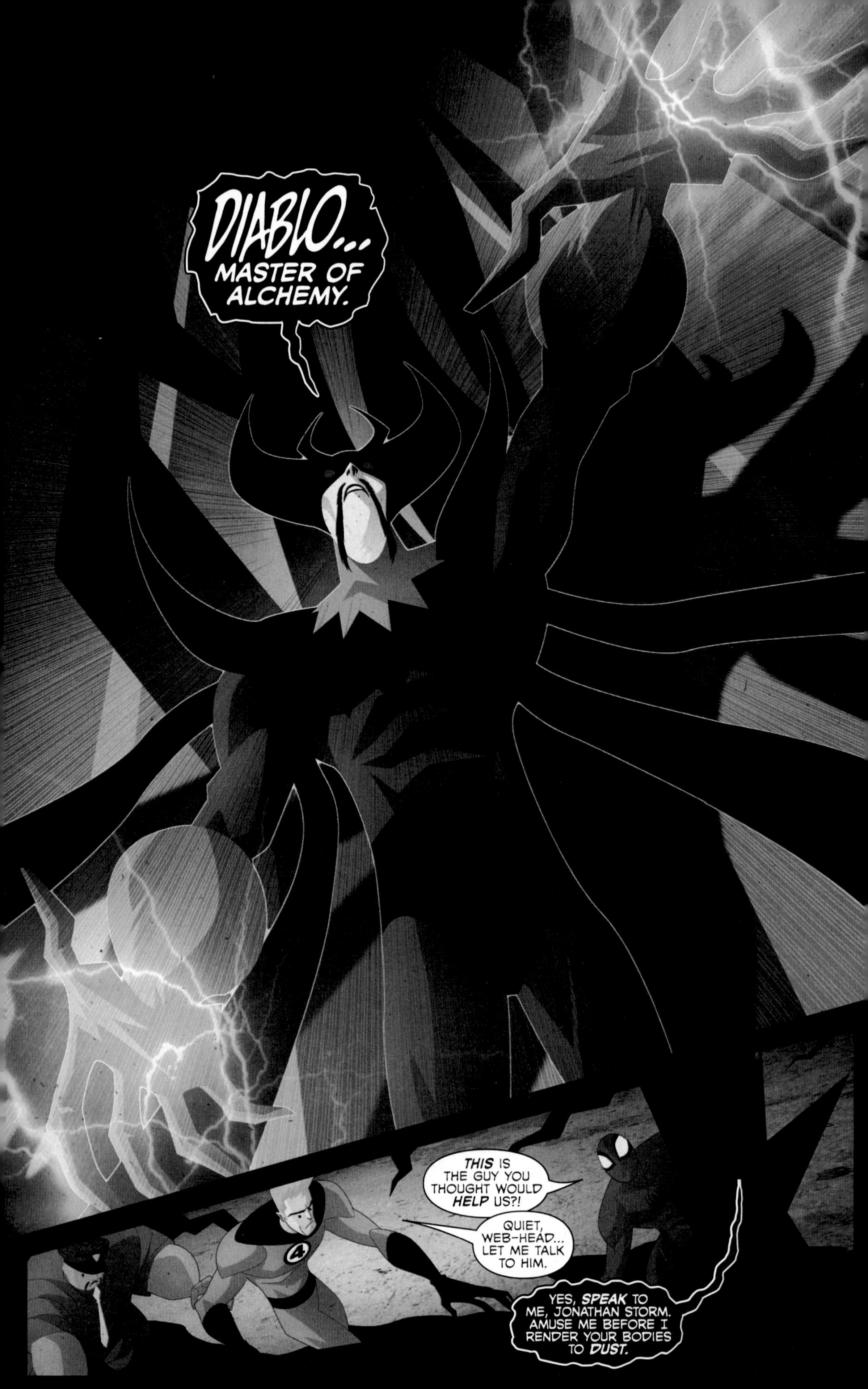
DIABLO... MASTER OF ALCHEMY.
THIS IS THE GUY YOU THOUGHT WOULD HELP US?!
QUIET, WEB-HEAD... LET ME TALK TO HIM.
YES, SPEAK TO ME, JONATHAN STORM. AMUSE ME BEFORE I RENDER YOUR BODIES TO DUST.

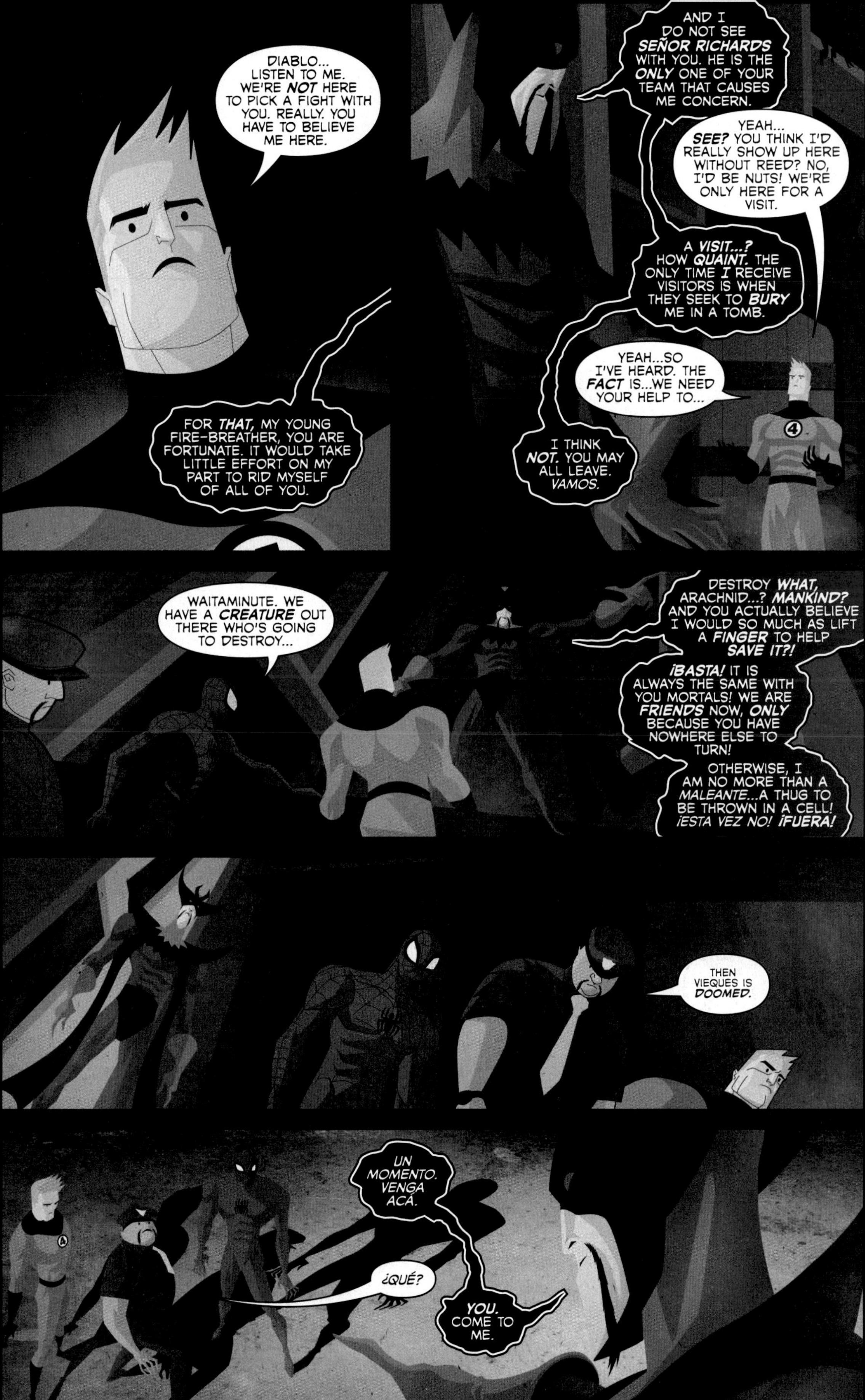
DIABLO... LISTEN TO ME. WE'RE NOT HERE TO PICK A FIGHT WITH YOU. REALLY. YOU HAVE TO BELIEVE ME HERE.
FOR THAT, MY YOUNG FIRE-BREATHER, YOU ARE FORTUNATE. IT WOULD TAKE LITTLE EFFORT ON MY PART TO RID MYSELF OF ALL OF YOU.
AND I DO NOT SEE SEÑOR RICHARDS WITH YOU. HE IS THE ONLY ONE OF YOUR TEAM THAT CAUSES ME CONCERN.
YEAH... SEE? YOU THINK I'D REALLY SHOW UP HERE WITHOUT REED? NO, I'D BE NUTS! WE'RE ONLY HERE FOR A VISIT.
A VISIT...? HOW QUAINT. THE ONLY TIME I RECEIVE VISITORS IS WHEN THEY SEEK TO BURY ME IN A TOMB.
YEAH...SO I'VE HEARD. THE FACT IS...WE NEED YOUR HELP TO...
I THINK NOT. YOU MAY ALL LEAVE. VAMOS.
WAITAMINUTE. WE HAVE A CREATURE OUT THERE WHO'S GOING TO DESTROY...
DESTROY WHAT, ARACHNID...? MANKIND? AND YOU ACTUALLY BELIEVE I WOULD SO MUCH AS LIFT A FINGER TO HELP SAVE IT?!
¡BASTA! IT IS ALWAYS THE SAME WITH YOU MORTALS! WE ARE FRIENDS NOW, ONLY BECAUSE YOU HAVE NOWHERE ELSE TO TURN!
OTHERWISE, I AM NO MORE THAN A MALEANTE...A THUG TO BE THROWN IN A CELL! ¡ESTA VEZ NO! ¡FUERA!
THEN VIEQUES IS DOOMED.
UN MOMENTO. VENGA ACÁ.
¿QUÉ?
YOU. COME TO ME.

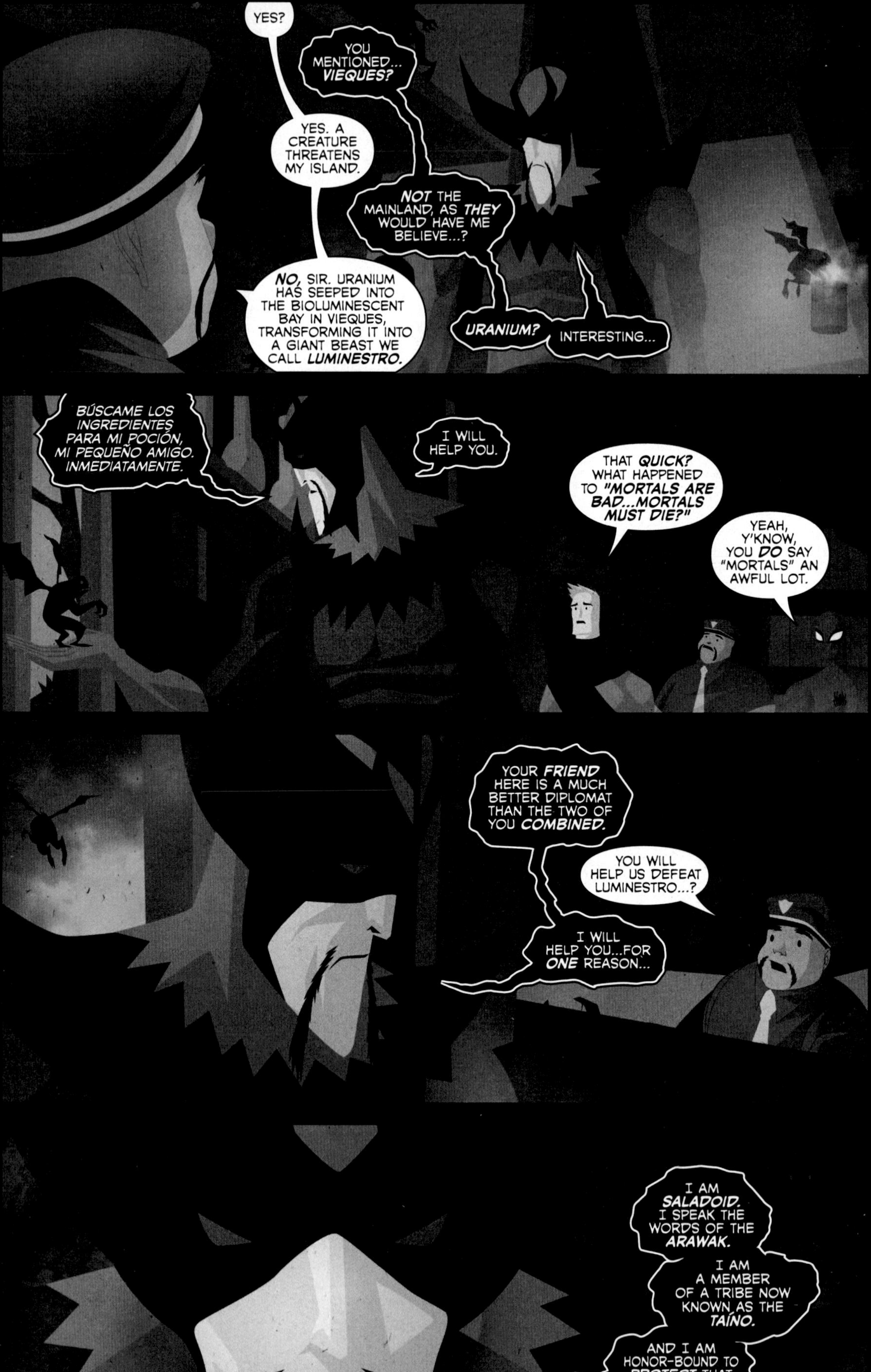
YES?
YOU MENTIONED... VIEQUES?
YES. A CREATURE THREATENS MY ISLAND.
NOT THE MAINLAND, AS THEY WOULD HAVE ME BELIEVE...?
NO, SIR. URANIUM HAS SEEPED INTO THE BIOLUMINESCENT BAY IN VIEQUES, TRANSFORMING IT INTO A GIANT BEAST WE CALL LUMINESTRO.
URANIUM?
INTERESTING...
BÚSCAME LOS INGREDIENTES PARA MI POCIÓN, MI PEQUEÑO AMIGO. INMEDIATAMENTE.
I WILL HELP YOU.
THAT QUICK? WHAT HAPPENED TO "MORTALS ARE BAD...MORTALS MUST DIE?"
YEAH, Y'KNOW, YOU DO SAY "MORTALS" AN AWFUL LOT.
YOUR FRIEND HERE IS A MUCH BETTER DIPLOMAT THAN THE TWO OF YOU COMBINED.
YOU WILL HELP US DEFEAT LUMINESTRO...?
I WILL HELP YOU...FOR ONE REASON...
I AM SALADOID. I SPEAK THE WORDS OF THE ARAWAK.
I AM A MEMBER OF A TRIBE NOW KNOWN AS THE TAÍNO.
AND I AM HONOR-BOUND TO PROTECT THAT LAND.

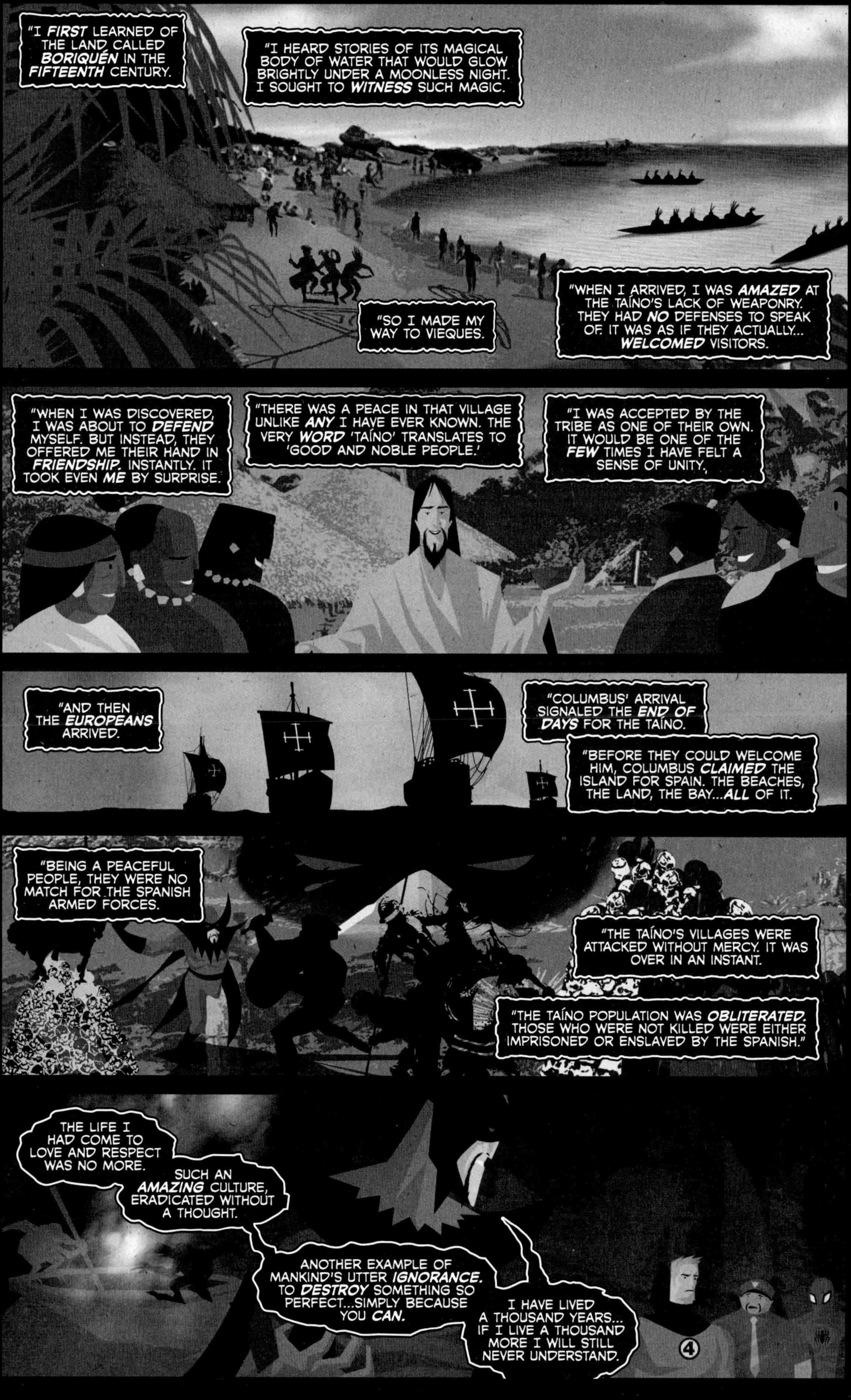
"I FIRST LEARNED OF THE LAND CALLED BORIQUÉN IN THE FIFTEENTH CENTURY.
"I HEARD STORIES OF ITS MAGICAL BODY OF WATER THAT WOULD GLOW BRIGHTLY UNDER A MOONLESS NIGHT. I SOUGHT TO WITNESS SUCH MAGIC.
"SO I MADE MY WAY TO VIEQUES.
"WHEN I ARRIVED, I WAS AMAZED AT THE TAÍNO'S LACK OF WEAPONRY. THEY HAD NO DEFENSES TO SPEAK OF. IT WAS AS IF THEY ACTUALLY... WELCOMED VISITORS.
"WHEN I WAS DISCOVERED, I WAS ABOUT TO DEFEND MYSELF. BUT INSTEAD, THEY OFFERED ME THEIR HAND IN FRIENDSHIP. INSTANTLY. IT TOOK EVEN ME BY SURPRISE.
"THERE WAS A PEACE IN THAT VILLAGE UNLIKE ANY I HAVE EVER KNOWN. THE VERY WORD 'TAÍNO' TRANSLATES TO 'GOOD AND NOBLE PEOPLE.'
"I WAS ACCEPTED BY THE TRIBE AS ONE OF THEIR OWN. IT WOULD BE ONE OF THE FEW TIMES I HAVE FELT A SENSE OF UNITY.
"AND THEN THE EUROPEANS ARRIVED.
"COLUMBUS' ARRIVAL SIGNALED THE END OF DAYS FOR THE TAÍNO.
"BEFORE THEY COULD WELCOME HIM, COLUMBUS CLAIMED THE ISLAND FOR SPAIN. THE BEACHES, THE LAND, THE BAY...ALL OF IT.
"BEING A PEACEFUL PEOPLE, THEY WERE NO MATCH FOR THE SPANISH ARMED FORCES.
"THE TAÍNO'S VILLAGES WERE ATTACKED WITHOUT MERCY. IT WAS OVER IN AN INSTANT.
"THE TAÍNO POPULATION WAS OBLITERATED. THOSE WHO WERE NOT KILLED WERE EITHER IMPRISONED OR ENSLAVED BY THE SPANISH."
THE LIFE I HAD COME TO LOVE AND RESPECT WAS NO MORE.
SUCH AN AMAZING CULTURE, ERADICATED WITHOUT A THOUGHT.
ANOTHER EXAMPLE OF MANKIND'S UTTER IGNORANCE. TO DESTROY SOMETHING SO PERFECT...SIMPLY BECAUSE YOU CAN.
I HAVE LIVED A THOUSAND YEARS... IF I LIVE A THOUSAND MORE I WILL STILL NEVER UNDERSTAND.

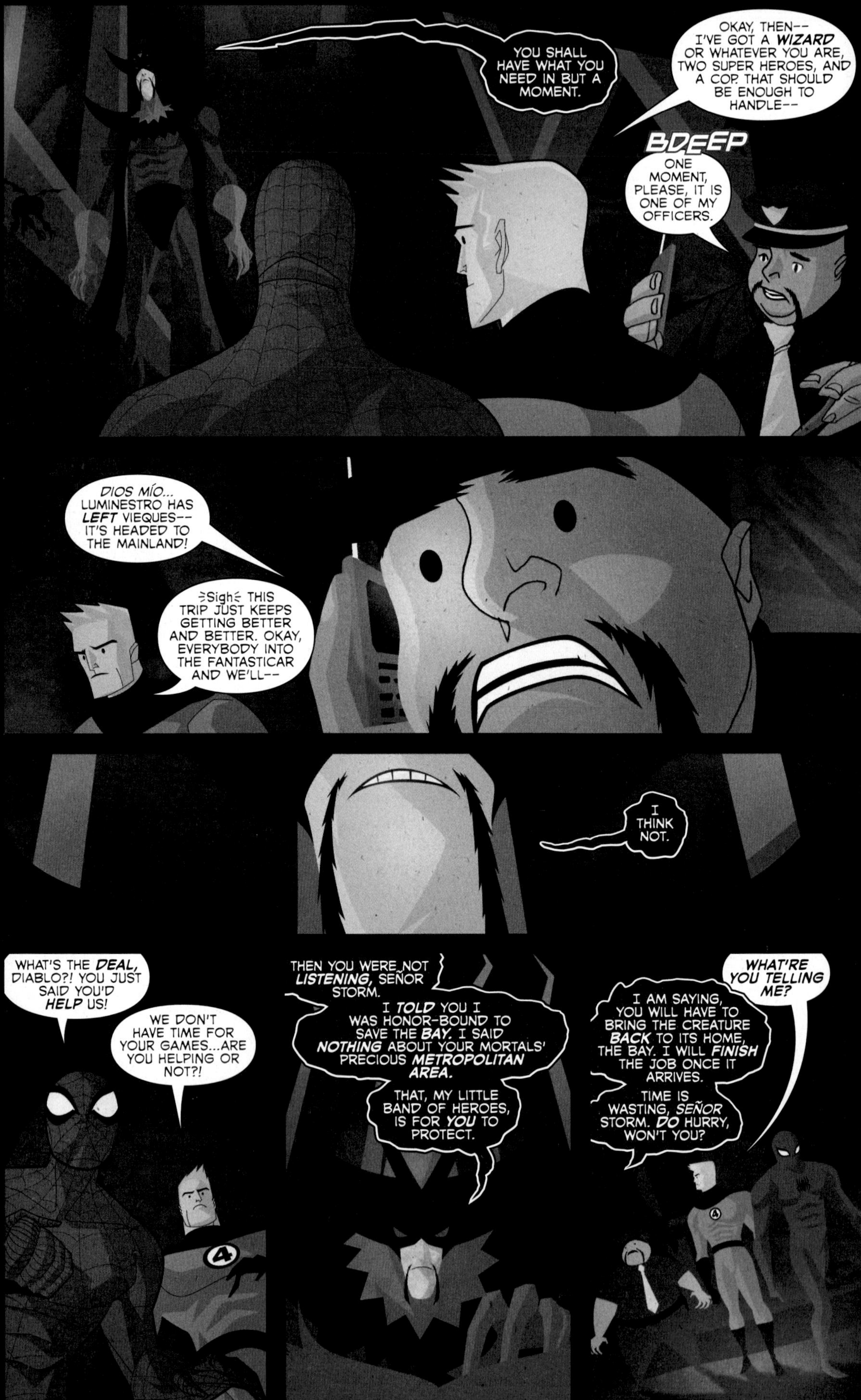
YOU SHALL HAVE WHAT YOU NEED IN BUT A MOMENT.
OKAY, THEN-- I'VE GOT A WIZARD OR WHATEVER YOU ARE, TWO SUPER HEROES, AND A COP. THAT SHOULD BE ENOUGH TO HANDLE--
BDEEP
ONE MOMENT, PLEASE, IT IS ONE OF MY OFFICERS.
DIOS MÍO... LUMINESTRO HAS LEFT VIEQUES-- IT'S HEADED TO THE MAINLAND!
≥Sigh≤ THIS TRIP JUST KEEPS GETTING BETTER AND BETTER. OKAY, EVERYBODY INTO THE FANTASTICAR AND WE'LL--
I THINK NOT.
WHAT'S THE DEAL, DIABLO?! YOU JUST SAID YOU'D HELP US!
WE DON'T HAVE TIME FOR YOUR GAMES...ARE YOU HELPING OR NOT?!
THEN YOU WERE NOT LISTENING, SEÑOR STORM.
I TOLD YOU I WAS HONOR-BOUND TO SAVE THE BAY. I SAID NOTHING ABOUT YOUR MORTALS' PRECIOUS METROPOLITAN AREA.
THAT, MY LITTLE BAND OF HEROES, IS FOR YOU TO PROTECT.
WHAT'RE YOU TELLING ME?
I AM SAYING, YOU WILL HAVE TO BRING THE CREATURE BACK TO ITS HOME, THE BAY. I WILL FINISH THE JOB ONCE IT ARRIVES.
TIME IS WASTING, SEÑOR STORM. DO HURRY, WON'T YOU?

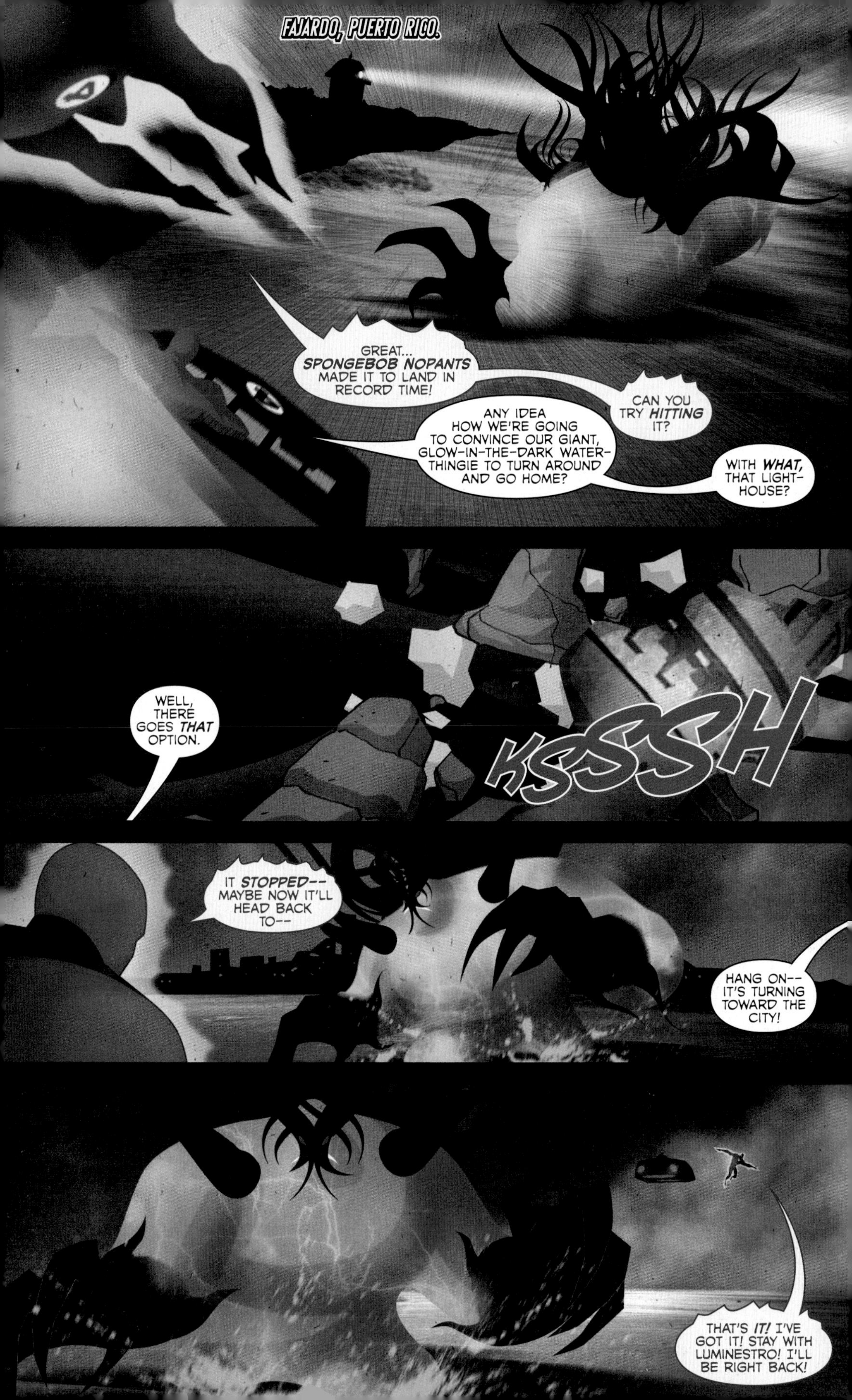
FAJARDO, PUERTO RICO.
GREAT... SPONGEBOB NOPANTS MADE IT TO LAND IN RECORD TIME!
CAN YOU TRY HITTING IT?
ANY IDEA HOW WE'RE GOING TO CONVINCE OUR GIANT, GLOW-IN-THE-DARK WATER-THINGIE TO TURN AROUND AND GO HOME?
WITH WHAT, THAT LIGHT-HOUSE?
WELL, THERE GOES THAT OPTION.
KSSSH
IT STOPPED-- MAYBE NOW IT'LL HEAD BACK TO--
HANG ON-- IT'S TURNING TOWARD THE CITY!
THAT'S IT! I'VE GOT IT! STAY WITH LUMINESTRO! I'LL BE RIGHT BACK!

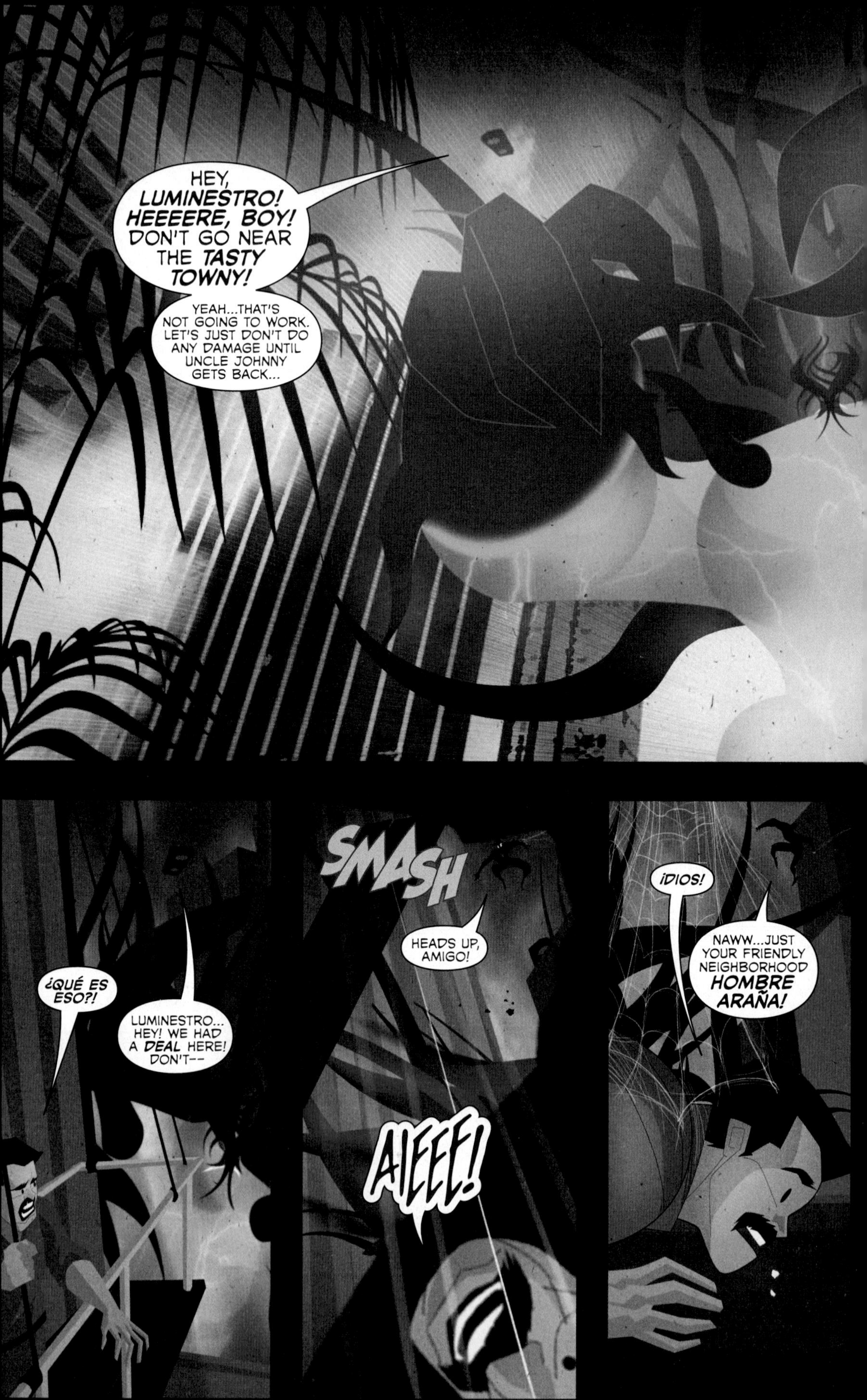
HEY, LUMINESTRO! HEEEERE, BOY! DON'T GO NEAR THE TASTY TOWNY!
YEAH...THAT'S NOT GOING TO WORK. LET'S JUST DON'T DO ANY DAMAGE UNTIL UNCLE JOHNNY GETS BACK...
¿QUÉ ES ESO?!
LUMINESTRO... HEY! WE HAD A DEAL HERE! DON'T--
SMASH
HEADS UP, AMIGO!
AIEEE!
¡DIOS!
NAWW...JUST YOUR FRIENDLY NEIGHBORHOOD HOMBRE ARAÑA!

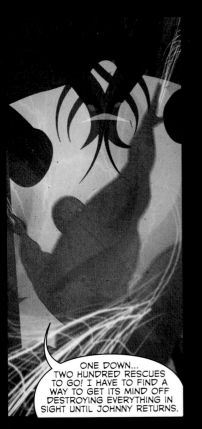

ONE DOWN... TWO HUNDRED RESCUES TO GO! I HAVE TO FIND A WAY TO GET ITS MIND OFF DESTROYING EVERYTHING IN SIGHT UNTIL JOHNNY RETURNS.

Hmmm...IF I'M LOOKING TO DISTRACT IT, MAYBE I SHOULD TAKE A CUE FROM THE MOSQUITOES AND BECOME AN ANNOYANCE.

THAT'S IT, WATERPUSS...TRY TO KEEP YOUR EYES ON THE DANCING SPIDEY! MAYBE I CAN MAKE YOU DIZZY...

C'MON FLAME-BRAIN...WHERE THE HECK ARE YOU?

JOHNNY! IT'S ABOUT TIME! YOU MIND TELLING ME...

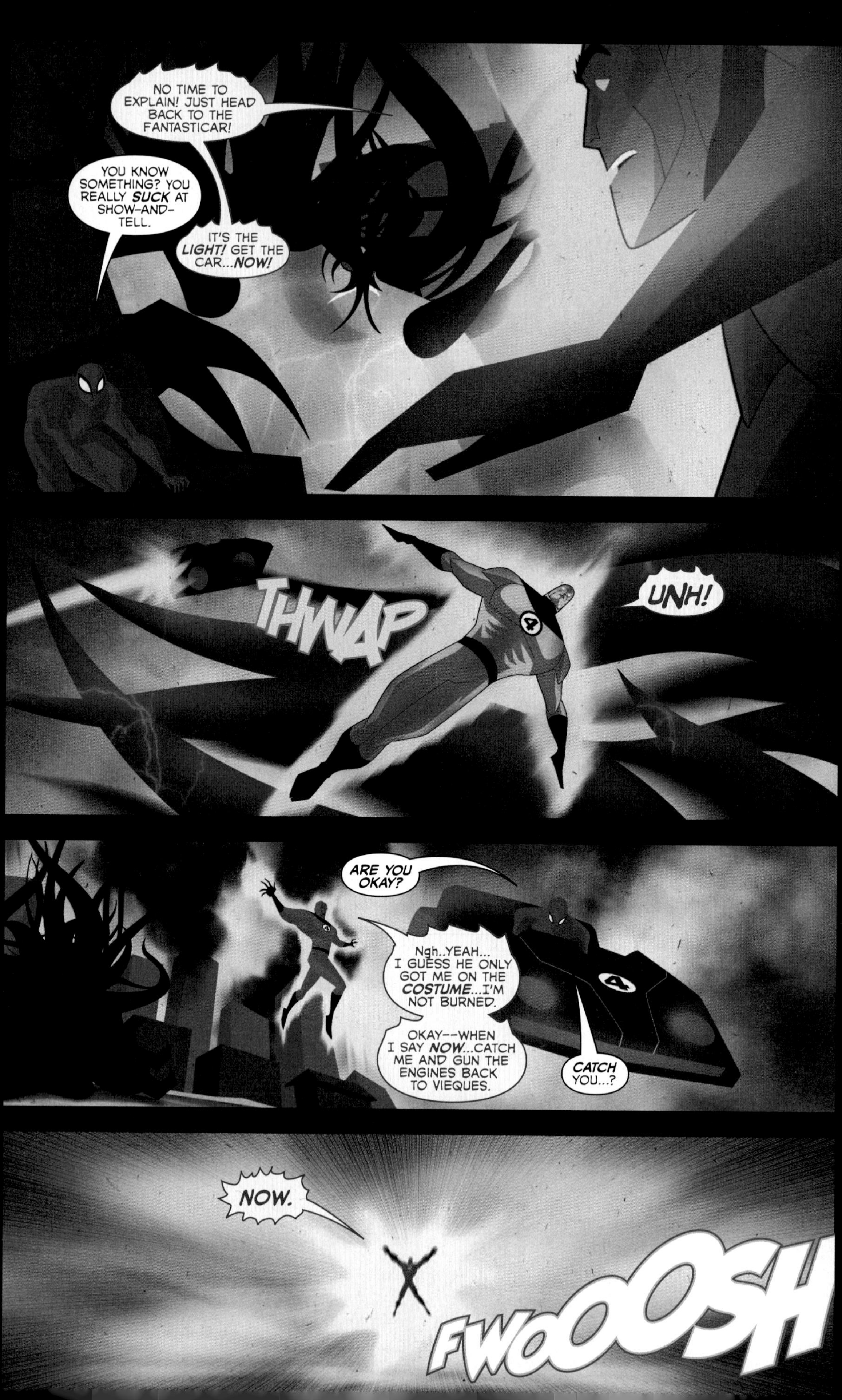
NO TIME TO EXPLAIN! JUST HEAD BACK TO THE FANTASTICAR!
YOU KNOW SOMETHING? YOU REALLY **SUCK** AT SHOW-AND-TELL.
IT'S THE **LIGHT!** GET THE CAR...**NOW!**
THWAP
UNH!
ARE YOU OKAY?
Ngh..YEAH... I GUESS HE ONLY GOT ME ON THE **COSTUME**...I'M NOT BURNED.
OKAY--WHEN I SAY **NOW**...CATCH ME AND GUN THE ENGINES BACK TO VIEQUES.
CATCH YOU...?
NOW.
FWOOOSH

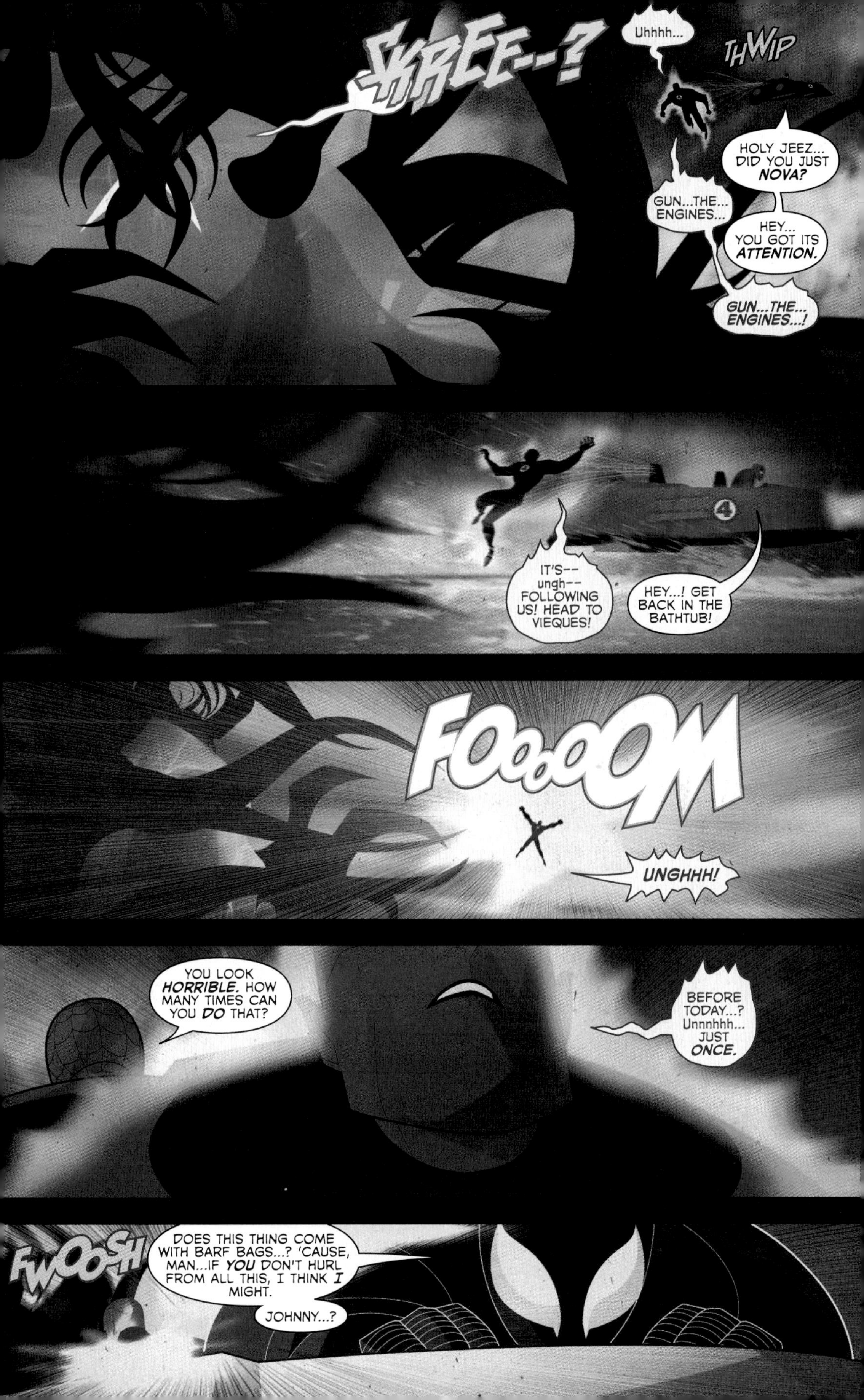
SKREE--?
Uhhhh...
THWIP
HOLY JEEZ... DID YOU JUST NOVA?
GUN...THE... ENGINES...
HEY... YOU GOT ITS ATTENTION.
GUN...THE... ENGINES...!
IT'S-- ungh-- FOLLOWING US! HEAD TO VIEQUES!
HEY...! GET BACK IN THE BATHTUB!
FOoooOM
UNGHHH!
YOU LOOK HORRIBLE. HOW MANY TIMES CAN YOU DO THAT?
BEFORE TODAY...? Unnnhhh... JUST ONCE.
FWOOSH
DOES THIS THING COME WITH BARF BAGS...? 'CAUSE, MAN...IF YOU DON'T HURL FROM ALL THIS, I THINK I MIGHT.
JOHNNY...?

Oh MAN-O-MAN-O-MAN...JOHNNY-BOY...COME BACK TO THE LIGHT!
Susie...? what aRe YOU doinG at th' prOm...?
YOU'RE KIDDING ME, RIGHT?
niGhty-nigHt, unca Benjy...
Ohhh... WE'RE DEAD.
HOLD ON TIGHT, WE'RE ALMOST THERE!
SKRREEEEEEEEEEEEEE
WE'RE NOT DEAD! WE MADE IT TO VIEQUES!
daddy...mAke... paNcakes...?
DADDY MAKE PANCAKES, BABY! LET'S LAND THIS THING AND WAKE YOU UP!
FWASH
FWASH

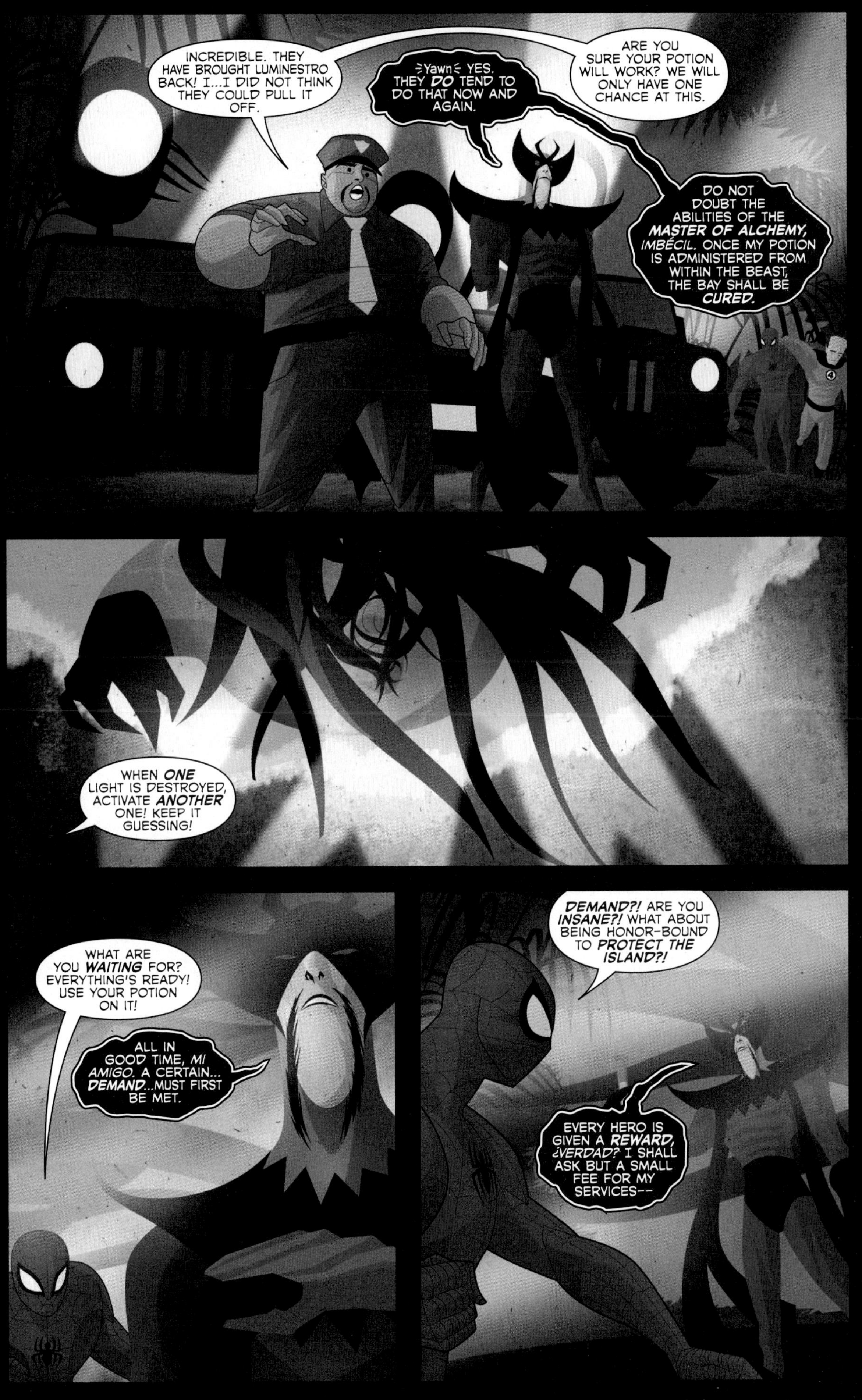
INCREDIBLE. THEY HAVE BROUGHT LUMINESTRO BACK! I...I DID NOT THINK THEY COULD PULL IT OFF.
≥Yawn≤ YES. THEY DO TEND TO DO THAT NOW AND AGAIN.
ARE YOU SURE YOUR POTION WILL WORK? WE WILL ONLY HAVE ONE CHANCE AT THIS.
DO NOT DOUBT THE ABILITIES OF THE MASTER OF ALCHEMY, IMBÉCIL. ONCE MY POTION IS ADMINISTERED FROM WITHIN THE BEAST, THE BAY SHALL BE CURED.
WHEN ONE LIGHT IS DESTROYED, ACTIVATE ANOTHER ONE! KEEP IT GUESSING!
WHAT ARE YOU WAITING FOR? EVERYTHING'S READY! USE YOUR POTION ON IT!
ALL IN GOOD TIME, MI AMIGO. A CERTAIN... DEMAND...MUST FIRST BE MET.
DEMAND?! ARE YOU INSANE?! WHAT ABOUT BEING HONOR-BOUND TO PROTECT THE ISLAND?!
EVERY HERO IS GIVEN A REWARD, ¿VERDAD? I SHALL ASK BUT A SMALL FEE FOR MY SERVICES--

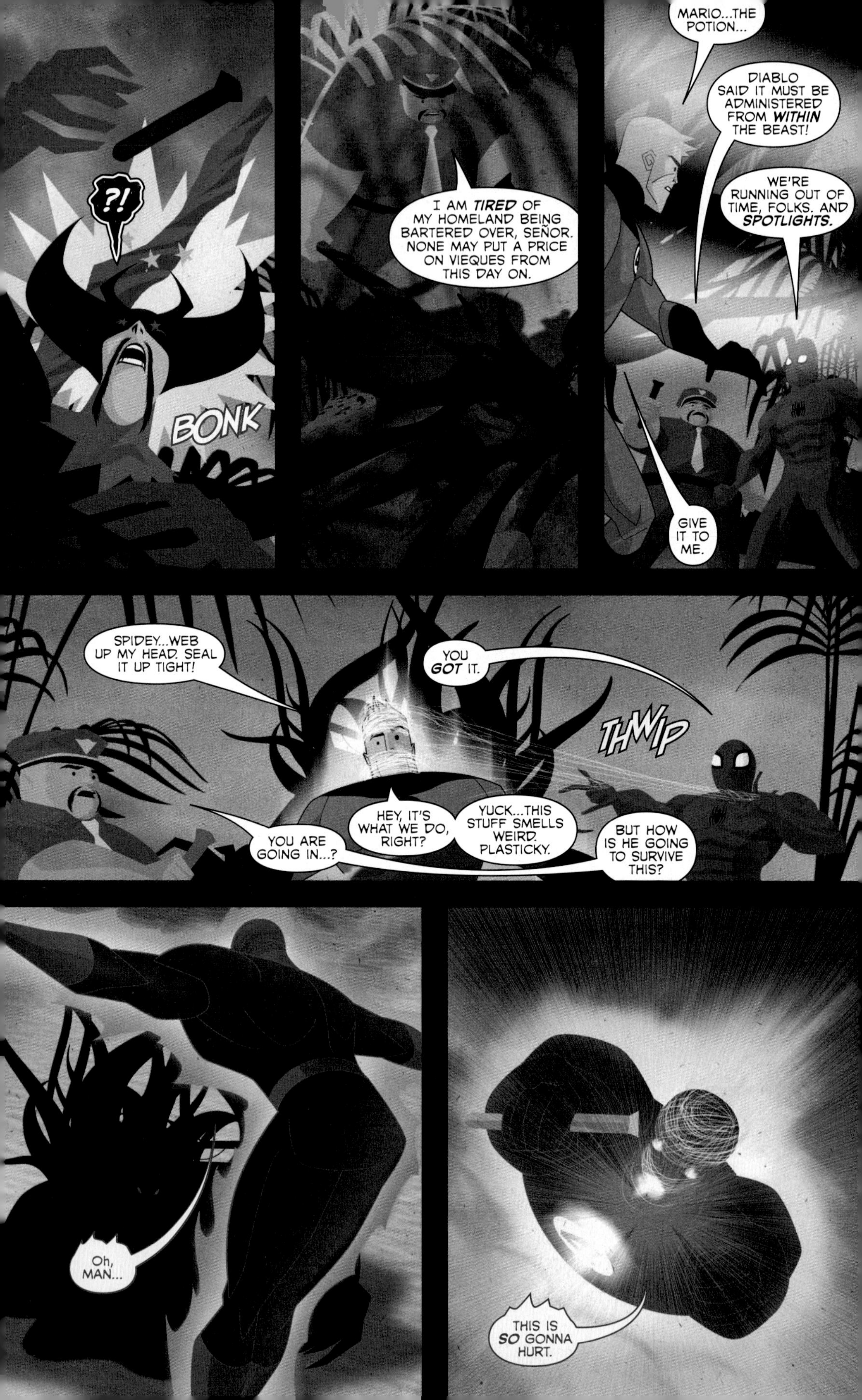
?!
BONK
I AM TIRED OF MY HOMELAND BEING BARTERED OVER, SEÑOR. NONE MAY PUT A PRICE ON VIEQUES FROM THIS DAY ON.
MARIO...THE POTION...
DIABLO SAID IT MUST BE ADMINISTERED FROM WITHIN THE BEAST!
WE'RE RUNNING OUT OF TIME, FOLKS. AND SPOTLIGHTS.
GIVE IT TO ME.
SPIDEY...WEB UP MY HEAD. SEAL IT UP TIGHT!
YOU GOT IT.
THWIP
YOU ARE GOING IN...?
HEY, IT'S WHAT WE DO, RIGHT?
YUCK...THIS STUFF SMELLS WEIRD. PLASTICKY.
BUT HOW IS HE GOING TO SURVIVE THIS?
Oh, MAN...
THIS IS SO GONNA HURT.

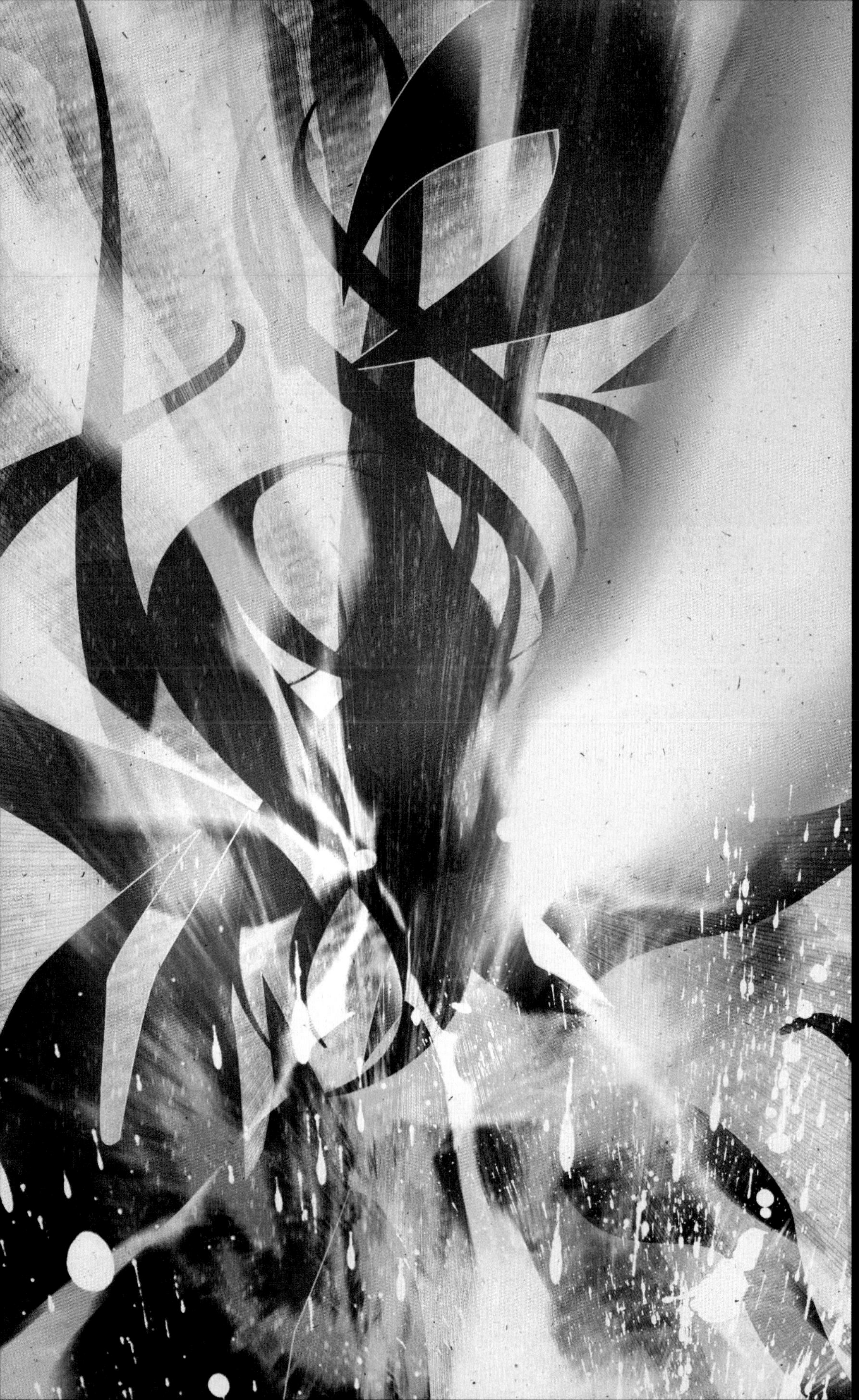

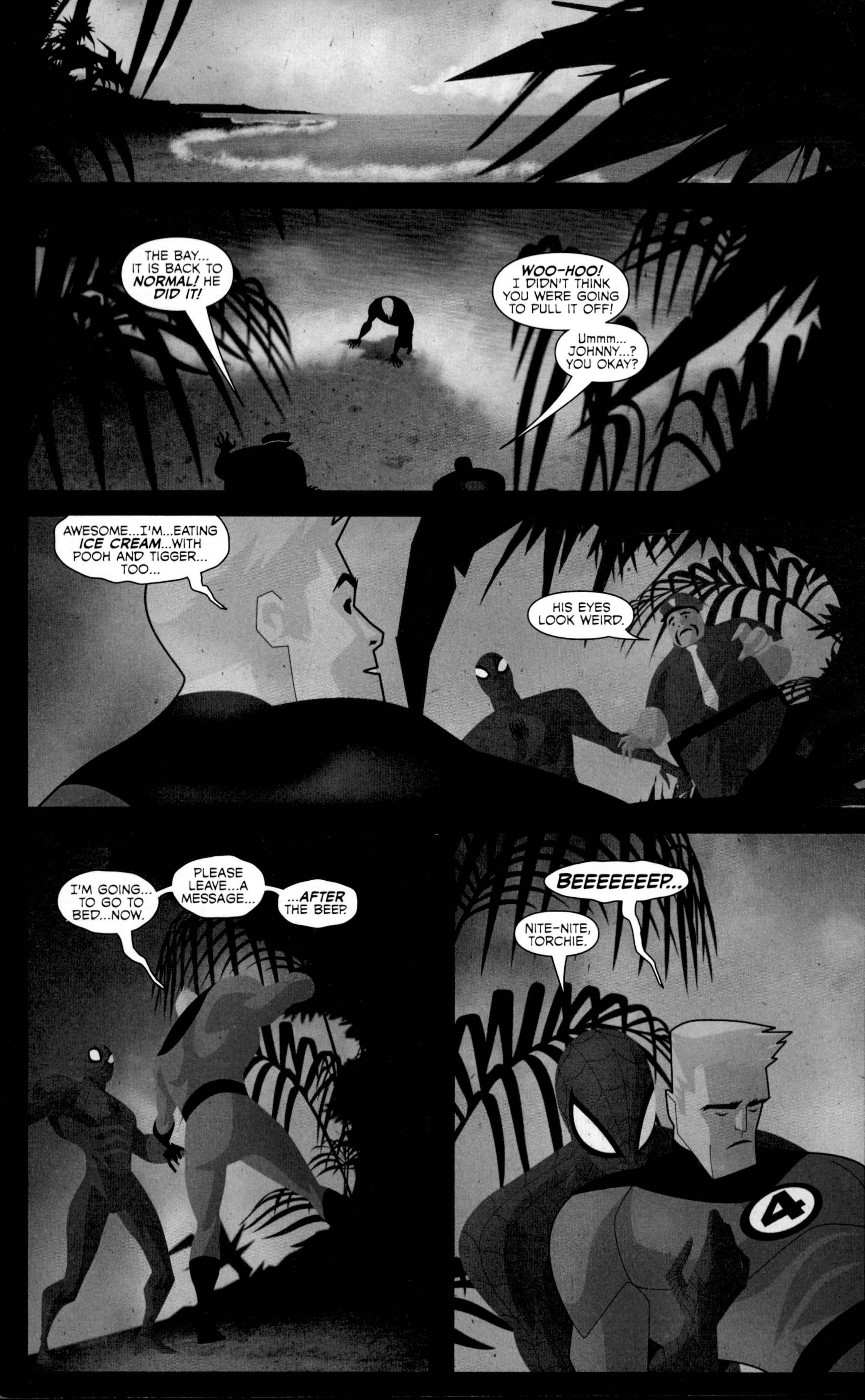
THE BAY... IT IS BACK TO NORMAL! HE DID IT!
WOO-HOO! I DIDN'T THINK YOU WERE GOING TO PULL IT OFF!
Ummm... JOHNNY...? YOU OKAY?
AWESOME...I'M...EATING ICE CREAM...WITH POOH AND TIGGER... TOO...
HIS EYES LOOK WEIRD.
I'M GOING... TO GO TO BED...NOW.
PLEASE LEAVE...A MESSAGE...
...AFTER THE BEEP.
BEEEEEEEP...
NITE-NITE, TORCHIE.

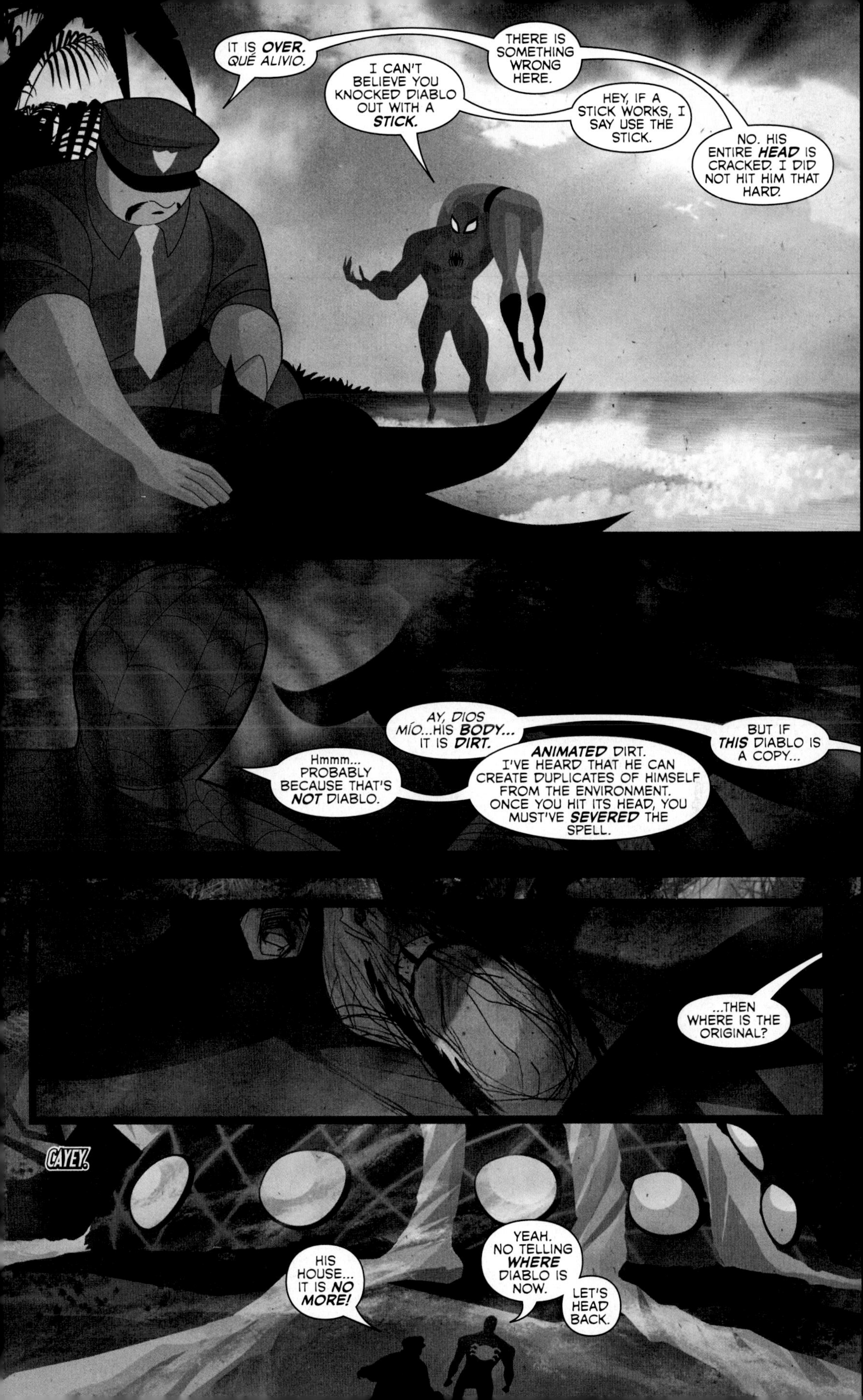
IT IS OVER. QUÉ ALIVIO.
THERE IS SOMETHING WRONG HERE.
I CAN'T BELIEVE YOU KNOCKED DIABLO OUT WITH A STICK.
HEY, IF A STICK WORKS, I SAY USE THE STICK.
NO. HIS ENTIRE HEAD IS CRACKED. I DID NOT HIT HIM THAT HARD.
AY, DIOS MÍO...HIS BODY... IT IS DIRT.
Hmmm... PROBABLY BECAUSE THAT'S NOT DIABLO.
ANIMATED DIRT. I'VE HEARD THAT HE CAN CREATE DUPLICATES OF HIMSELF FROM THE ENVIRONMENT. ONCE YOU HIT ITS HEAD, YOU MUST'VE SEVERED THE SPELL.
BUT IF THIS DIABLO IS A COPY...
...THEN WHERE IS THE ORIGINAL?
CAYEY.
HIS HOUSE... IT IS NO MORE!
YEAH. NO TELLING WHERE DIABLO IS NOW.
LET'S HEAD BACK.

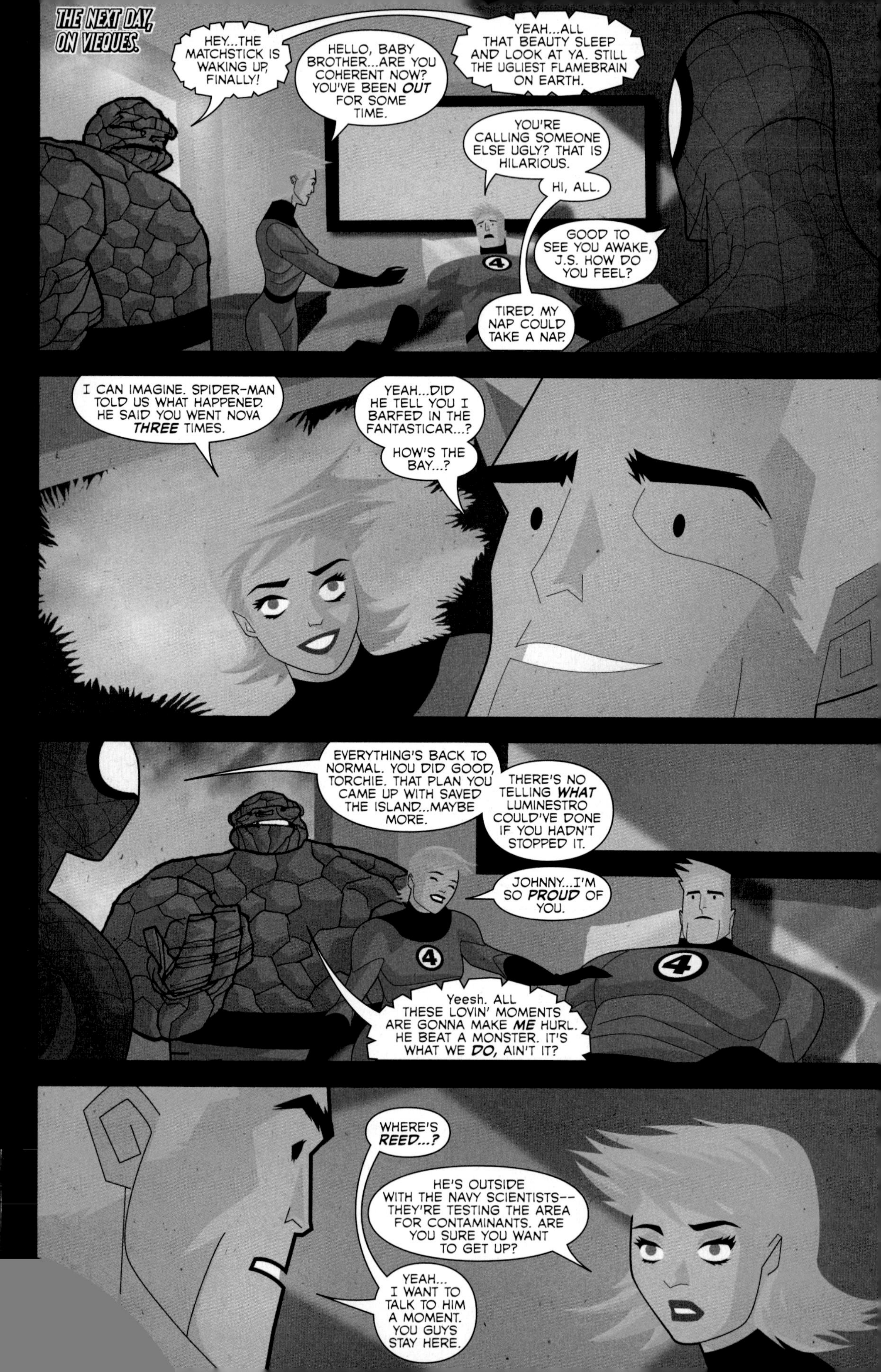
THE NEXT DAY, ON VIEQUES.
HEY...THE MATCHSTICK IS WAKING UP, FINALLY!
HELLO, BABY BROTHER...ARE YOU COHERENT NOW? YOU'VE BEEN OUT FOR SOME TIME.
YEAH...ALL THAT BEAUTY SLEEP AND LOOK AT YA. STILL THE UGLIEST FLAMEBRAIN ON EARTH.
YOU'RE CALLING SOMEONE ELSE UGLY? THAT IS HILARIOUS.
HI, ALL.
GOOD TO SEE YOU AWAKE, J.S. HOW DO YOU FEEL?
TIRED. MY NAP COULD TAKE A NAP.
I CAN IMAGINE. SPIDER-MAN TOLD US WHAT HAPPENED. HE SAID YOU WENT NOVA THREE TIMES.
YEAH...DID HE TELL YOU I BARFED IN THE FANTASTICAR...?
HOW'S THE BAY...?
EVERYTHING'S BACK TO NORMAL. YOU DID GOOD, TORCHIE. THAT PLAN YOU CAME UP WITH SAVED THE ISLAND...MAYBE MORE.
THERE'S NO TELLING WHAT LUMINESTRO COULD'VE DONE IF YOU HADN'T STOPPED IT.
JOHNNY...I'M SO PROUD OF YOU.
Yeesh. ALL THESE LOVIN' MOMENTS ARE GONNA MAKE ME HURL. HE BEAT A MONSTER. IT'S WHAT WE DO, AIN'T IT?
WHERE'S REED...?
HE'S OUTSIDE WITH THE NAVY SCIENTISTS-- THEY'RE TESTING THE AREA FOR CONTAMINANTS. ARE YOU SURE YOU WANT TO GET UP?
YEAH... I WANT TO TALK TO HIM A MOMENT. YOU GUYS STAY HERE.

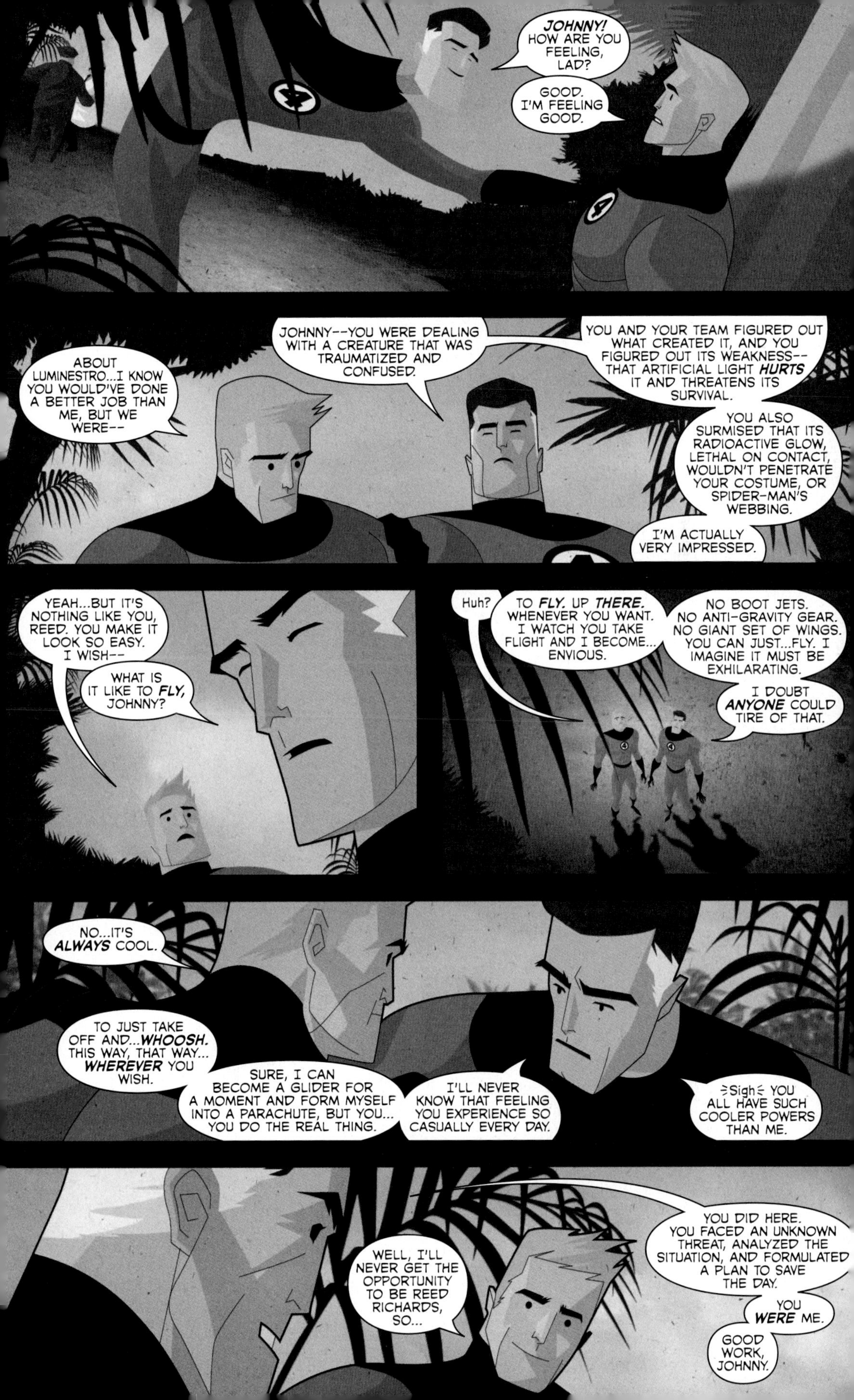
JOHNNY! HOW ARE YOU FEELING, LAD?
GOOD. I'M FEELING GOOD.
ABOUT LUMINESTRO...I KNOW YOU WOULD'VE DONE A BETTER JOB THAN ME, BUT WE WERE--
JOHNNY--YOU WERE DEALING WITH A CREATURE THAT WAS TRAUMATIZED AND CONFUSED.
YOU AND YOUR TEAM FIGURED OUT WHAT CREATED IT, AND YOU FIGURED OUT ITS WEAKNESS--THAT ARTIFICIAL LIGHT HURTS IT AND THREATENS ITS SURVIVAL.
YOU ALSO SURMISED THAT ITS RADIOACTIVE GLOW, LETHAL ON CONTACT, WOULDN'T PENETRATE YOUR COSTUME, OR SPIDER-MAN'S WEBBING.
I'M ACTUALLY VERY IMPRESSED.
YEAH...BUT IT'S NOTHING LIKE YOU, REED. YOU MAKE IT LOOK SO EASY. I WISH--
WHAT IS IT LIKE TO FLY, JOHNNY?
Huh?
TO FLY. UP THERE. WHENEVER YOU WANT. I WATCH YOU TAKE FLIGHT AND I BECOME... ENVIOUS.
NO BOOT JETS. NO ANTI-GRAVITY GEAR. NO GIANT SET OF WINGS. YOU CAN JUST...FLY. I IMAGINE IT MUST BE EXHILARATING.
I DOUBT ANYONE COULD TIRE OF THAT.
NO...IT'S ALWAYS COOL.
TO JUST TAKE OFF AND...WHOOSH. THIS WAY, THAT WAY... WHEREVER YOU WISH.
SURE, I CAN BECOME A GLIDER FOR A MOMENT AND FORM MYSELF INTO A PARACHUTE, BUT YOU... YOU DO THE REAL THING.
I'LL NEVER KNOW THAT FEELING YOU EXPERIENCE SO CASUALLY EVERY DAY.
Sigh YOU ALL HAVE SUCH COOLER POWERS THAN ME.
WELL, I'LL NEVER GET THE OPPORTUNITY TO BE REED RICHARDS, SO...
YOU DID HERE. YOU FACED AN UNKNOWN THREAT, ANALYZED THE SITUATION, AND FORMULATED A PLAN TO SAVE THE DAY.
YOU WERE ME.
GOOD WORK, JOHNNY.

LOOK AT YOU.

LOOK AT ME, WHAT?

YOU. YOU LOOK LIKE DADDY WATCHED YOU CATCH THE WINNING TOUCHDOWN.

YEAH...heh. I GUESS IT *DOES* KINDA FEEL THAT WAY.

GET THIS-- *REED* SAID HE WAS *IMPRESSED* WITH ME.

GET OUT. REALLY? HOW DID *THAT* FEEL?

WEIRD. COOL. GREAT. AND *WEIRD.* AWESOME.

I'M GLAD I CAME ALONG. THIS PLACE IS GORGEOUS.

YEAH...*SPEAKING* OF GORGEOUS, WHAT SAY WE DITCH THE FANTASTICOS OVER THERE AND TAKE IN A GAME OF BEACH VOLLEYBALL?

LEAD ON, JOHNNY STORM... LEAD ON!

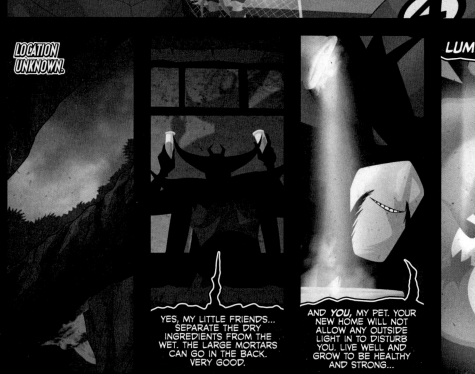

LOCATION UNKNOWN.

LUMINESTRO!

YES, MY LITTLE FRIENDS... SEPARATE THE DRY INGREDIENTS FROM THE WET. THE LARGE MORTARS CAN GO IN THE BACK. VERY GOOD.

AND *YOU*, MY PET. YOUR NEW HOME WILL NOT ALLOW ANY OUTSIDE LIGHT IN TO DISTURB YOU. LIVE WELL AND GROW TO BE HEALTHY AND STRONG...

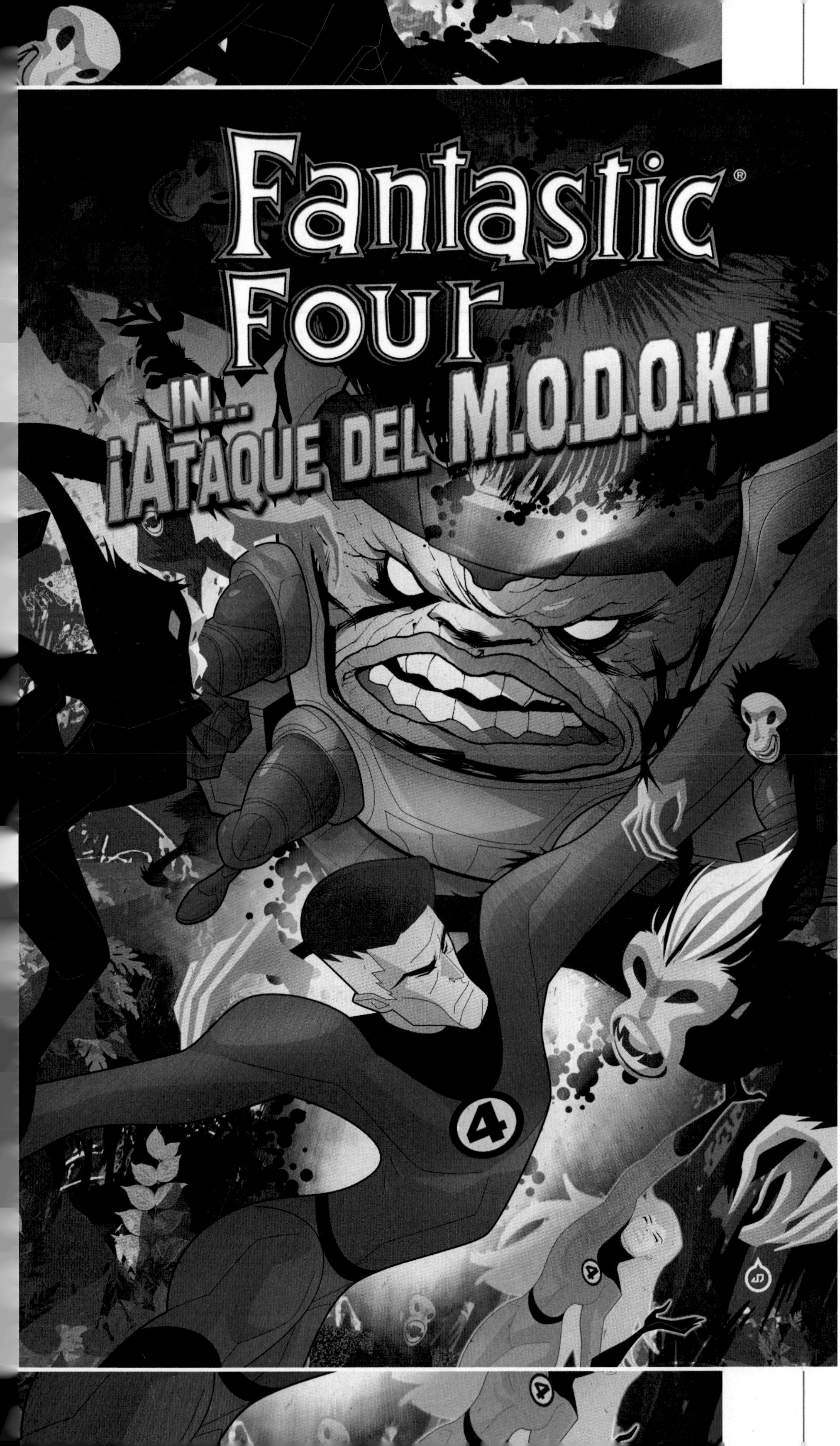
Fantastic Four®
IN...
¡ATAQUE DEL M.O.D.O.K.!

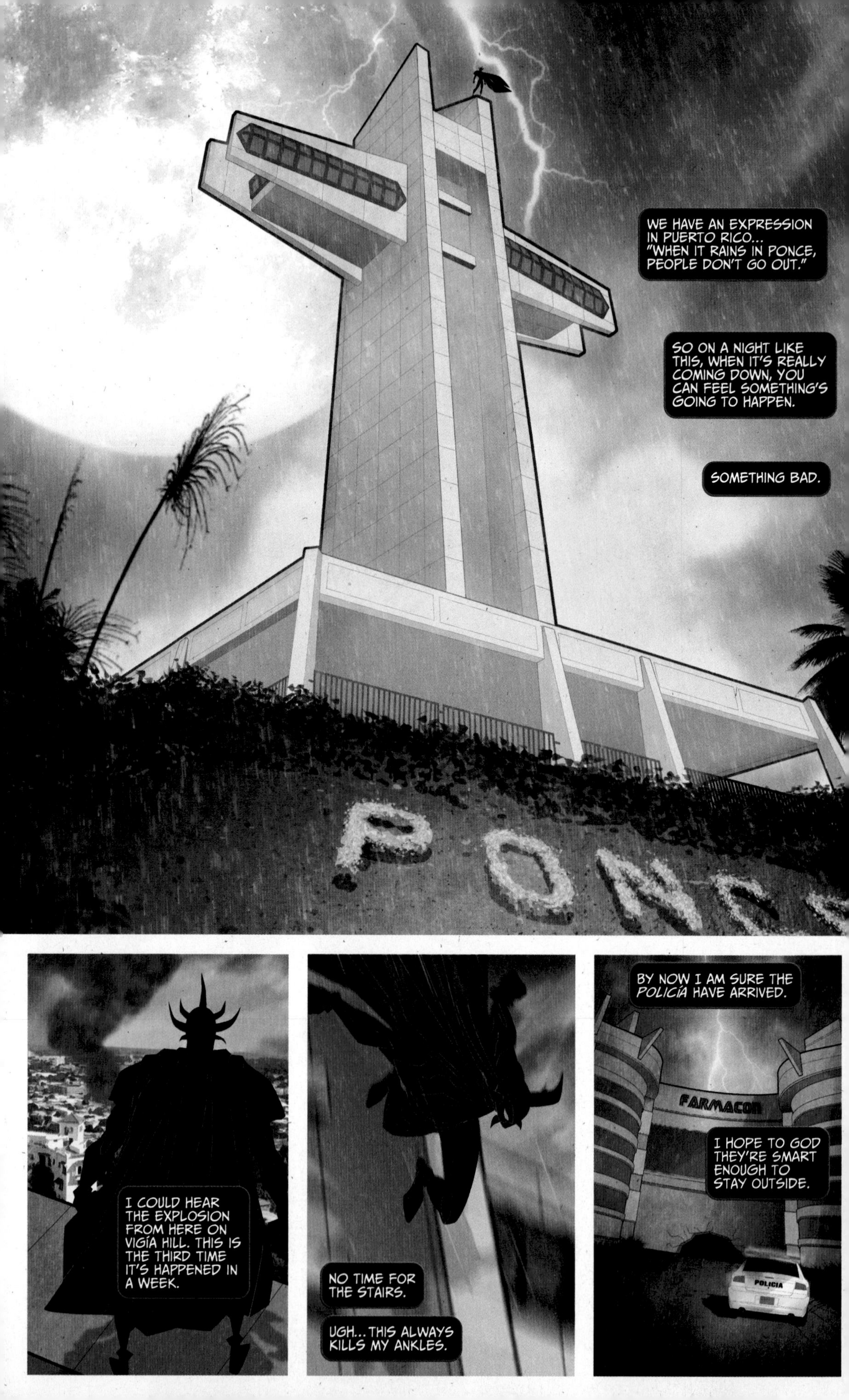
WE HAVE AN EXPRESSION IN PUERTO RICO... "WHEN IT RAINS IN PONCE, PEOPLE DON'T GO OUT."
SO ON A NIGHT LIKE THIS, WHEN IT'S REALLY COMING DOWN, YOU CAN FEEL SOMETHING'S GOING TO HAPPEN.
SOMETHING BAD.
I COULD HEAR THE EXPLOSION FROM HERE ON VIGÍA HILL. THIS IS THE THIRD TIME IT'S HAPPENED IN A WEEK.
NO TIME FOR THE STAIRS.
UGH... THIS ALWAYS KILLS MY ANKLES.
BY NOW I AM SURE THE *POLICÍA* HAVE ARRIVED.
FARMACOR
I HOPE TO GOD THEY'RE SMART ENOUGH TO STAY OUTSIDE.
POLICIA

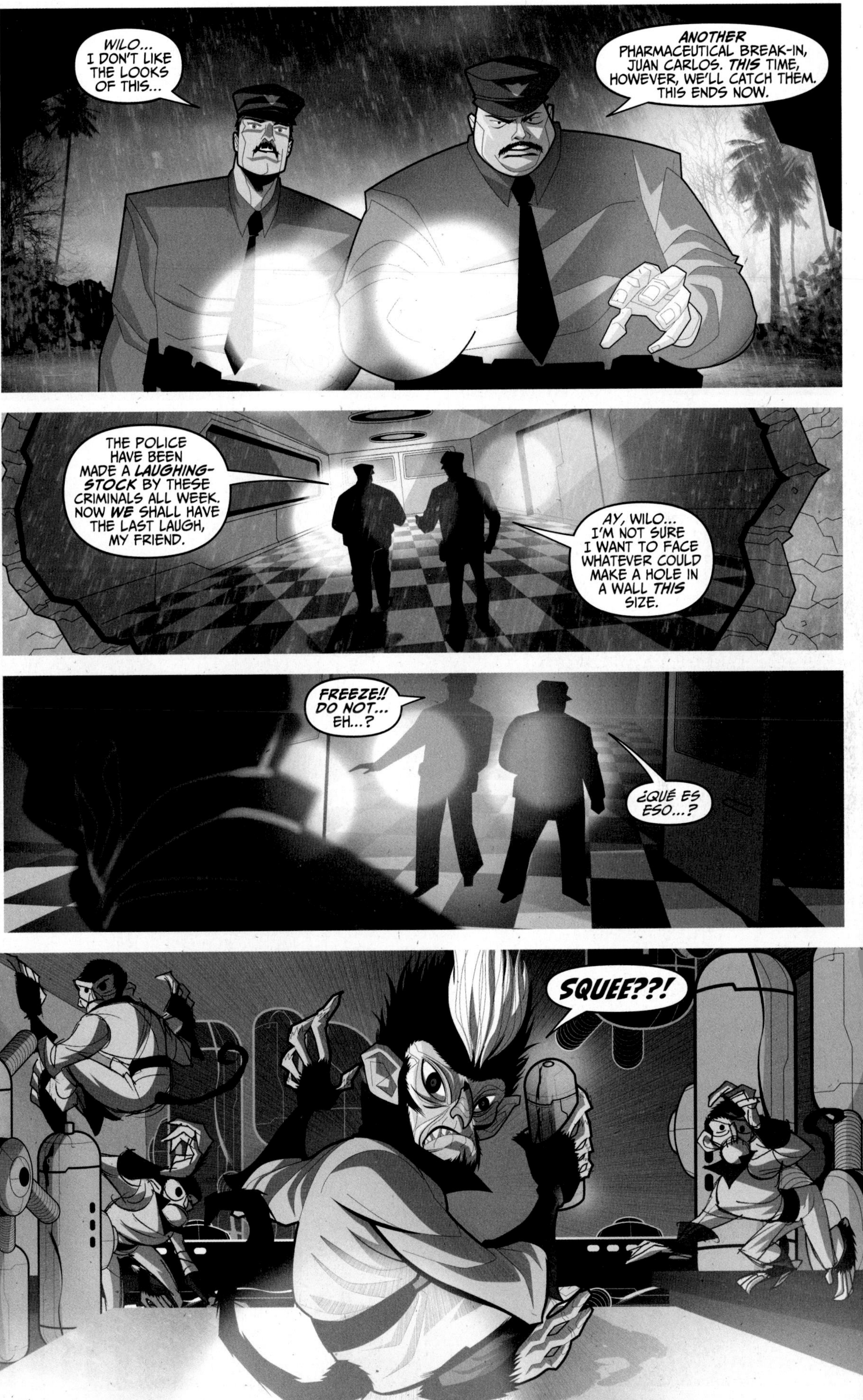
WILO... I DON'T LIKE THE LOOKS OF THIS...
ANOTHER PHARMACEUTICAL BREAK-IN, JUAN CARLOS. THIS TIME, HOWEVER, WE'LL CATCH THEM. THIS ENDS NOW.
THE POLICE HAVE BEEN MADE A LAUGHING-STOCK BY THESE CRIMINALS ALL WEEK. NOW WE SHALL HAVE THE LAST LAUGH, MY FRIEND.
AY, WILO... I'M NOT SURE I WANT TO FACE WHATEVER COULD MAKE A HOLE IN A WALL THIS SIZE.
FREEZE!! DO NOT... EH...?
¿QUÉ ES ESO...?
SQUEE??!

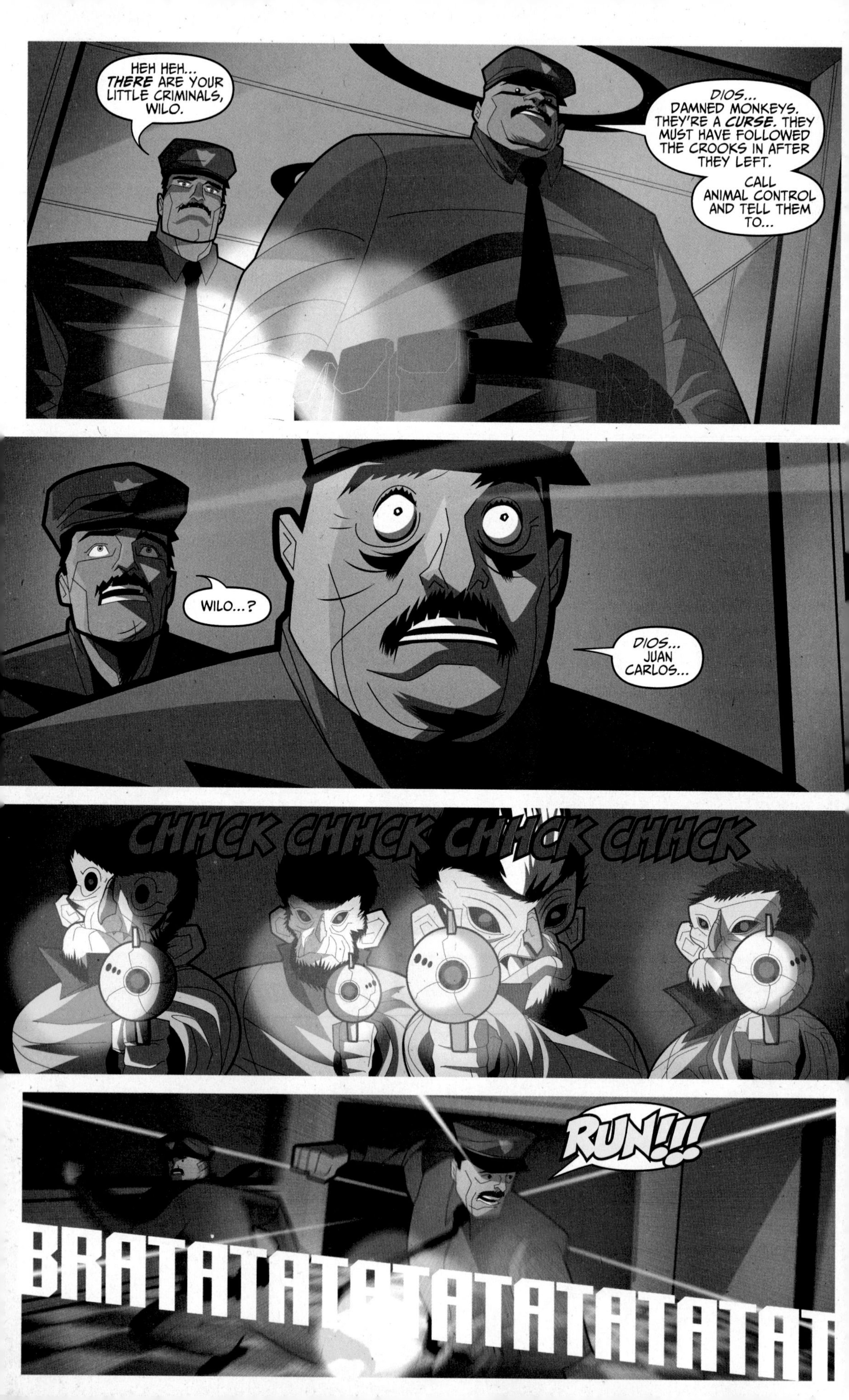

HEH HEH... *THERE* ARE YOUR LITTLE CRIMINALS, WILO.
DIOS... DAMNED MONKEYS. THEY'RE A *CURSE*. THEY MUST HAVE FOLLOWED THE CROOKS IN AFTER THEY LEFT.
CALL ANIMAL CONTROL AND TELL THEM TO...
WILO...?
DIOS... JUAN CARLOS...
CHHCK CHHCK CHHCK CHHCK
RUN!!!
BRATATATATATATATATATAT

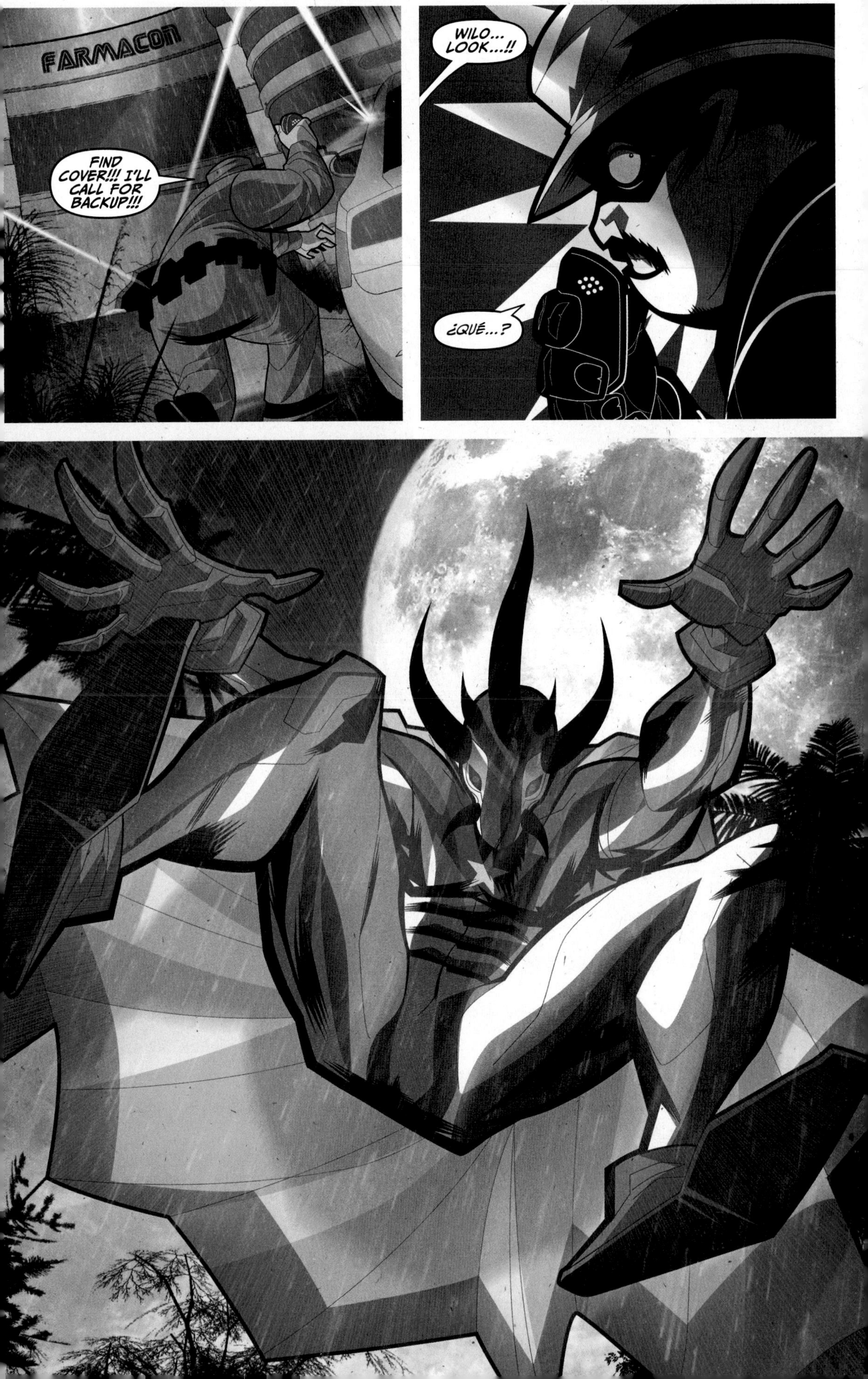
FARMACON
FIND COVER!!! I'LL CALL FOR BACKUP!!!
WILO... LOOK...!!
¿QUÉ...?

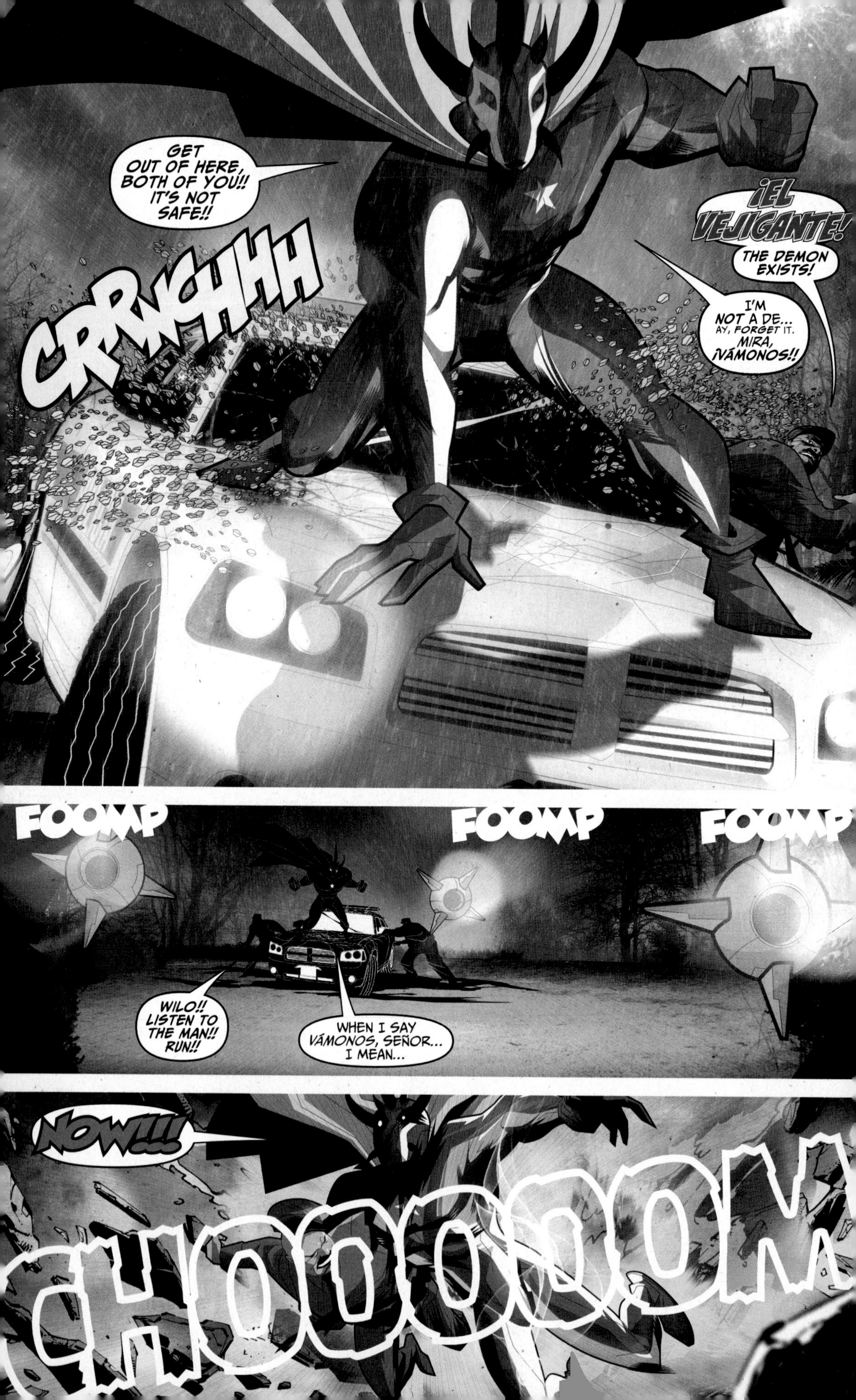
GET OUT OF HERE, BOTH OF YOU!! IT'S NOT SAFE!!
CRNCHHH
¡EL VEJIGANTE!
THE DEMON EXISTS!
I'M NOT A DE... AY, FORGET IT. MIRA, ¡VÁMONOS!!
FOOMP
FOOMP
FOOMP
WILO!! LISTEN TO THE MAN!! RUN!!
WHEN I SAY VÁMONOS, SEÑOR... I MEAN...
NOW!!!
CHOOOOOOM

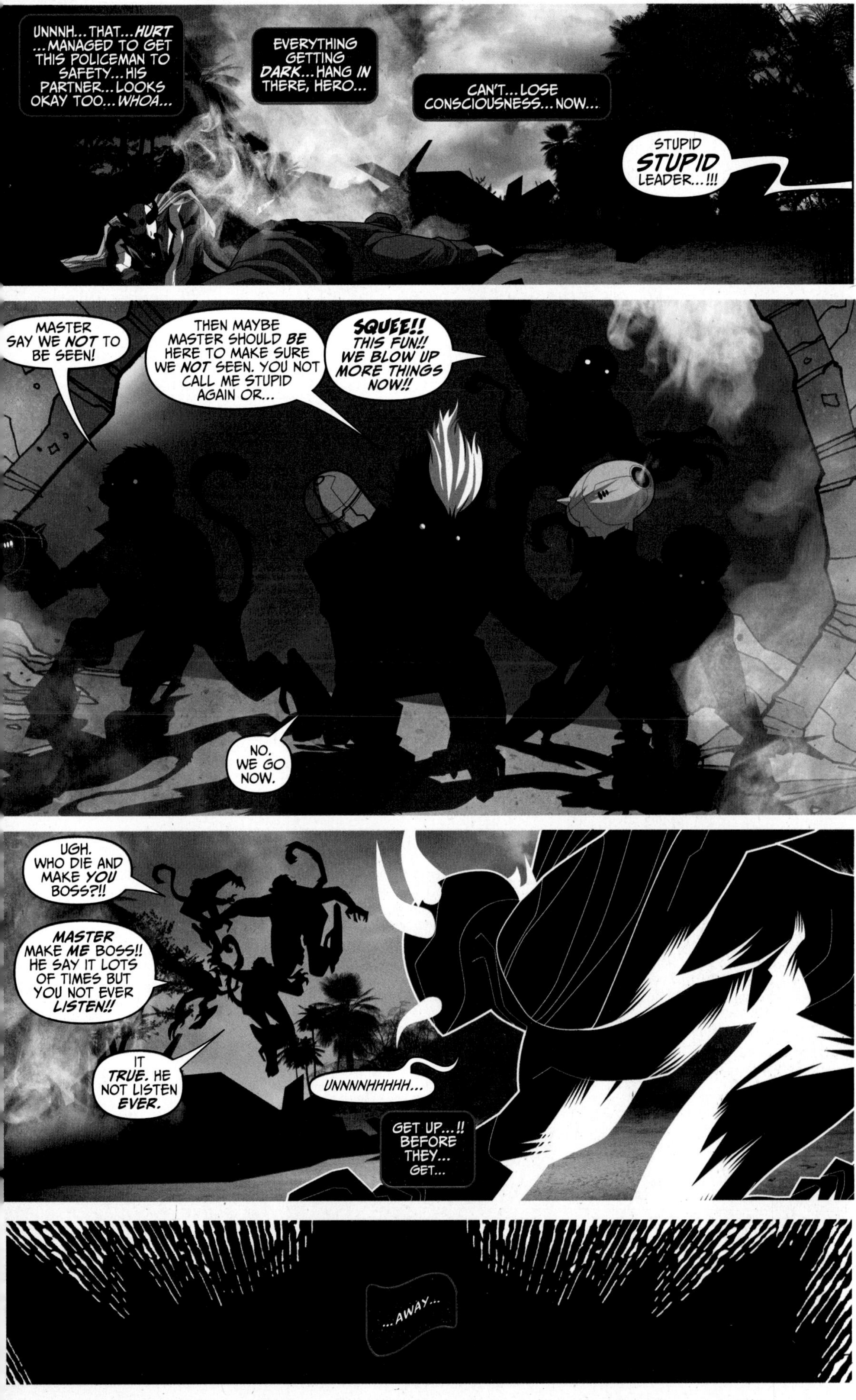
UNNNH... THAT... HURT ...MANAGED TO GET THIS POLICEMAN TO SAFETY... HIS PARTNER... LOOKS OKAY TOO... WHOA...
EVERYTHING GETTING DARK... HANG IN THERE, HERO...
CAN'T... LOSE CONSCIOUSNESS... NOW...
STUPID STUPID LEADER...!!!
MASTER SAY WE NOT TO BE SEEN!
THEN MAYBE MASTER SHOULD BE HERE TO MAKE SURE WE NOT SEEN. YOU NOT CALL ME STUPID AGAIN OR...
SQUEE!! THIS FUN!! WE BLOW UP MORE THINGS NOW!!
NO. WE GO NOW.
UGH. WHO DIE AND MAKE YOU BOSS?!!
MASTER MAKE ME BOSS!! HE SAY IT LOTS OF TIMES BUT YOU NOT EVER LISTEN!!
IT TRUE. HE NOT LISTEN EVER.
UNNNNHHHHH...
GET UP...!! BEFORE THEY... GET...
...AWAY...

ANYTHING ON LAST NIGHT'S *REFINERY EXPLOSION* IN CATAÑO...?

ONLY THE EXPLOSION *ITSELF,* NOT THE ACTUAL *CAUSE.*

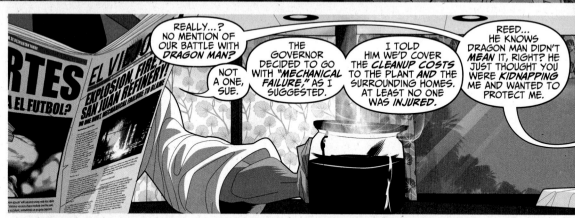

REALLY...? NO MENTION OF OUR BATTLE WITH *DRAGON MAN?*

NOT A ONE, SUE.

THE GOVERNOR DECIDED TO GO WITH *"MECHANICAL FAILURE,"* AS I SUGGESTED.

I TOLD HIM WE'D COVER THE *CLEANUP COSTS* TO THE PLANT *AND* THE SURROUNDING HOMES. AT LEAST NO ONE WAS *INJURED.*

REED... HE KNOWS DRAGON MAN DIDN'T *MEAN* IT, RIGHT? HE JUST THOUGHT YOU WERE *KIDNAPPING* ME AND WANTED TO PROTECT ME.

I FULLY EXPLAINED DRAGON MAN'S CONNECTION TO YOU, DARLING. I JUST WISH HE'D LET US ENJOY A *VACATION* NOW AND THEN.

REFILL...?

I FIND IT CUTE. AND *¡SÍ, GRACIAS!*

...

SO...

IT'S *YOUR* TURN TO ASK.

I THOUGHT IT WAS YOUR TURN.

NNNNOPE. I ASKED *MY* QUESTION BACK IN THE *FANTASTICAR,* REMEMBER..?

"WHO'S YOUR FAVORITE *MATHEMATICIAN?"*

AH, YES. JOHANN CARL FRIEDRICH GAUSS.

SO... MY TURN...

MAKE IT A *GOOD* ONE, DEAR. THIS WILL BE *NUMBER TWENTY.*

YOUR *FINAL* QUESTION.

HMMMM... LET ME *THINK* THEN...

TOO MANY CHOICES...?

OH, I ALREADY *HAVE* IT. IF YOU'RE WILLING TO *ANSWER,* THAT IS.

OH, YOU *SOOOO* DON'T KNOW ME, DARLING. I'LL ANSWER *ANYTHING* YOU ASK.

OKAY. *HERE* IT IS. IT'S *SIMPLE.* DO YOU RECALL THE *MOMENT* YOU REALIZED I WAS THE *ONE* FOR YOU?

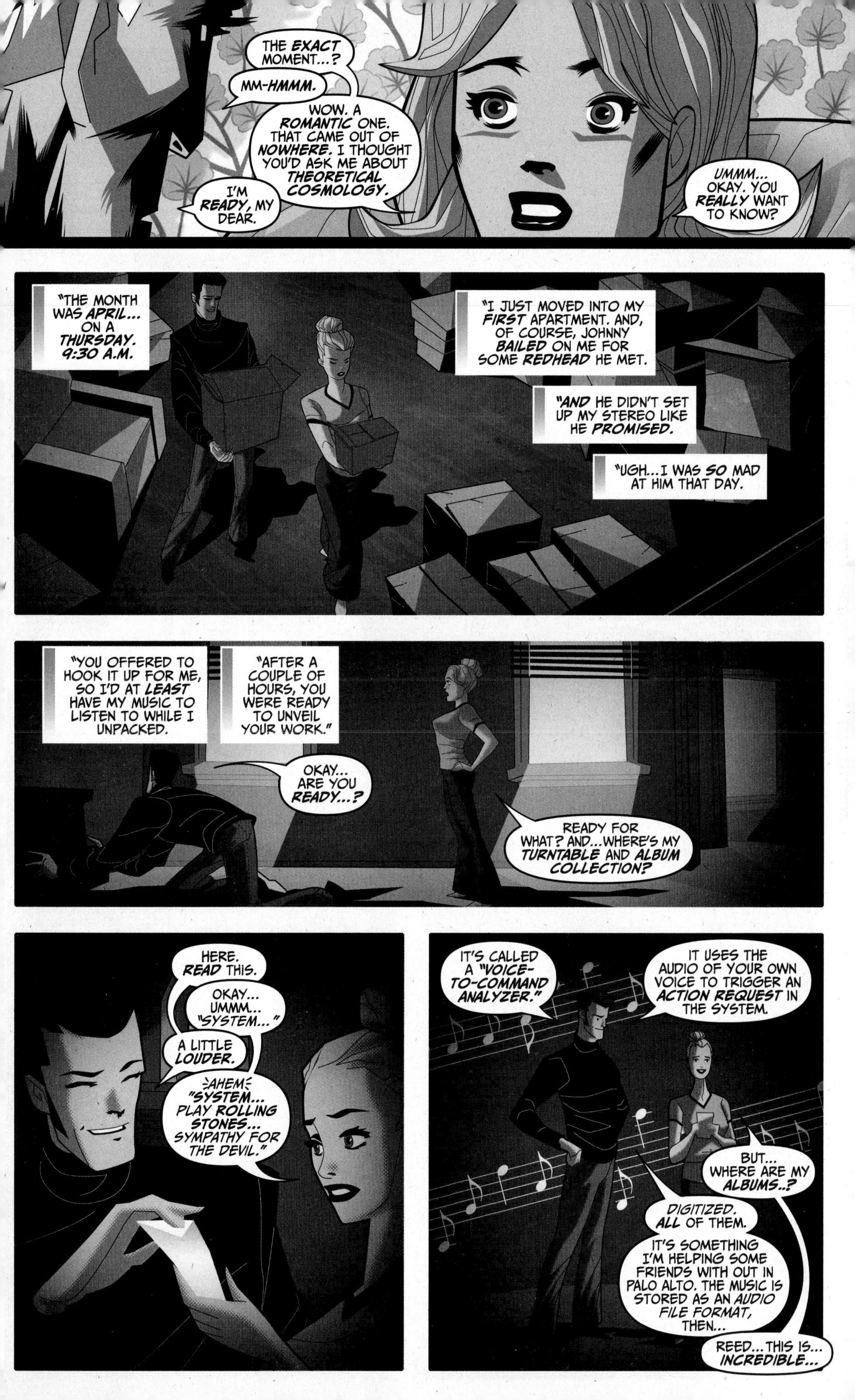
THE EXACT MOMENT...?
MM-HMMM.
WOW. A ROMANTIC ONE. THAT CAME OUT OF NOWHERE. I THOUGHT YOU'D ASK ME ABOUT THEORETICAL COSMOLOGY.
I'M READY, MY DEAR.
UMMM... OKAY. YOU REALLY WANT TO KNOW?
"THE MONTH WAS APRIL... ON A THURSDAY. 9:30 A.M.
"I JUST MOVED INTO MY FIRST APARTMENT. AND, OF COURSE, JOHNNY BAILED ON ME FOR SOME REDHEAD HE MET.
"AND HE DIDN'T SET UP MY STEREO LIKE HE PROMISED.
"UGH...I WAS SO MAD AT HIM THAT DAY.
"YOU OFFERED TO HOOK IT UP FOR ME, SO I'D AT LEAST HAVE MY MUSIC TO LISTEN TO WHILE I UNPACKED.
"AFTER A COUPLE OF HOURS, YOU WERE READY TO UNVEIL YOUR WORK."
OKAY... ARE YOU READY...?
READY FOR WHAT? AND...WHERE'S MY TURNTABLE AND ALBUM COLLECTION?
HERE. READ THIS.
OKAY... UMMM... "SYSTEM..."
A LITTLE LOUDER.
AHEM "SYSTEM... PLAY ROLLING STONES... SYMPATHY FOR THE DEVIL."
IT'S CALLED A "VOICE-TO-COMMAND ANALYZER."
IT USES THE AUDIO OF YOUR OWN VOICE TO TRIGGER AN ACTION REQUEST IN THE SYSTEM.
BUT... WHERE ARE MY ALBUMS..?
DIGITIZED. ALL OF THEM.
IT'S SOMETHING I'M HELPING SOME FRIENDS WITH OUT IN PALO ALTO. THE MUSIC IS STORED AS AN AUDIO FILE FORMAT, THEN...
REED... THIS IS... INCREDIBLE...

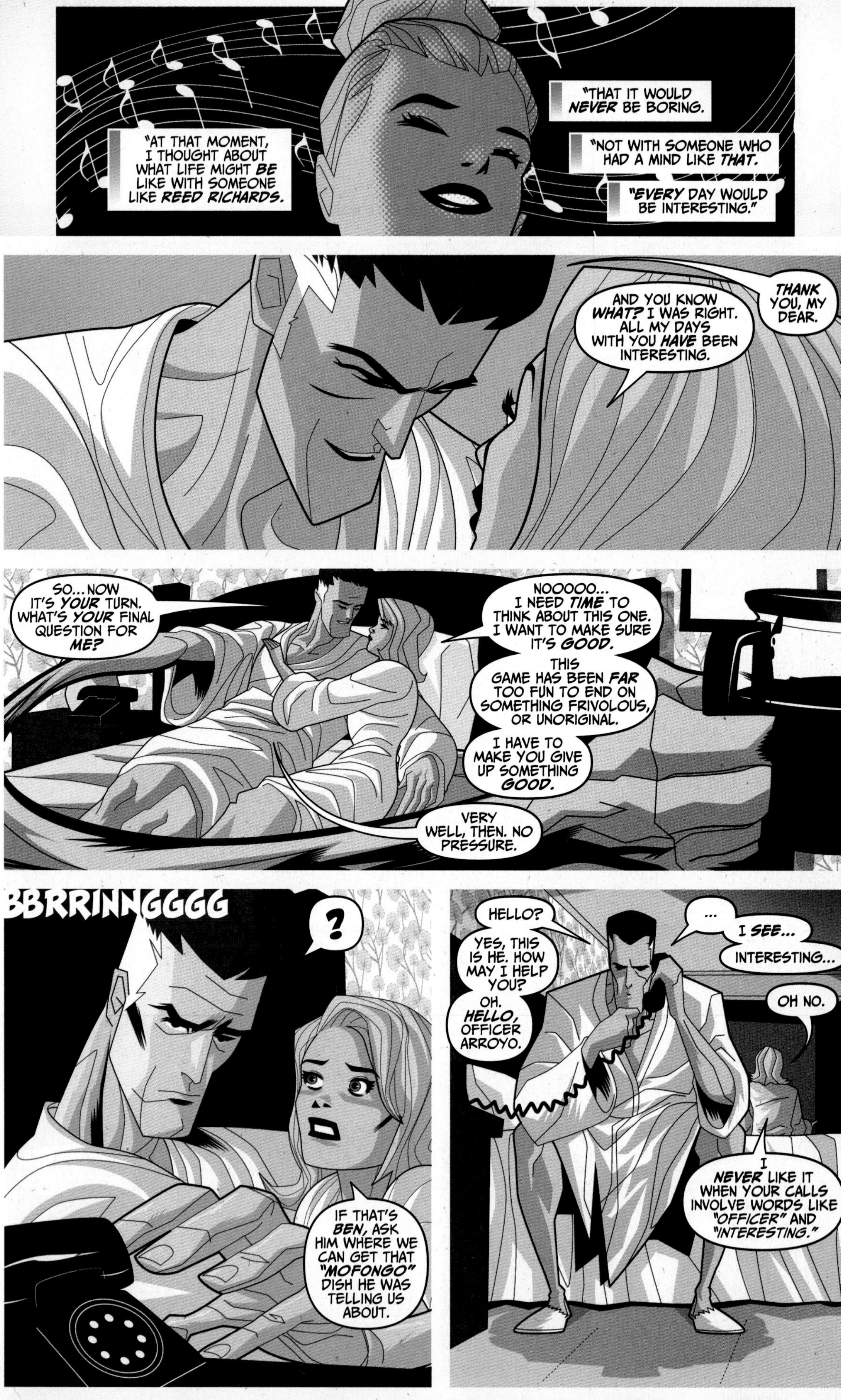
"AT THAT MOMENT, I THOUGHT ABOUT WHAT LIFE MIGHT BE LIKE WITH SOMEONE LIKE REED RICHARDS.
"THAT IT WOULD NEVER BE BORING.
"NOT WITH SOMEONE WHO HAD A MIND LIKE THAT.
"EVERY DAY WOULD BE INTERESTING."
AND YOU KNOW WHAT? I WAS RIGHT. ALL MY DAYS WITH YOU HAVE BEEN INTERESTING.
THANK YOU, MY DEAR.
SO...NOW IT'S YOUR TURN. WHAT'S YOUR FINAL QUESTION FOR ME?
NOOOOO... I NEED TIME TO THINK ABOUT THIS ONE. I WANT TO MAKE SURE IT'S GOOD.
THIS GAME HAS BEEN FAR TOO FUN TO END ON SOMETHING FRIVOLOUS, OR UNORIGINAL.
I HAVE TO MAKE YOU GIVE UP SOMETHING GOOD.
VERY WELL, THEN. NO PRESSURE.
BBRRINNGGGG
?
IF THAT'S BEN, ASK HIM WHERE WE CAN GET THAT "MOFONGO" DISH HE WAS TELLING US ABOUT.
HELLO?
YES, THIS IS HE. HOW MAY I HELP YOU?
OH. HELLO, OFFICER ARROYO.
...
I SEE...
INTERESTING...
OH NO.
I NEVER LIKE IT WHEN YOUR CALLS INVOLVE WORDS LIKE "OFFICER" AND "INTERESTING."

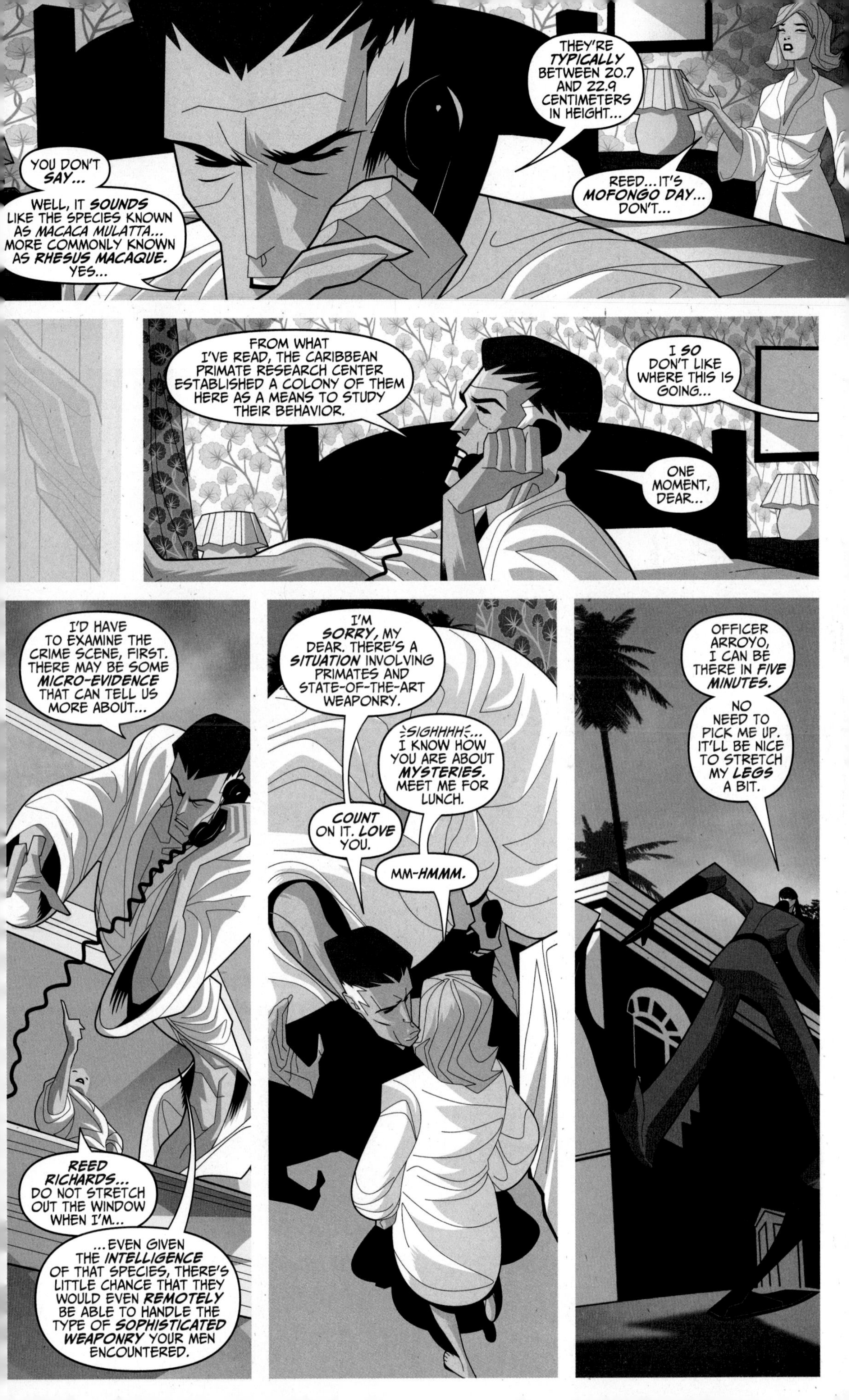
YOU DON'T SAY...
WELL, IT SOUNDS LIKE THE SPECIES KNOWN AS MACACA MULATTA... MORE COMMONLY KNOWN AS RHESUS MACAQUE. YES...
THEY'RE TYPICALLY BETWEEN 20.7 AND 22.9 CENTIMETERS IN HEIGHT...
REED... IT'S MOFONGO DAY... DON'T...
FROM WHAT I'VE READ, THE CARIBBEAN PRIMATE RESEARCH CENTER ESTABLISHED A COLONY OF THEM HERE AS A MEANS TO STUDY THEIR BEHAVIOR.
I SO DON'T LIKE WHERE THIS IS GOING...
ONE MOMENT, DEAR...
I'D HAVE TO EXAMINE THE CRIME SCENE, FIRST. THERE MAY BE SOME MICRO-EVIDENCE THAT CAN TELL US MORE ABOUT...
REED RICHARDS... DO NOT STRETCH OUT THE WINDOW WHEN I'M...
...EVEN GIVEN THE INTELLIGENCE OF THAT SPECIES, THERE'S LITTLE CHANCE THAT THEY WOULD EVEN REMOTELY BE ABLE TO HANDLE THE TYPE OF SOPHISTICATED WEAPONRY YOUR MEN ENCOUNTERED.
I'M SORRY, MY DEAR. THERE'S A SITUATION INVOLVING PRIMATES AND STATE-OF-THE-ART WEAPONRY.
SIGHHHH... I KNOW HOW YOU ARE ABOUT MYSTERIES. MEET ME FOR LUNCH.
COUNT ON IT. LOVE YOU.
MM-HMMM.
OFFICER ARROYO, I CAN BE THERE IN FIVE MINUTES.
NO NEED TO PICK ME UP. IT'LL BE NICE TO STRETCH MY LEGS A BIT.

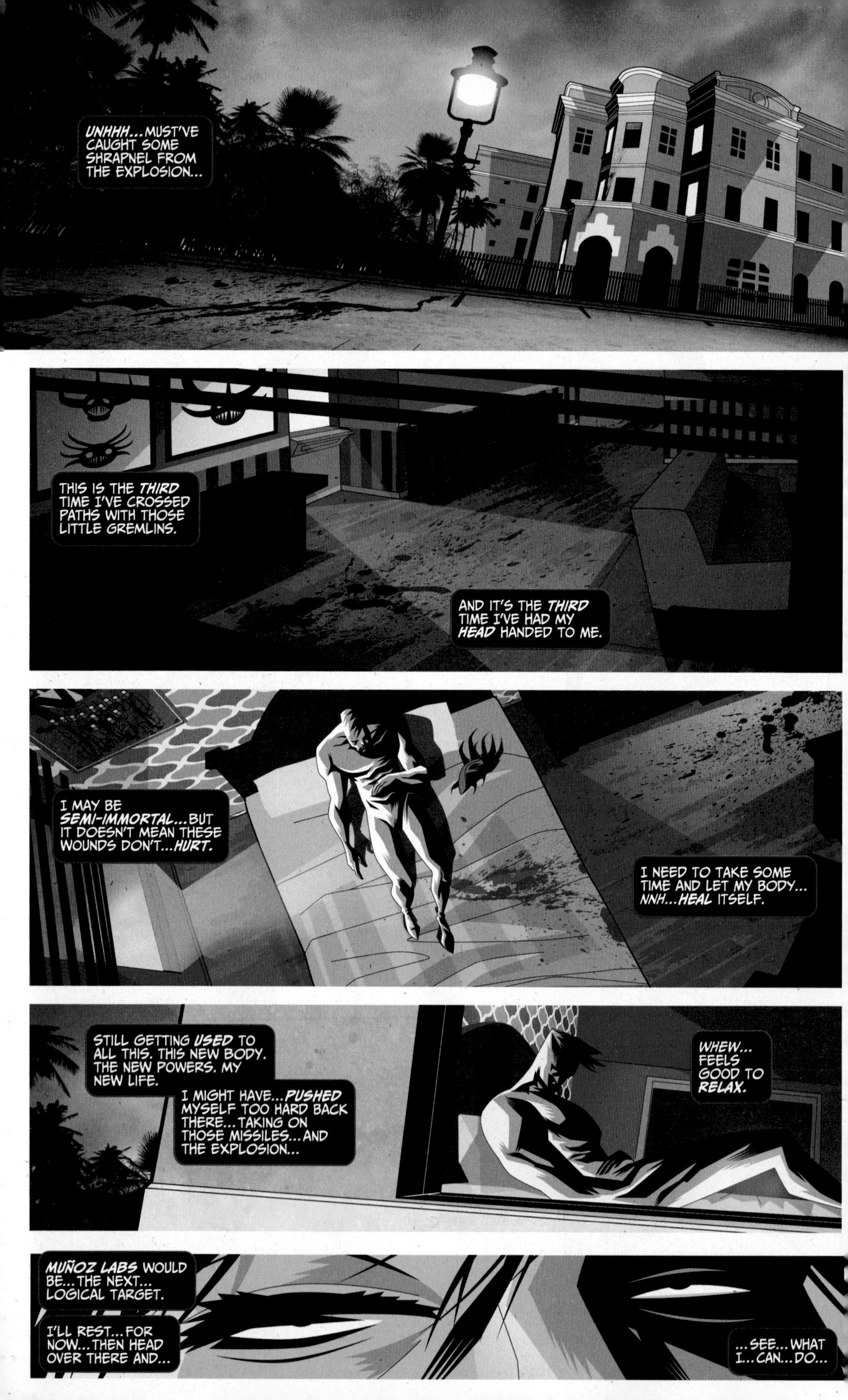
UNHHH... MUST'VE CAUGHT SOME SHRAPNEL FROM THE EXPLOSION...
THIS IS THE THIRD TIME I'VE CROSSED PATHS WITH THOSE LITTLE GREMLINS.
AND IT'S THE THIRD TIME I'VE HAD MY HEAD HANDED TO ME.
I MAY BE SEMI-IMMORTAL... BUT IT DOESN'T MEAN THESE WOUNDS DON'T... HURT.
I NEED TO TAKE SOME TIME AND LET MY BODY... NNH... HEAL ITSELF.
STILL GETTING USED TO ALL THIS. THIS NEW BODY. THE NEW POWERS. MY NEW LIFE.
I MIGHT HAVE... PUSHED MYSELF TOO HARD BACK THERE... TAKING ON THOSE MISSILES... AND THE EXPLOSION...
WHEW... FEELS GOOD TO RELAX.
MUÑOZ LABS WOULD BE... THE NEXT... LOGICAL TARGET.
I'LL REST... FOR NOW... THEN HEAD OVER THERE AND...
...SEE... WHAT I... CAN... DO...

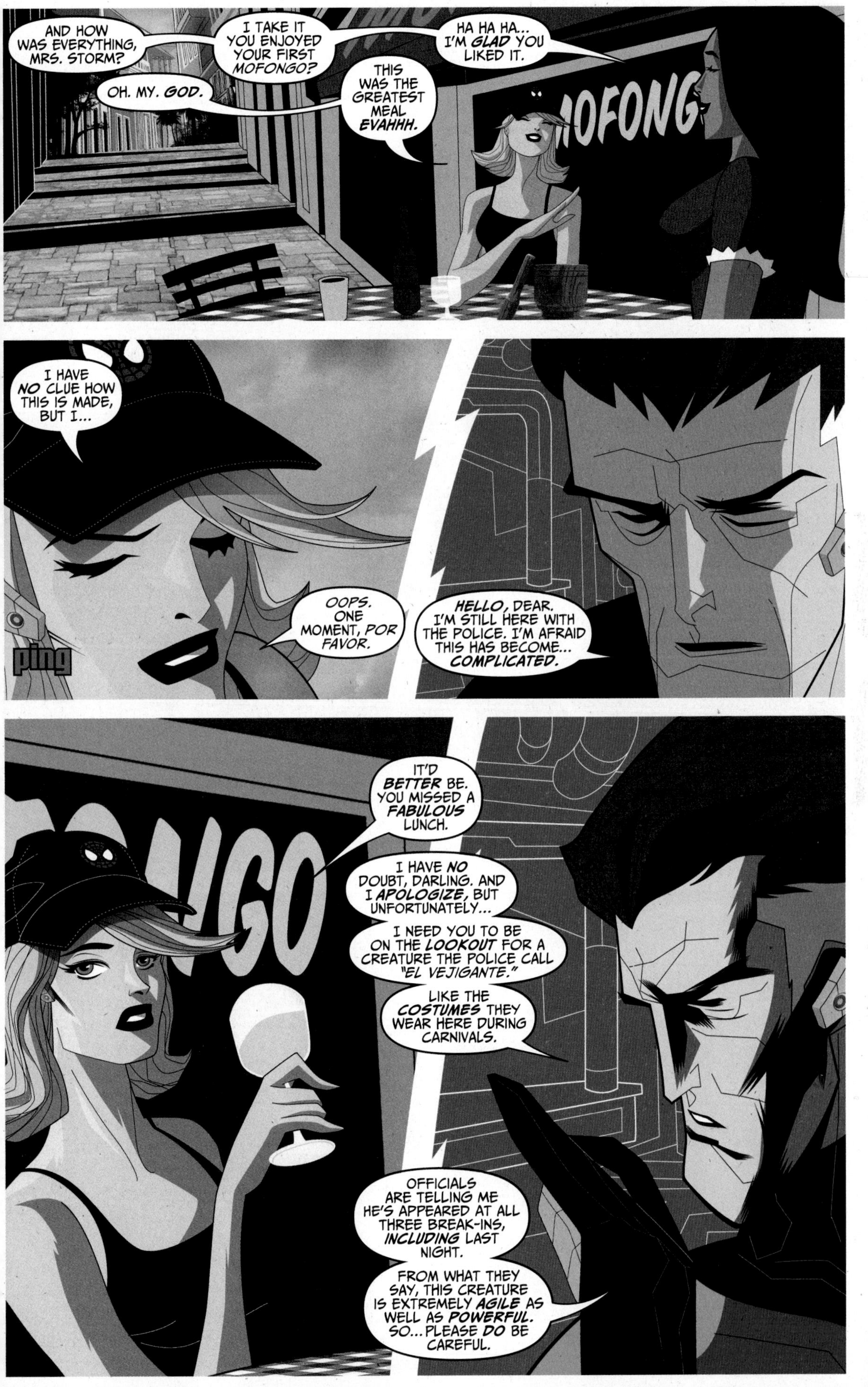
AND HOW WAS EVERYTHING, MRS. STORM?
OH. MY. GOD.
I TAKE IT YOU ENJOYED YOUR FIRST MOFONGO?
THIS WAS THE GREATEST MEAL EVAHHH.
HA HA HA... I'M GLAD YOU LIKED IT.
MOFONG
I HAVE NO CLUE HOW THIS IS MADE, BUT I...
ping
OOPS. ONE MOMENT, POR FAVOR.
HELLO, DEAR. I'M STILL HERE WITH THE POLICE. I'M AFRAID THIS HAS BECOME... COMPLICATED.
UGO
IT'D BETTER BE. YOU MISSED A FABULOUS LUNCH.
I HAVE NO DOUBT, DARLING. AND I APOLOGIZE, BUT UNFORTUNATELY...
I NEED YOU TO BE ON THE LOOKOUT FOR A CREATURE THE POLICE CALL "EL VEJIGANTE."
LIKE THE COSTUMES THEY WEAR HERE DURING CARNIVALS.
OFFICIALS ARE TELLING ME HE'S APPEARED AT ALL THREE BREAK-INS, INCLUDING LAST NIGHT.
FROM WHAT THEY SAY, THIS CREATURE IS EXTREMELY AGILE AS WELL AS POWERFUL. SO...PLEASE DO BE CAREFUL.

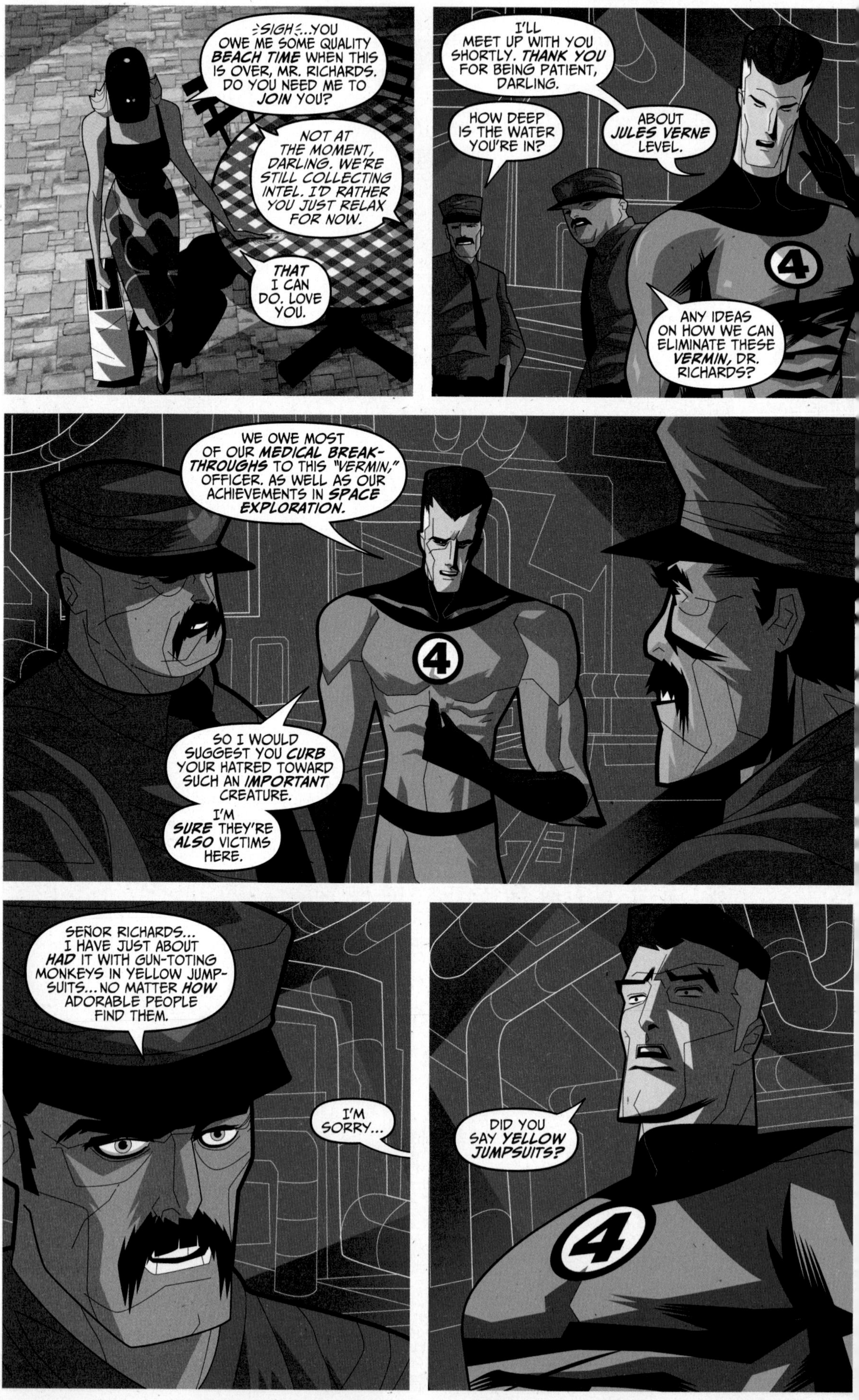

SIGH...YOU OWE ME SOME QUALITY BEACH TIME WHEN THIS IS OVER, MR. RICHARDS. DO YOU NEED ME TO JOIN YOU?
NOT AT THE MOMENT, DARLING. WE'RE STILL COLLECTING INTEL. I'D RATHER YOU JUST RELAX FOR NOW.
THAT I CAN DO. LOVE YOU.
I'LL MEET UP WITH YOU SHORTLY. THANK YOU FOR BEING PATIENT, DARLING.
HOW DEEP IS THE WATER YOU'RE IN?
ABOUT JULES VERNE LEVEL.
ANY IDEAS ON HOW WE CAN ELIMINATE THESE VERMIN, DR. RICHARDS?
WE OWE MOST OF OUR MEDICAL BREAK-THROUGHS TO THIS "VERMIN," OFFICER. AS WELL AS OUR ACHIEVEMENTS IN SPACE EXPLORATION.
SO I WOULD SUGGEST YOU CURB YOUR HATRED TOWARD SUCH AN IMPORTANT CREATURE.
I'M SURE THEY'RE ALSO VICTIMS HERE.
SEÑOR RICHARDS... I HAVE JUST ABOUT HAD IT WITH GUN-TOTING MONKEYS IN YELLOW JUMP-SUITS...NO MATTER HOW ADORABLE PEOPLE FIND THEM.
I'M SORRY...
DID YOU SAY YELLOW JUMPSUITS?

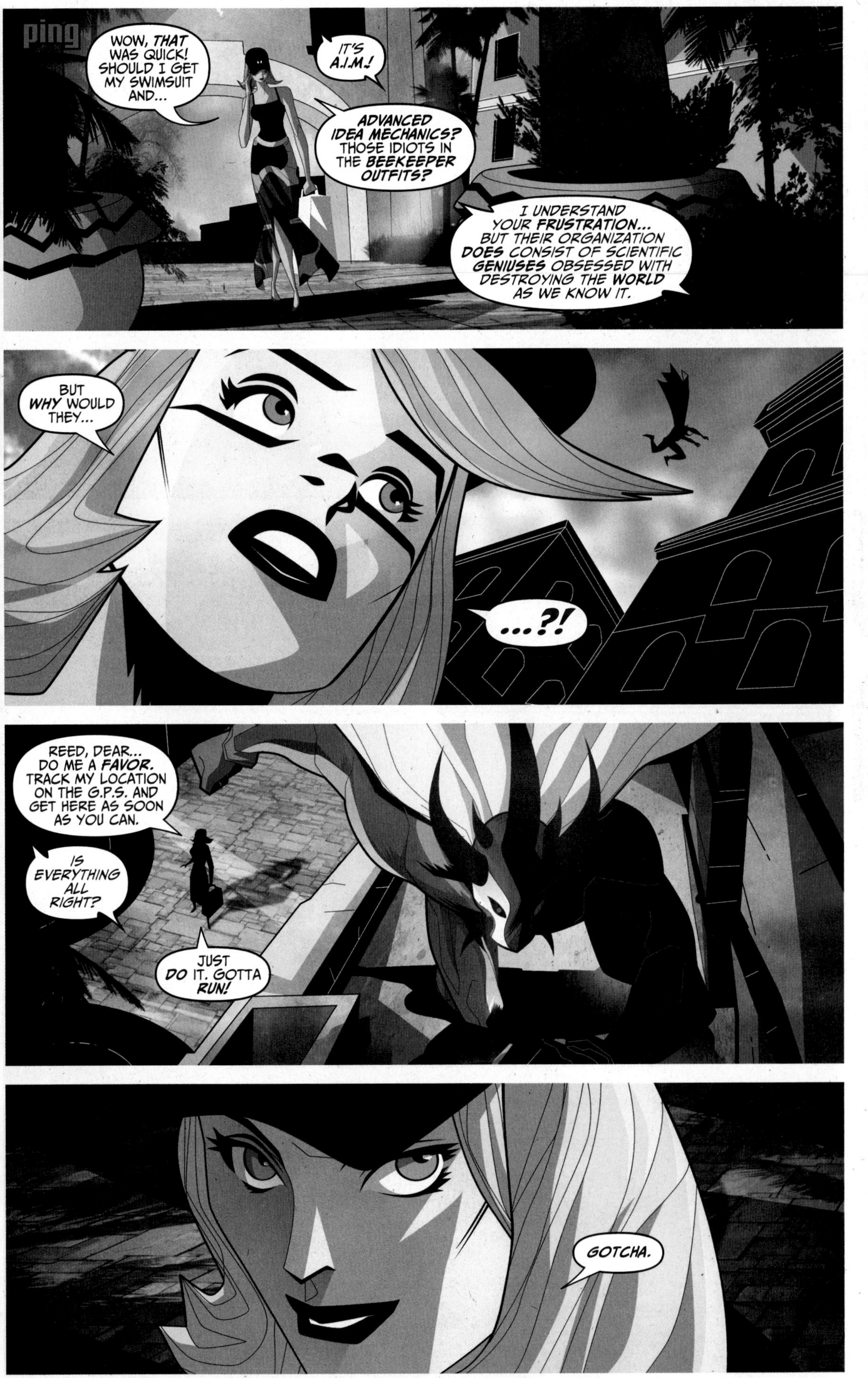
WOW, THAT WAS QUICK! SHOULD I GET MY SWIMSUIT AND...
IT'S A.I.M.!
ADVANCED IDEA MECHANICS? THOSE IDIOTS IN THE BEEKEEPER OUTFITS?
I UNDERSTAND YOUR FRUSTRATION... BUT THEIR ORGANIZATION DOES CONSIST OF SCIENTIFIC GENIUSES OBSESSED WITH DESTROYING THE WORLD AS WE KNOW IT.
BUT WHY WOULD THEY...
...?!
REED, DEAR... DO ME A FAVOR. TRACK MY LOCATION ON THE G.P.S. AND GET HERE AS SOON AS YOU CAN.
IS EVERYTHING ALL RIGHT?
JUST DO IT. GOTTA RUN!
GOTCHA.

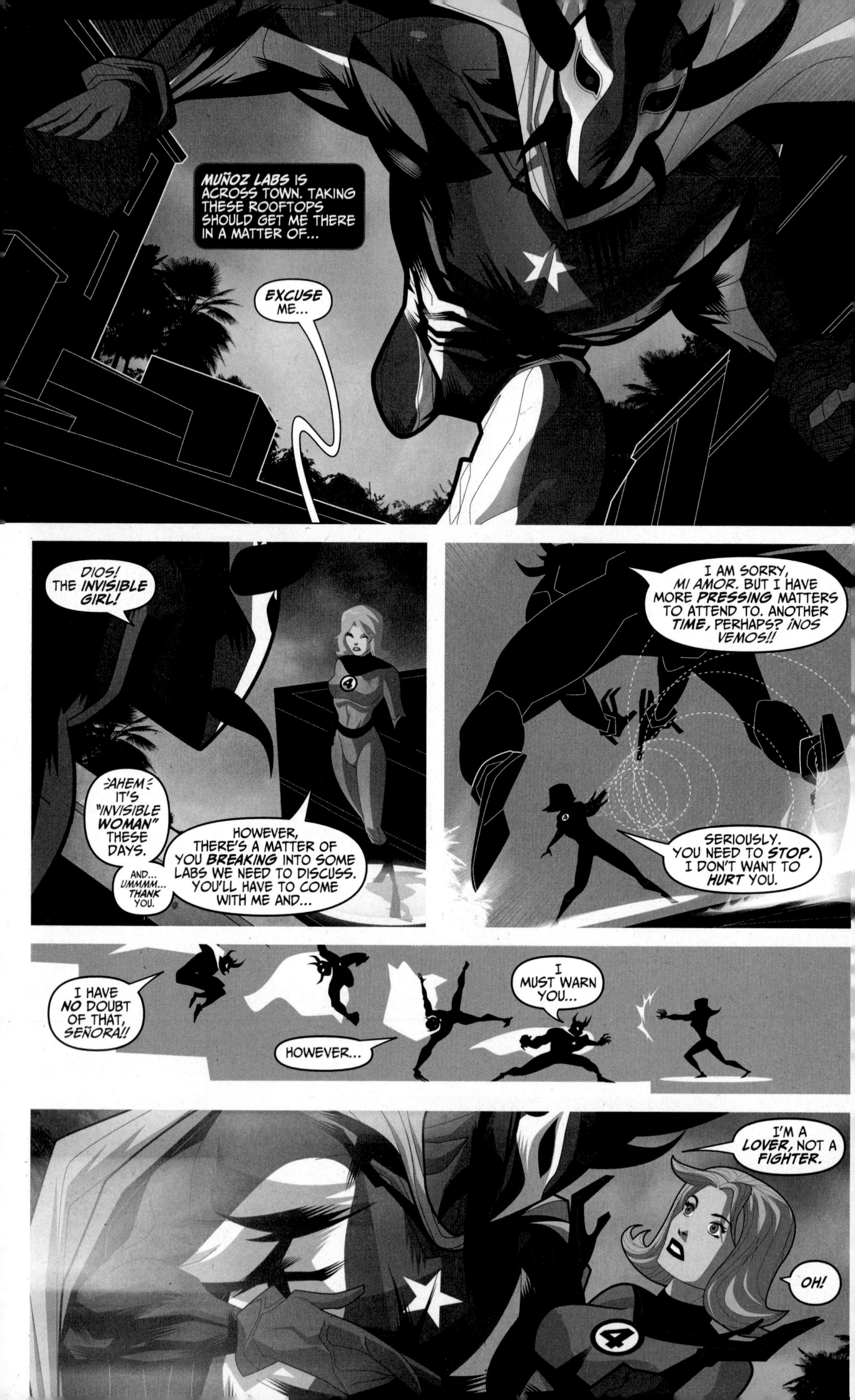
MUÑOZ LABS IS ACROSS TOWN. TAKING THESE ROOFTOPS SHOULD GET ME THERE IN A MATTER OF...
EXCUSE ME...
DIOS! THE INVISIBLE GIRL!
AHEM IT'S "INVISIBLE WOMAN" THESE DAYS.
AND... UMMMM... THANK YOU.
HOWEVER, THERE'S A MATTER OF YOU BREAKING INTO SOME LABS WE NEED TO DISCUSS. YOU'LL HAVE TO COME WITH ME AND...
I AM SORRY, MI AMOR. BUT I HAVE MORE PRESSING MATTERS TO ATTEND TO. ANOTHER TIME, PERHAPS? ¡NOS VEMOS!!
SERIOUSLY. YOU NEED TO STOP. I DON'T WANT TO HURT YOU.
I HAVE NO DOUBT OF THAT, SEÑORA!!
HOWEVER...
I MUST WARN YOU...
I'M A LOVER, NOT A FIGHTER.
OH!

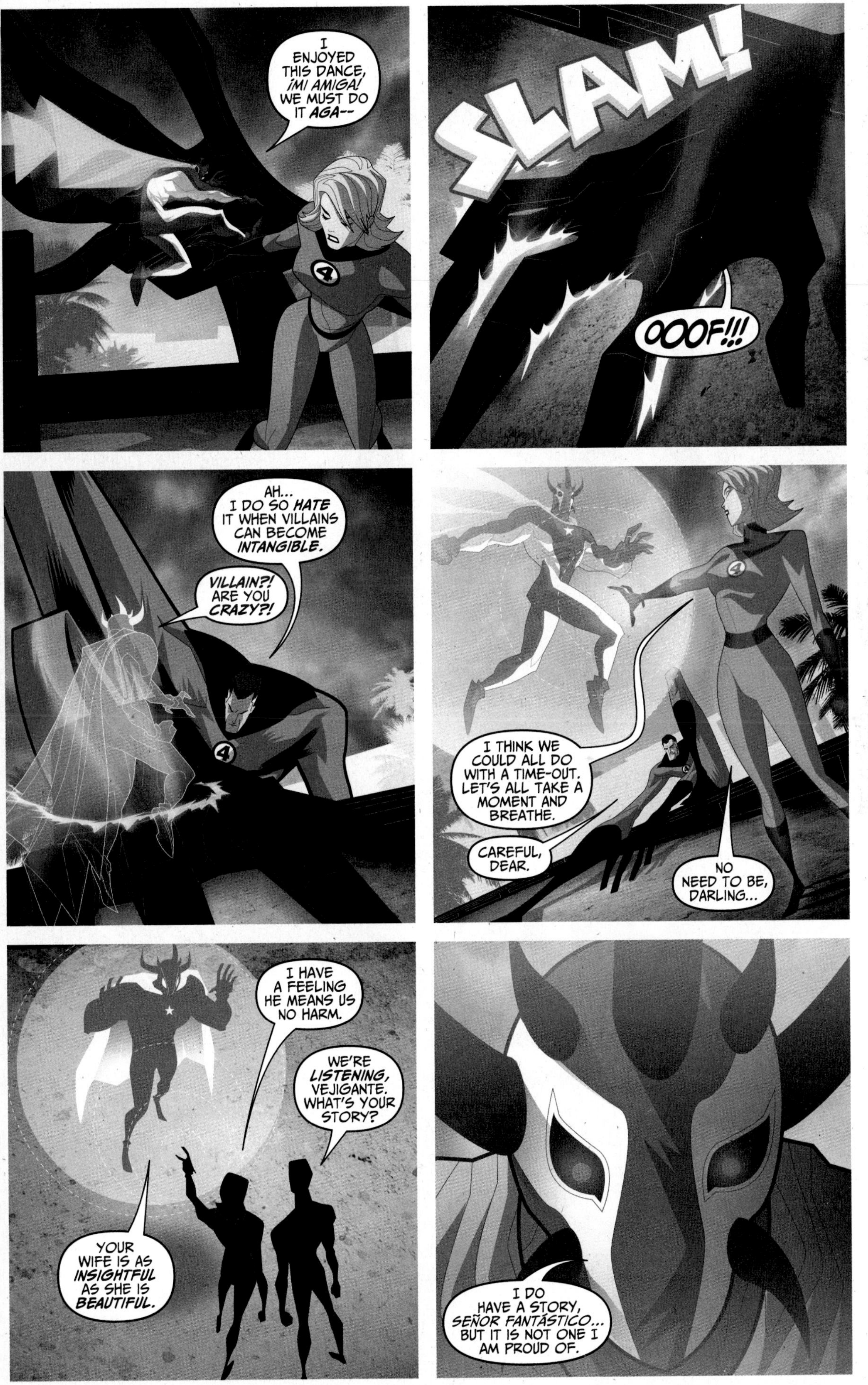
I ENJOYED THIS DANCE, ¡MI AMIGA! WE MUST DO IT AGA--
SLAM!
OOOF!!!
AH... I DO SO HATE IT WHEN VILLAINS CAN BECOME INTANGIBLE.
VILLAIN?! ARE YOU CRAZY?!
I THINK WE COULD ALL DO WITH A TIME-OUT. LET'S ALL TAKE A MOMENT AND BREATHE.
CAREFUL, DEAR.
NO NEED TO BE, DARLING...
I HAVE A FEELING HE MEANS US NO HARM.
WE'RE LISTENING, VEJIGANTE. WHAT'S YOUR STORY?
YOUR WIFE IS AS INSIGHTFUL AS SHE IS BEAUTIFUL.
I DO HAVE A STORY, SEÑOR FANTÁSTICO... BUT IT IS NOT ONE I AM PROUD OF.

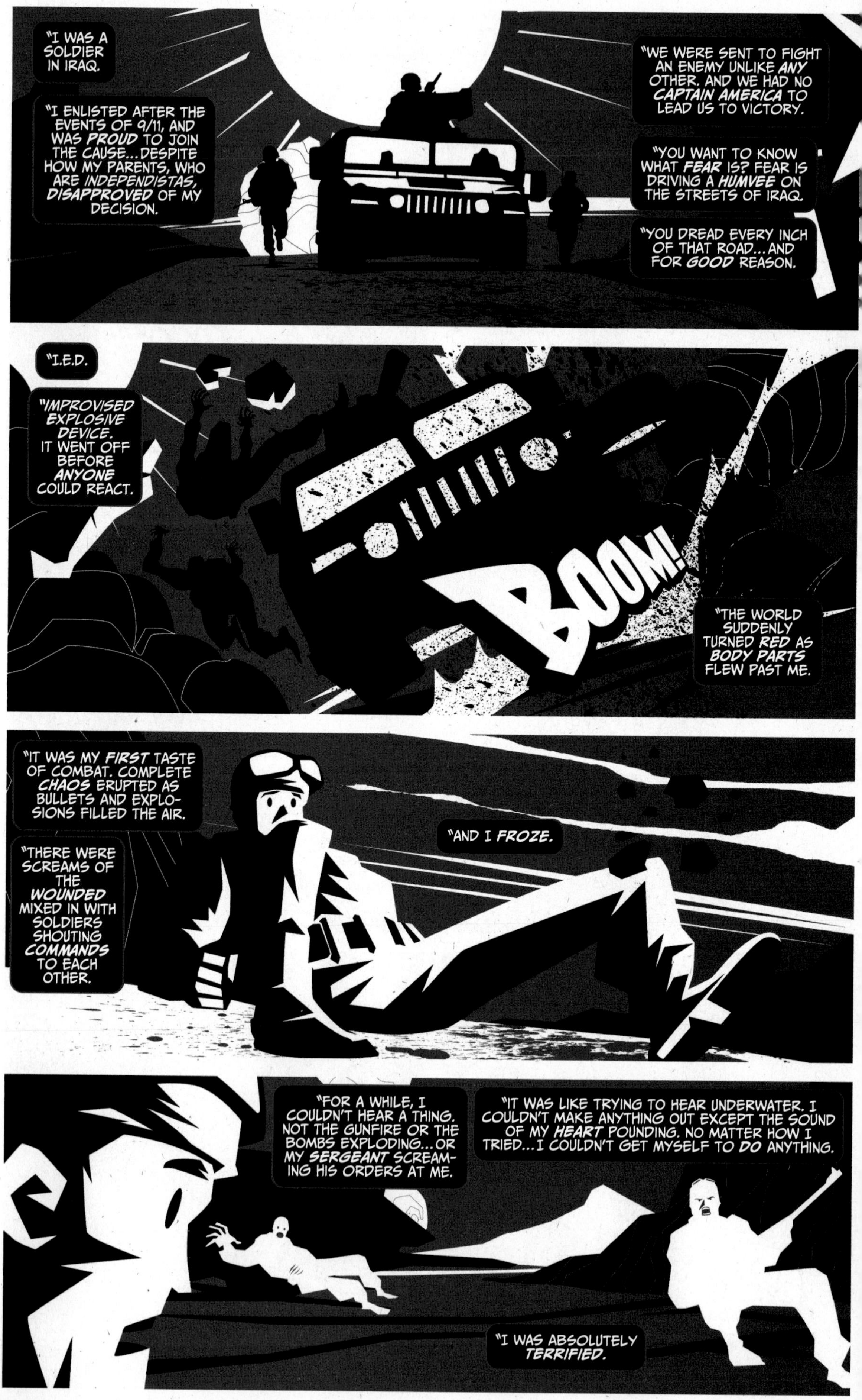
"I WAS A SOLDIER IN IRAQ.
"I ENLISTED AFTER THE EVENTS OF 9/11, AND WAS PROUD TO JOIN THE CAUSE...DESPITE HOW MY PARENTS, WHO ARE INDEPENDISTAS, DISAPPROVED OF MY DECISION.
"WE WERE SENT TO FIGHT AN ENEMY UNLIKE ANY OTHER. AND WE HAD NO CAPTAIN AMERICA TO LEAD US TO VICTORY.
"YOU WANT TO KNOW WHAT FEAR IS? FEAR IS DRIVING A HUMVEE ON THE STREETS OF IRAQ.
"YOU DREAD EVERY INCH OF THAT ROAD...AND FOR GOOD REASON.
"I.E.D.
"IMPROVISED EXPLOSIVE DEVICE. IT WENT OFF BEFORE ANYONE COULD REACT.
BOOM!
"THE WORLD SUDDENLY TURNED RED AS BODY PARTS FLEW PAST ME.
"IT WAS MY FIRST TASTE OF COMBAT. COMPLETE CHAOS ERUPTED AS BULLETS AND EXPLOSIONS FILLED THE AIR.
"THERE WERE SCREAMS OF THE WOUNDED MIXED IN WITH SOLDIERS SHOUTING COMMANDS TO EACH OTHER.
"AND I FROZE.
"FOR A WHILE, I COULDN'T HEAR A THING. NOT THE GUNFIRE OR THE BOMBS EXPLODING...OR MY SERGEANT SCREAMING HIS ORDERS AT ME.
"IT WAS LIKE TRYING TO HEAR UNDERWATER. I COULDN'T MAKE ANYTHING OUT EXCEPT THE SOUND OF MY HEART POUNDING. NO MATTER HOW I TRIED...I COULDN'T GET MYSELF TO DO ANYTHING.
"I WAS ABSOLUTELY TERRIFIED.

"THEN...SUDDENLY... MY HEARING CAME *BACK* TO ME...

"TO A MOST TERRIFYING SOUND.

"R.P.G.'S.

"*THREE* OF THEM.

"I SHOULD HAVE *HELPED* MY SERGEANT WITH THE WOUNDED. SHOULD HAVE HELPED THEM GET TO *SAFETY.*

"BUT MY *SURVIVAL INSTINCTS* TOOK OVER. AND I FLED. AS *FAST* AS MY LEGS COULD *CARRY* ME.

"I *MADE* IT TO SAFETY.

"MY TEAM, HOWEVER...

"GONE.

"*NONE* SURVIVED.

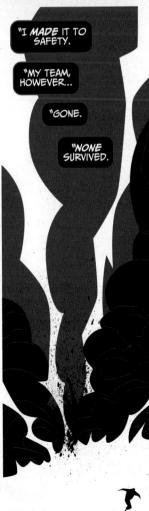

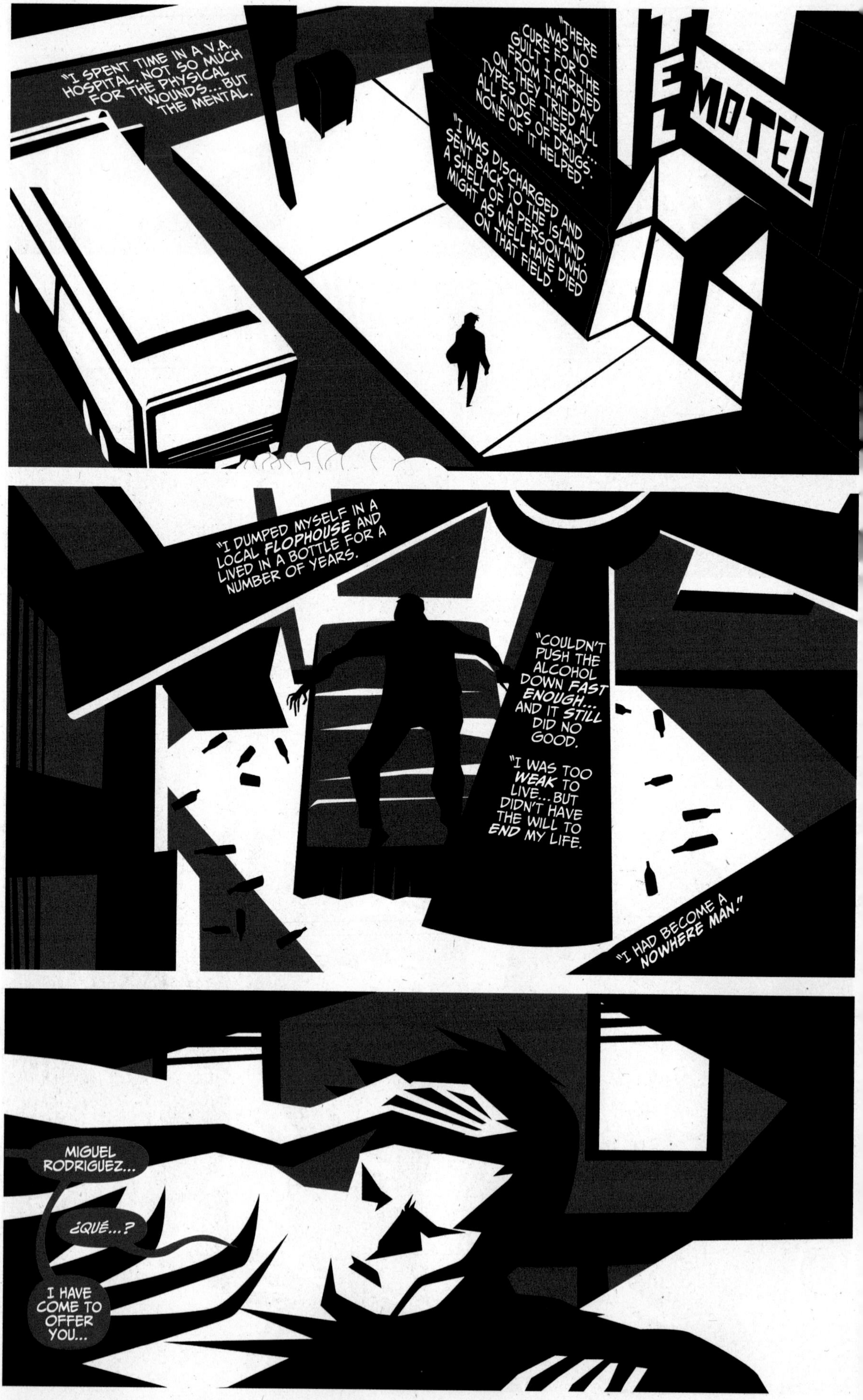
"I SPENT TIME IN A V.A. HOSPITAL. NOT SO MUCH FOR THE PHYSICAL WOUNDS... BUT THE MENTAL.
"THERE WAS NO CURE FOR THE GUILT I CARRIED FROM THAT DAY ON. THEY TRIED ALL TYPES OF THERAPY... ALL KINDS OF DRUGS... NONE OF IT HELPED.
"I WAS DISCHARGED AND SENT BACK TO THE ISLAND. A SHELL OF A PERSON WHO MIGHT AS WELL HAVE DIED ON THAT FIELD.
MOTEL
"I DUMPED MYSELF IN A LOCAL FLOPHOUSE AND LIVED IN A BOTTLE FOR A NUMBER OF YEARS.
"COULDN'T PUSH THE ALCOHOL DOWN FAST ENOUGH... AND IT STILL DID NO GOOD.
"I WAS TOO WEAK TO LIVE... BUT DIDN'T HAVE THE WILL TO END MY LIFE.
"I HAD BECOME A NOWHERE MAN."
MIGUEL RODRIGUEZ...
¿QUÉ...?
I HAVE COME TO OFFER YOU...

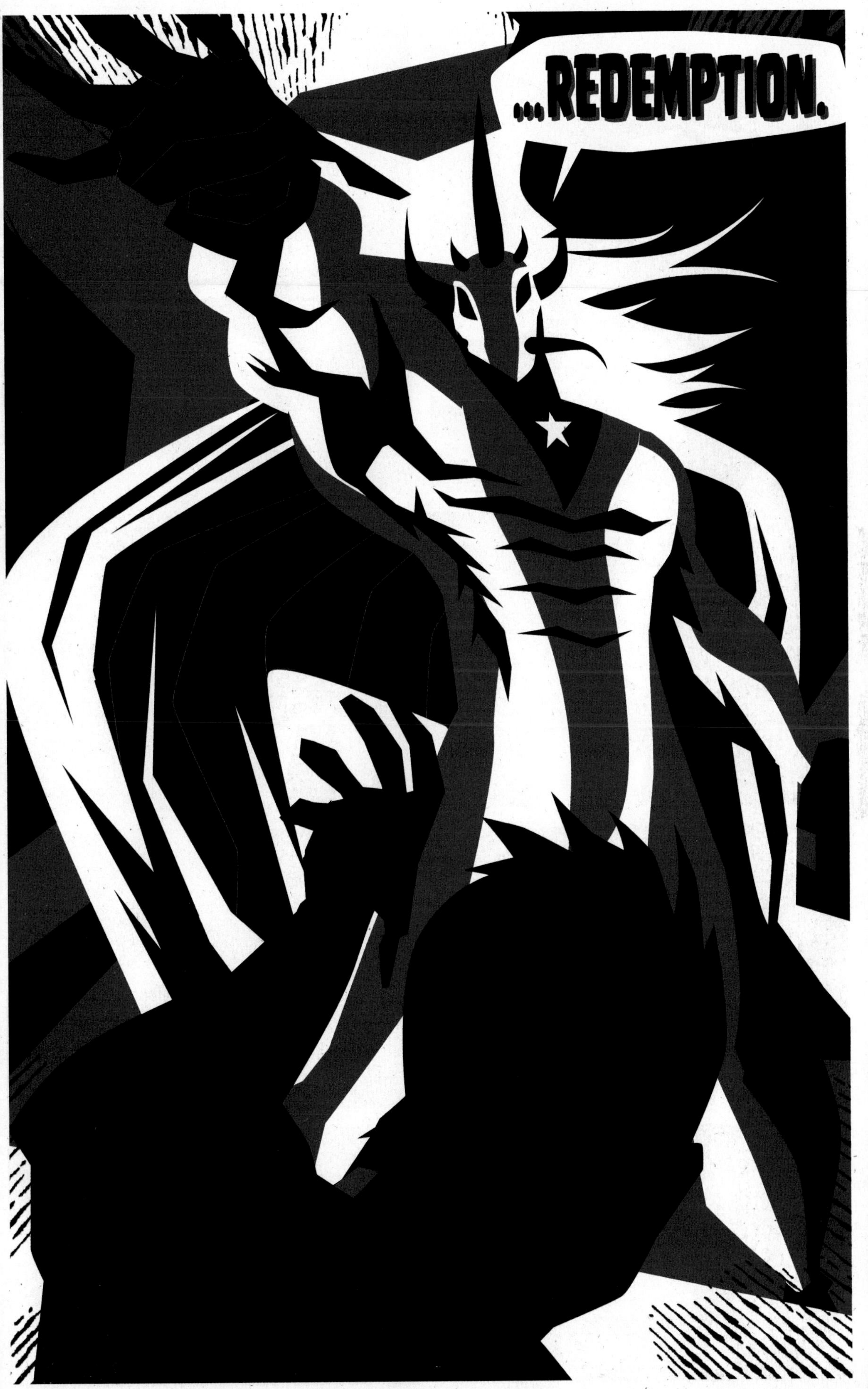
...REDEMPTION.

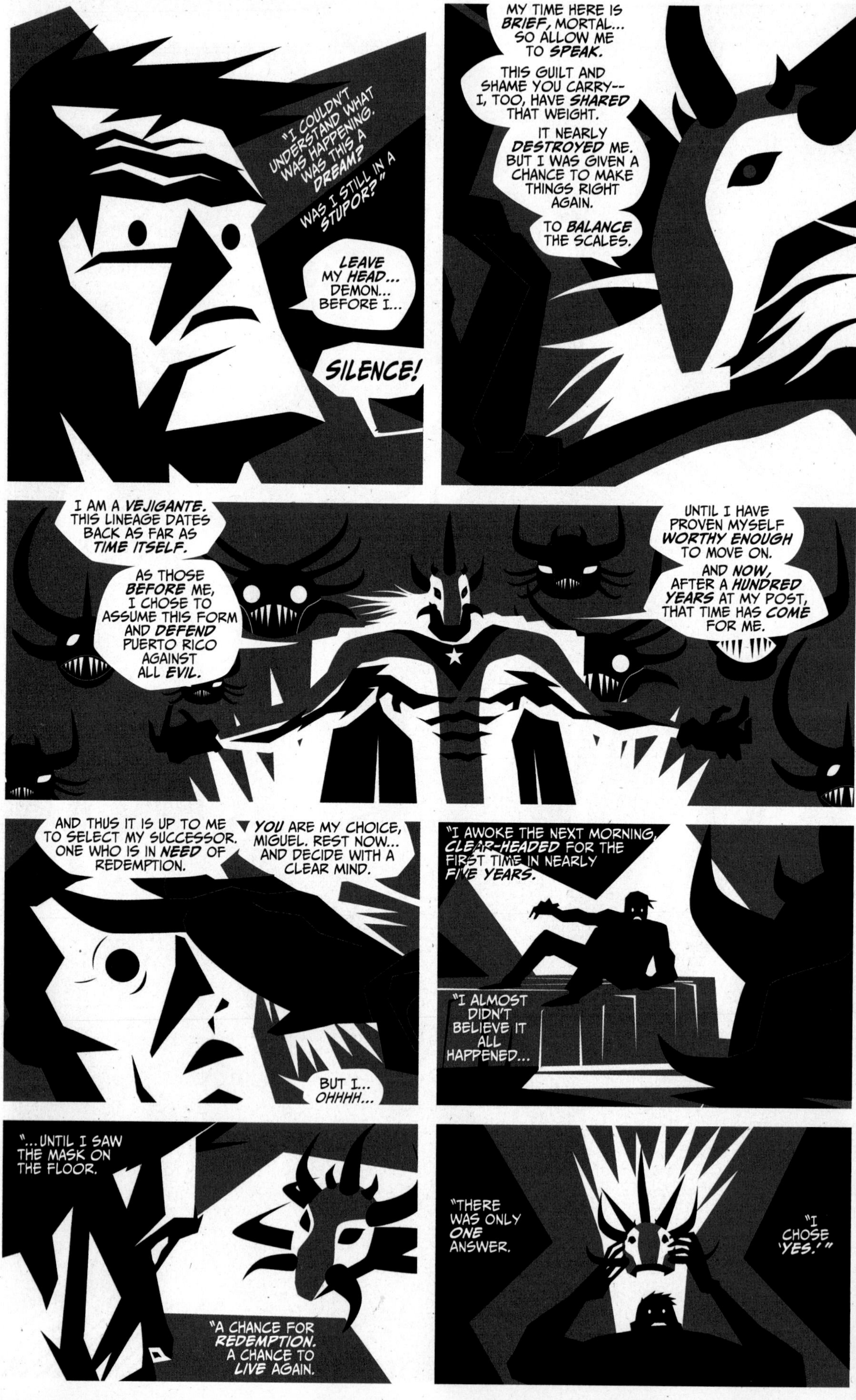
"I COULDN'T UNDERSTAND WHAT WAS HAPPENING. WAS THIS A DREAM?
WAS I STILL IN A STUPOR?"
LEAVE MY HEAD... DEMON... BEFORE I...
SILENCE!
MY TIME HERE IS BRIEF, MORTAL... SO ALLOW ME TO SPEAK.
THIS GUILT AND SHAME YOU CARRY-- I, TOO, HAVE SHARED THAT WEIGHT.
IT NEARLY DESTROYED ME. BUT I WAS GIVEN A CHANCE TO MAKE THINGS RIGHT AGAIN.
TO BALANCE THE SCALES.
I AM A VEJIGANTE. THIS LINEAGE DATES BACK AS FAR AS TIME ITSELF.
AS THOSE BEFORE ME, I CHOSE TO ASSUME THIS FORM AND DEFEND PUERTO RICO AGAINST ALL EVIL.
UNTIL I HAVE PROVEN MYSELF WORTHY ENOUGH TO MOVE ON.
AND NOW, AFTER A HUNDRED YEARS AT MY POST, THAT TIME HAS COME FOR ME.
AND THUS IT IS UP TO ME TO SELECT MY SUCCESSOR. ONE WHO IS IN NEED OF REDEMPTION.
YOU ARE MY CHOICE, MIGUEL. REST NOW... AND DECIDE WITH A CLEAR MIND.
BUT I... OHHHH...
"I AWOKE THE NEXT MORNING, CLEAR-HEADED FOR THE FIRST TIME IN NEARLY FIVE YEARS.
"I ALMOST DIDN'T BELIEVE IT ALL HAPPENED...
"...UNTIL I SAW THE MASK ON THE FLOOR.
"A CHANCE FOR REDEMPTION. A CHANCE TO LIVE AGAIN.
"THERE WAS ONLY ONE ANSWER.
"I CHOSE 'YES.'"

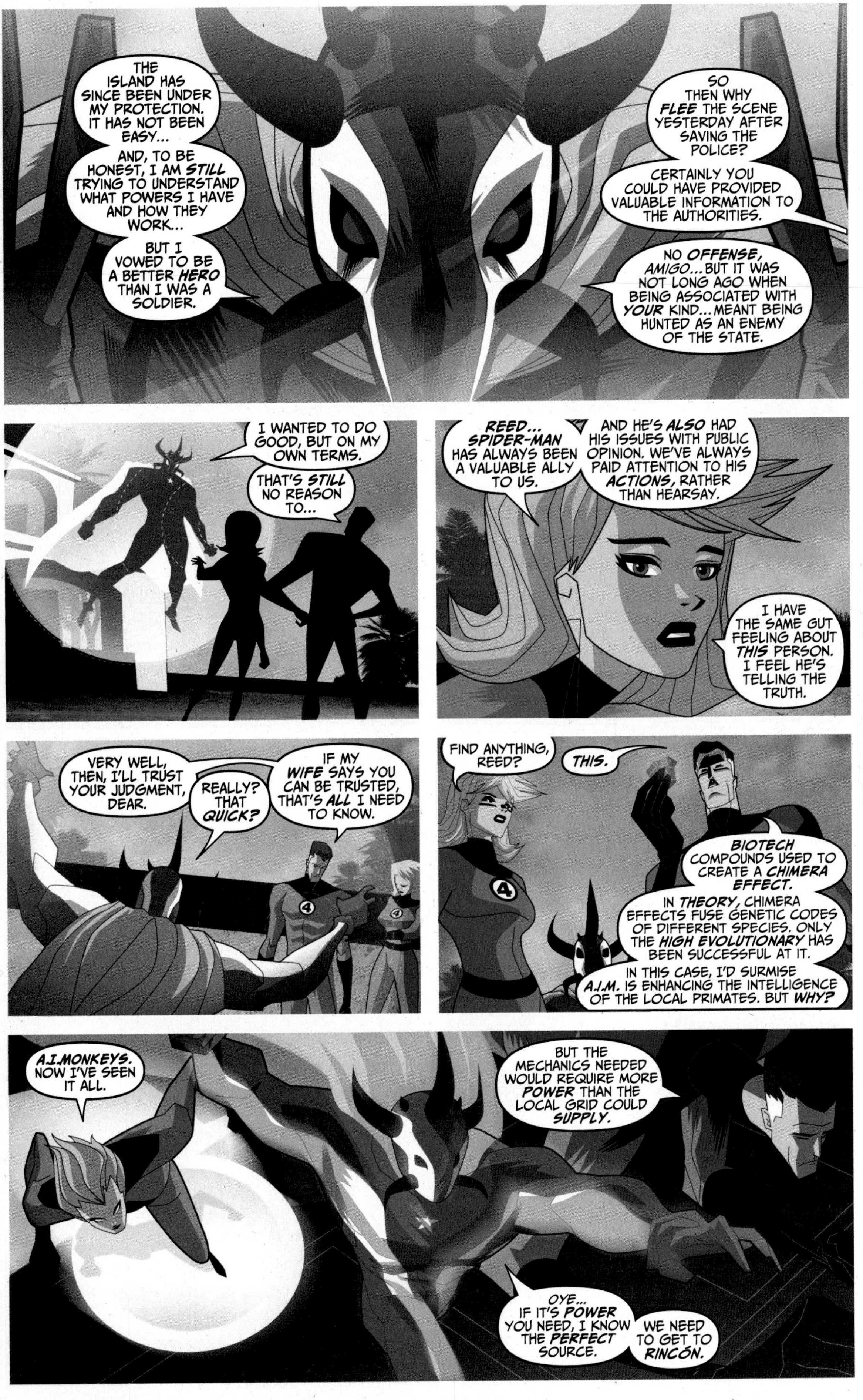
THE ISLAND HAS SINCE BEEN UNDER MY PROTECTION. IT HAS NOT BEEN EASY...
AND, TO BE HONEST, I AM STILL TRYING TO UNDERSTAND WHAT POWERS I HAVE AND HOW THEY WORK...
BUT I VOWED TO BE A BETTER HERO THAN I WAS A SOLDIER.
SO THEN WHY FLEE THE SCENE YESTERDAY AFTER SAVING THE POLICE?
CERTAINLY YOU COULD HAVE PROVIDED VALUABLE INFORMATION TO THE AUTHORITIES.
NO OFFENSE, AMIGO... BUT IT WAS NOT LONG AGO WHEN BEING ASSOCIATED WITH YOUR KIND... MEANT BEING HUNTED AS AN ENEMY OF THE STATE.
I WANTED TO DO GOOD, BUT ON MY OWN TERMS.
THAT'S STILL NO REASON TO...
REED... SPIDER-MAN HAS ALWAYS BEEN A VALUABLE ALLY TO US.
AND HE'S ALSO HAD HIS ISSUES WITH PUBLIC OPINION. WE'VE ALWAYS PAID ATTENTION TO HIS ACTIONS, RATHER THAN HEARSAY.
I HAVE THE SAME GUT FEELING ABOUT THIS PERSON. I FEEL HE'S TELLING THE TRUTH.
VERY WELL, THEN, I'LL TRUST YOUR JUDGMENT, DEAR.
REALLY? THAT QUICK?
IF MY WIFE SAYS YOU CAN BE TRUSTED, THAT'S ALL I NEED TO KNOW.
FIND ANYTHING, REED?
THIS.
BIOTECH COMPOUNDS USED TO CREATE A CHIMERA EFFECT.
IN THEORY, CHIMERA EFFECTS FUSE GENETIC CODES OF DIFFERENT SPECIES. ONLY THE HIGH EVOLUTIONARY HAS BEEN SUCCESSFUL AT IT.
IN THIS CASE, I'D SURMISE A.I.M. IS ENHANCING THE INTELLIGENCE OF THE LOCAL PRIMATES. BUT WHY?
A.I.MONKEYS. NOW I'VE SEEN IT ALL.
BUT THE MECHANICS NEEDED WOULD REQUIRE MORE POWER THAN THE LOCAL GRID COULD SUPPLY.
OYE... IF IT'S POWER YOU NEED, I KNOW THE PERFECT SOURCE.
WE NEED TO GET TO RINCÓN.

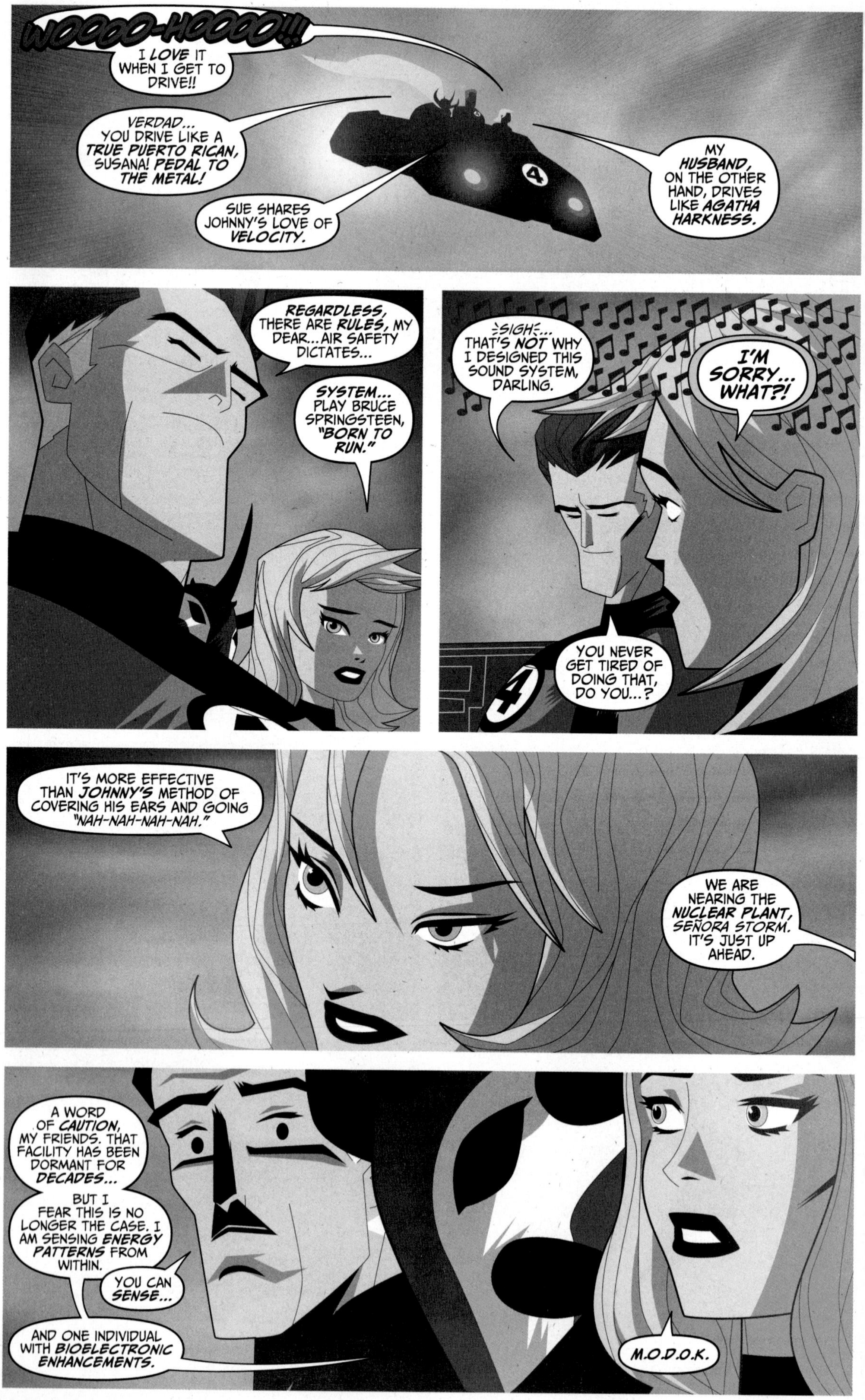
WOOOO-HOOOO!!!
I LOVE IT WHEN I GET TO DRIVE!!
VERDAD... YOU DRIVE LIKE A TRUE PUERTO RICAN, SUSANA! PEDAL TO THE METAL!
SUE SHARES JOHNNY'S LOVE OF VELOCITY.
MY HUSBAND, ON THE OTHER HAND, DRIVES LIKE AGATHA HARKNESS.
REGARDLESS, THERE ARE RULES, MY DEAR...AIR SAFETY DICTATES...
SYSTEM... PLAY BRUCE SPRINGSTEEN, "BORN TO RUN."
SIGH... THAT'S NOT WHY I DESIGNED THIS SOUND SYSTEM, DARLING.
I'M SORRY... WHAT?!
YOU NEVER GET TIRED OF DOING THAT, DO YOU...?
IT'S MORE EFFECTIVE THAN JOHNNY'S METHOD OF COVERING HIS EARS AND GOING "NAH-NAH-NAH-NAH."
WE ARE NEARING THE NUCLEAR PLANT, SEÑORA STORM. IT'S JUST UP AHEAD.
A WORD OF CAUTION, MY FRIENDS. THAT FACILITY HAS BEEN DORMANT FOR DECADES...
BUT I FEAR THIS IS NO LONGER THE CASE. I AM SENSING ENERGY PATTERNS FROM WITHIN.
YOU CAN SENSE...
AND ONE INDIVIDUAL WITH BIOELECTRONIC ENHANCEMENTS.
M.O.D.O.K.

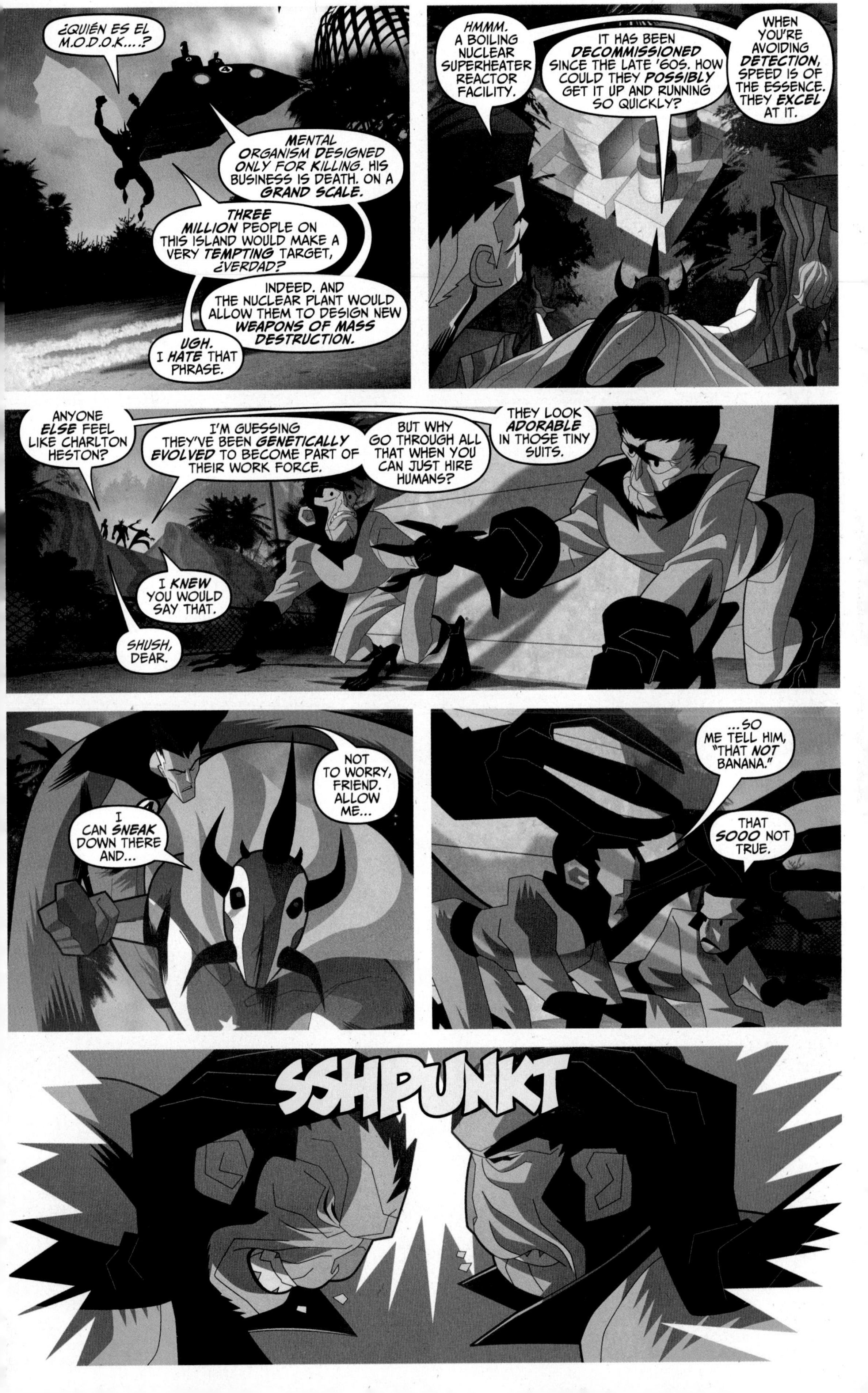
¿QUIÉN ES EL M.O.D.O.K....?
MENTAL ORGANISM DESIGNED ONLY FOR KILLING. HIS BUSINESS IS DEATH. ON A GRAND SCALE.
THREE MILLION PEOPLE ON THIS ISLAND WOULD MAKE A VERY TEMPTING TARGET, ¿VERDAD?
INDEED. AND THE NUCLEAR PLANT WOULD ALLOW THEM TO DESIGN NEW WEAPONS OF MASS DESTRUCTION.
UGH. I HATE THAT PHRASE.
HMMM. A BOILING NUCLEAR SUPERHEATER REACTOR FACILITY.
IT HAS BEEN DECOMMISSIONED SINCE THE LATE '60S. HOW COULD THEY POSSIBLY GET IT UP AND RUNNING SO QUICKLY?
WHEN YOU'RE AVOIDING DETECTION, SPEED IS OF THE ESSENCE. THEY EXCEL AT IT.
ANYONE ELSE FEEL LIKE CHARLTON HESTON?
I'M GUESSING THEY'VE BEEN GENETICALLY EVOLVED TO BECOME PART OF THEIR WORK FORCE.
BUT WHY GO THROUGH ALL THAT WHEN YOU CAN JUST HIRE HUMANS?
THEY LOOK ADORABLE IN THOSE TINY SUITS.
I KNEW YOU WOULD SAY THAT.
SHUSH, DEAR.
I CAN SNEAK DOWN THERE AND...
NOT TO WORRY, FRIEND. ALLOW ME...
...SO ME TELL HIM, "THAT NOT BANANA."
THAT SOOO NOT TRUE.
SSHPUNKT

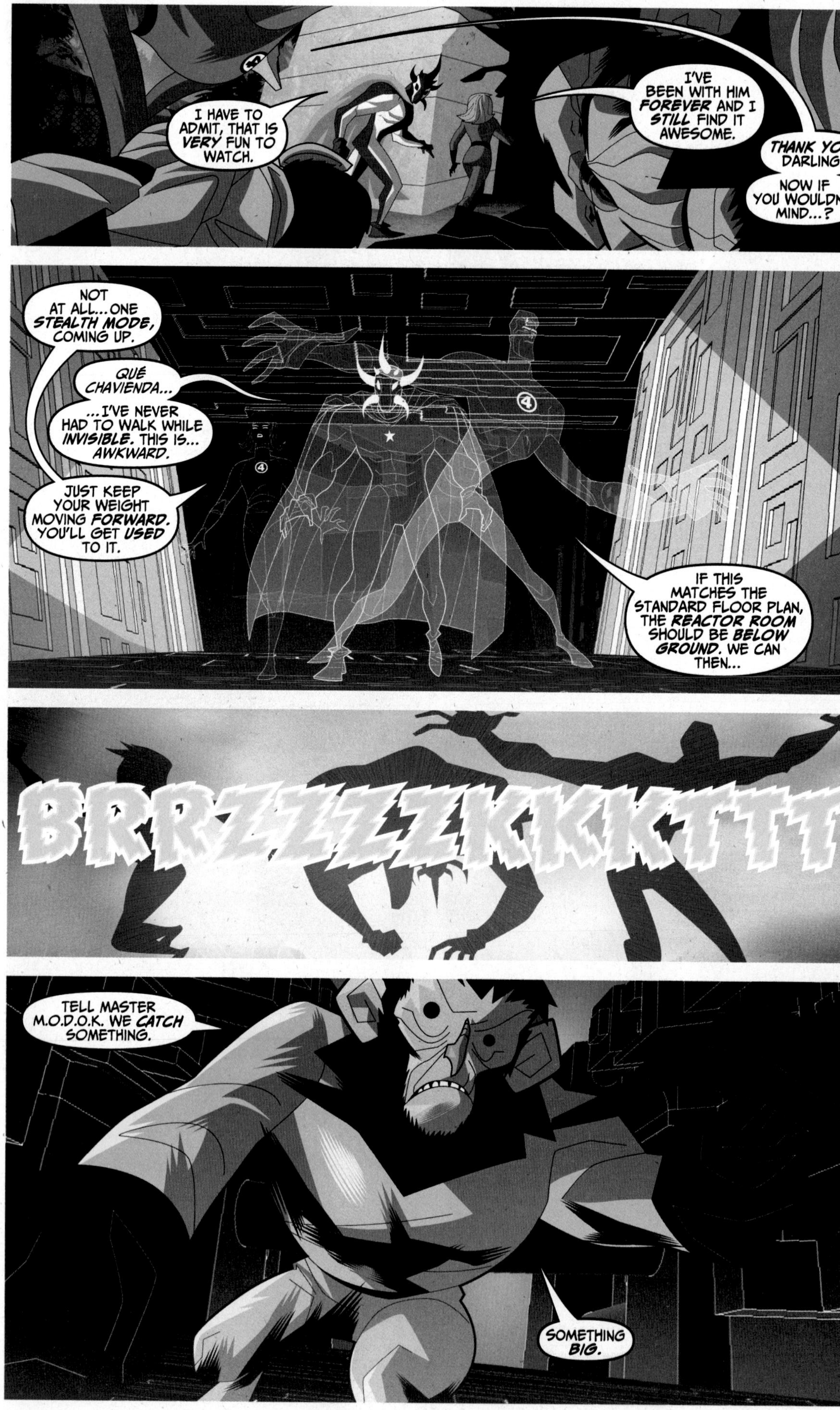
I HAVE TO ADMIT, THAT IS VERY FUN TO WATCH.
I'VE BEEN WITH HIM FOREVER AND I STILL FIND IT AWESOME.
THANK YOU, DARLING.
NOW IF YOU WOULDN'T MIND...?
NOT AT ALL...ONE STEALTH MODE, COMING UP.
QUÉ CHAVIENDA...
...I'VE NEVER HAD TO WALK WHILE INVISIBLE. THIS IS... AWKWARD.
JUST KEEP YOUR WEIGHT MOVING FORWARD. YOU'LL GET USED TO IT.
IF THIS MATCHES THE STANDARD FLOOR PLAN, THE REACTOR ROOM SHOULD BE BELOW GROUND. WE CAN THEN...
BRRZZZZKKKKTTT
TELL MASTER M.O.D.O.K. WE CATCH SOMETHING.
SOMETHING BIG.

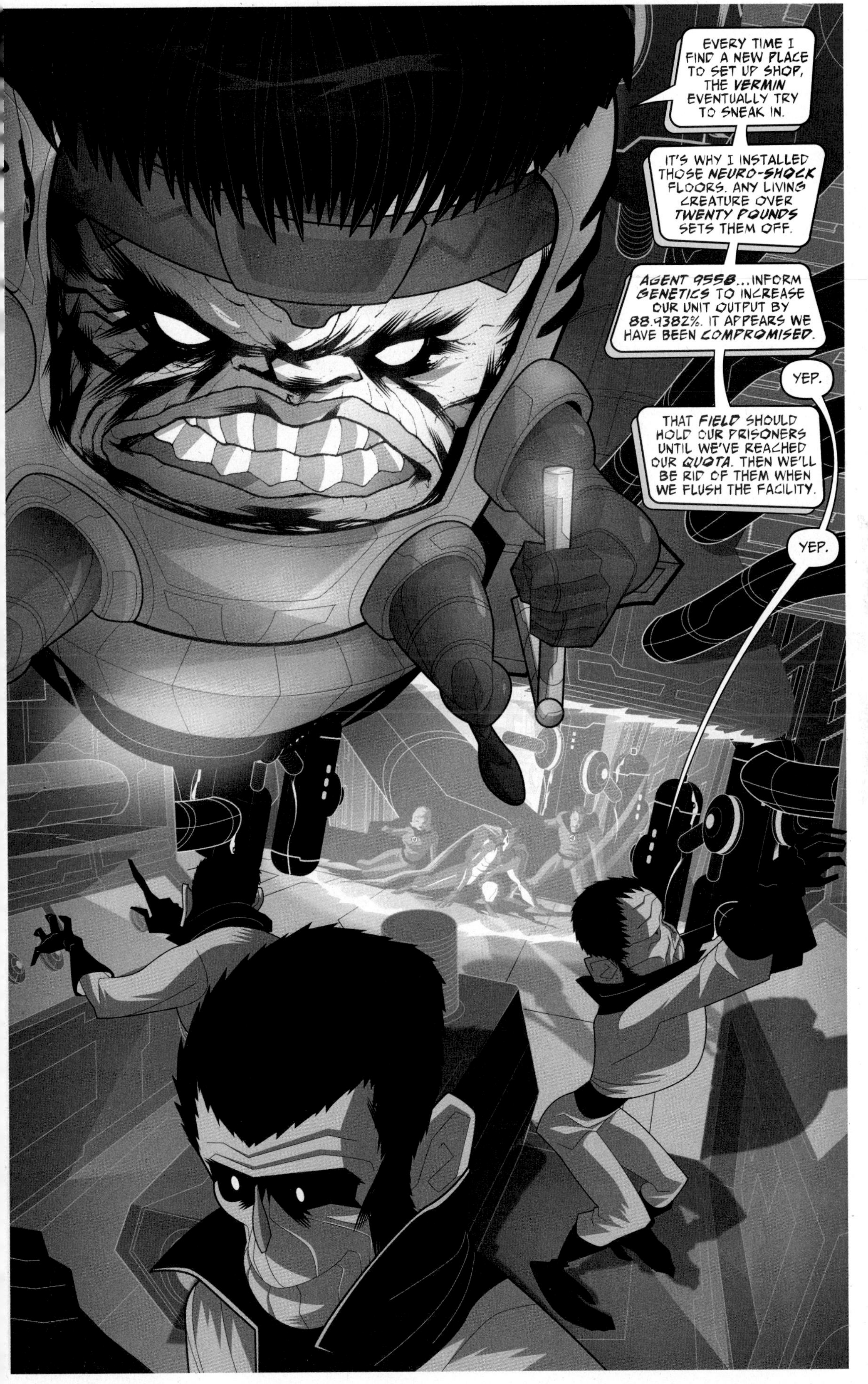
EVERY TIME I FIND A NEW PLACE TO SET UP SHOP, THE VERMIN EVENTUALLY TRY TO SNEAK IN.
IT'S WHY I INSTALLED THOSE NEURO-SHOCK FLOORS. ANY LIVING CREATURE OVER TWENTY POUNDS SETS THEM OFF.
AGENT 9558...INFORM GENETICS TO INCREASE OUR UNIT OUTPUT BY 88.9382%. IT APPEARS WE HAVE BEEN COMPROMISED.
YEP.
THAT FIELD SHOULD HOLD OUR PRISONERS UNTIL WE'VE REACHED OUR QUOTA. THEN WE'LL BE RID OF THEM WHEN WE FLUSH THE FACILITY.
YEP.

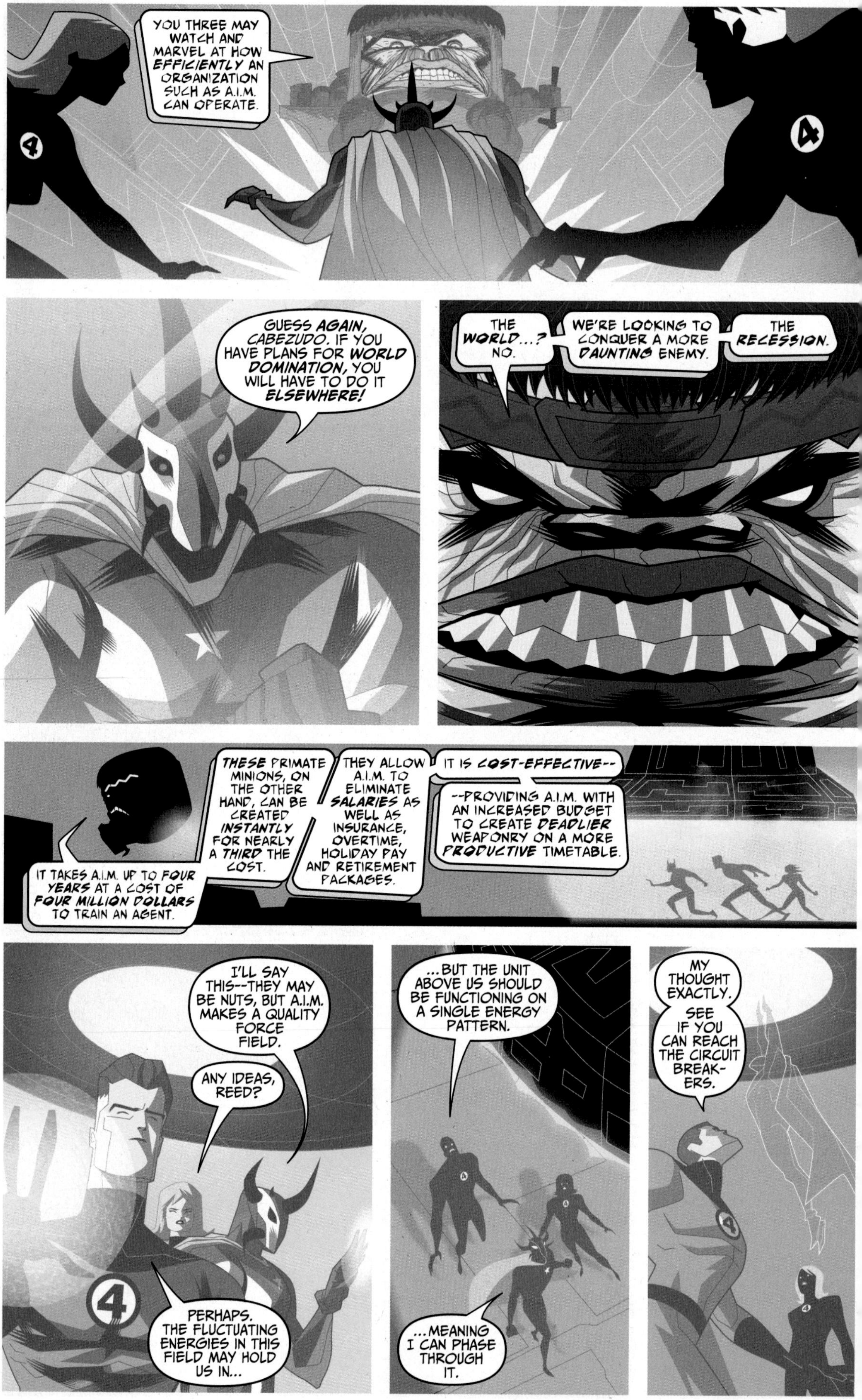
YOU THREE MAY WATCH AND MARVEL AT HOW EFFICIENTLY AN ORGANIZATION SUCH AS A.I.M. CAN OPERATE.
GUESS AGAIN, CABEZUDO. IF YOU HAVE PLANS FOR WORLD DOMINATION, YOU WILL HAVE TO DO IT ELSEWHERE!
THE WORLD...? NO.
WE'RE LOOKING TO CONQUER A MORE DAUNTING ENEMY.
THE RECESSION.
IT TAKES A.I.M. UP TO FOUR YEARS AT A COST OF FOUR MILLION DOLLARS TO TRAIN AN AGENT.
THESE PRIMATE MINIONS, ON THE OTHER HAND, CAN BE CREATED INSTANTLY FOR NEARLY A THIRD THE COST.
THEY ALLOW A.I.M. TO ELIMINATE SALARIES AS WELL AS INSURANCE, OVERTIME, HOLIDAY PAY AND RETIREMENT PACKAGES.
IT IS COST-EFFECTIVE--
--PROVIDING A.I.M. WITH AN INCREASED BUDGET TO CREATE DEADLIER WEAPONRY ON A MORE PRODUCTIVE TIMETABLE.
I'LL SAY THIS--THEY MAY BE NUTS, BUT A.I.M. MAKES A QUALITY FORCE FIELD.
ANY IDEAS, REED?
PERHAPS. THE FLUCTUATING ENERGIES IN THIS FIELD MAY HOLD US IN...
...BUT THE UNIT ABOVE US SHOULD BE FUNCTIONING ON A SINGLE ENERGY PATTERN.
...MEANING I CAN PHASE THROUGH IT.
MY THOUGHT EXACTLY.
SEE IF YOU CAN REACH THE CIRCUIT BREAKERS.

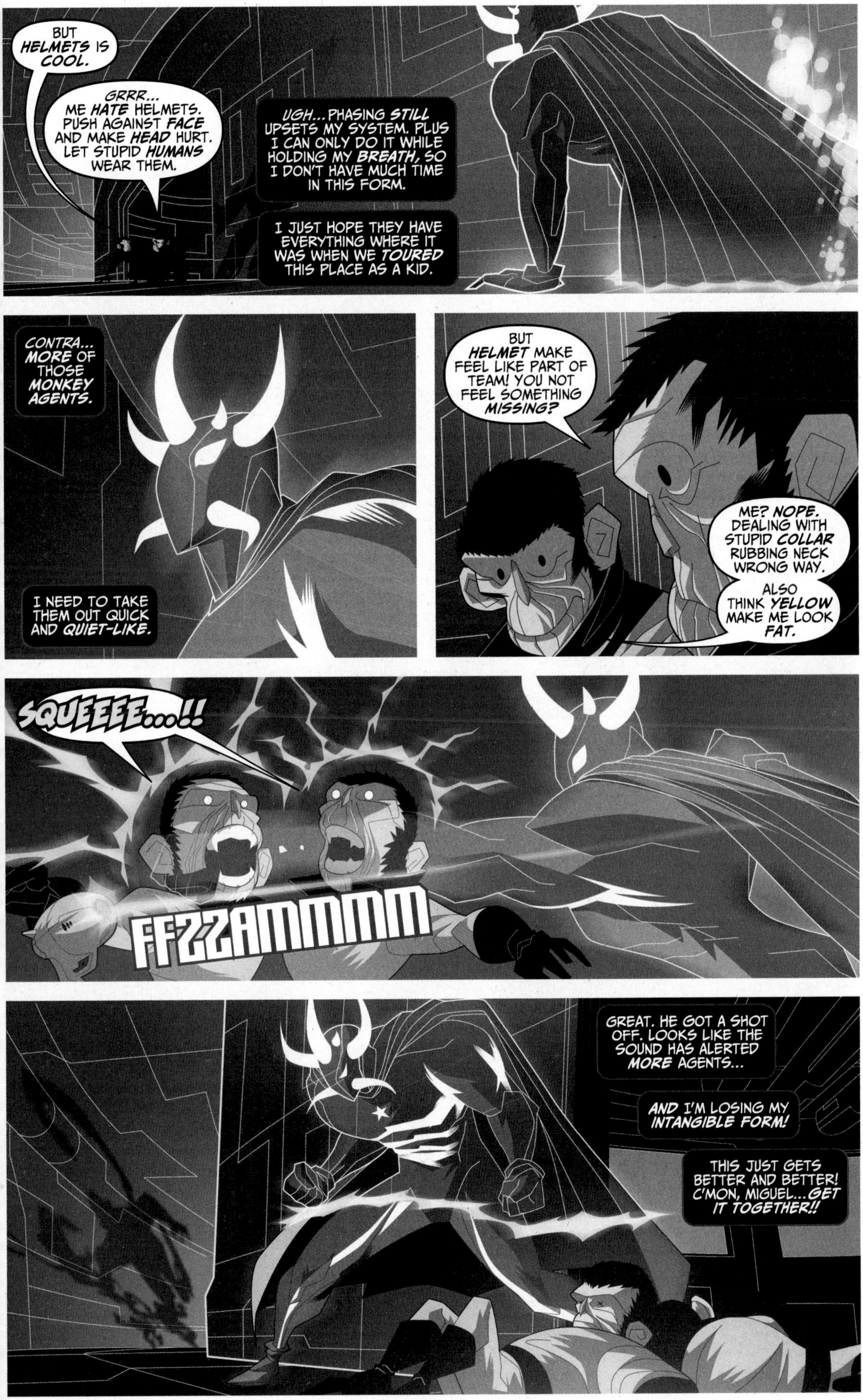
BUT HELMETS IS COOL.
GRRR... ME HATE HELMETS. PUSH AGAINST FACE AND MAKE HEAD HURT. LET STUPID HUMANS WEAR THEM.
UGH...PHASING STILL UPSETS MY SYSTEM. PLUS I CAN ONLY DO IT WHILE HOLDING MY BREATH, SO I DON'T HAVE MUCH TIME IN THIS FORM.
I JUST HOPE THEY HAVE EVERYTHING WHERE IT WAS WHEN WE TOURED THIS PLACE AS A KID.
CONTRA... MORE OF THOSE MONKEY AGENTS.
I NEED TO TAKE THEM OUT QUICK AND QUIET-LIKE.
BUT HELMET MAKE FEEL LIKE PART OF TEAM! YOU NOT FEEL SOMETHING MISSING?
ME? NOPE. DEALING WITH STUPID COLLAR RUBBING NECK WRONG WAY.
ALSO THINK YELLOW MAKE ME LOOK FAT.
SQUEEEE...!!
FFZZAMMMMM
GREAT. HE GOT A SHOT OFF. LOOKS LIKE THE SOUND HAS ALERTED MORE AGENTS...
AND I'M LOSING MY INTANGIBLE FORM!
THIS JUST GETS BETTER AND BETTER! C'MON, MIGUEL...GET IT TOGETHER!!

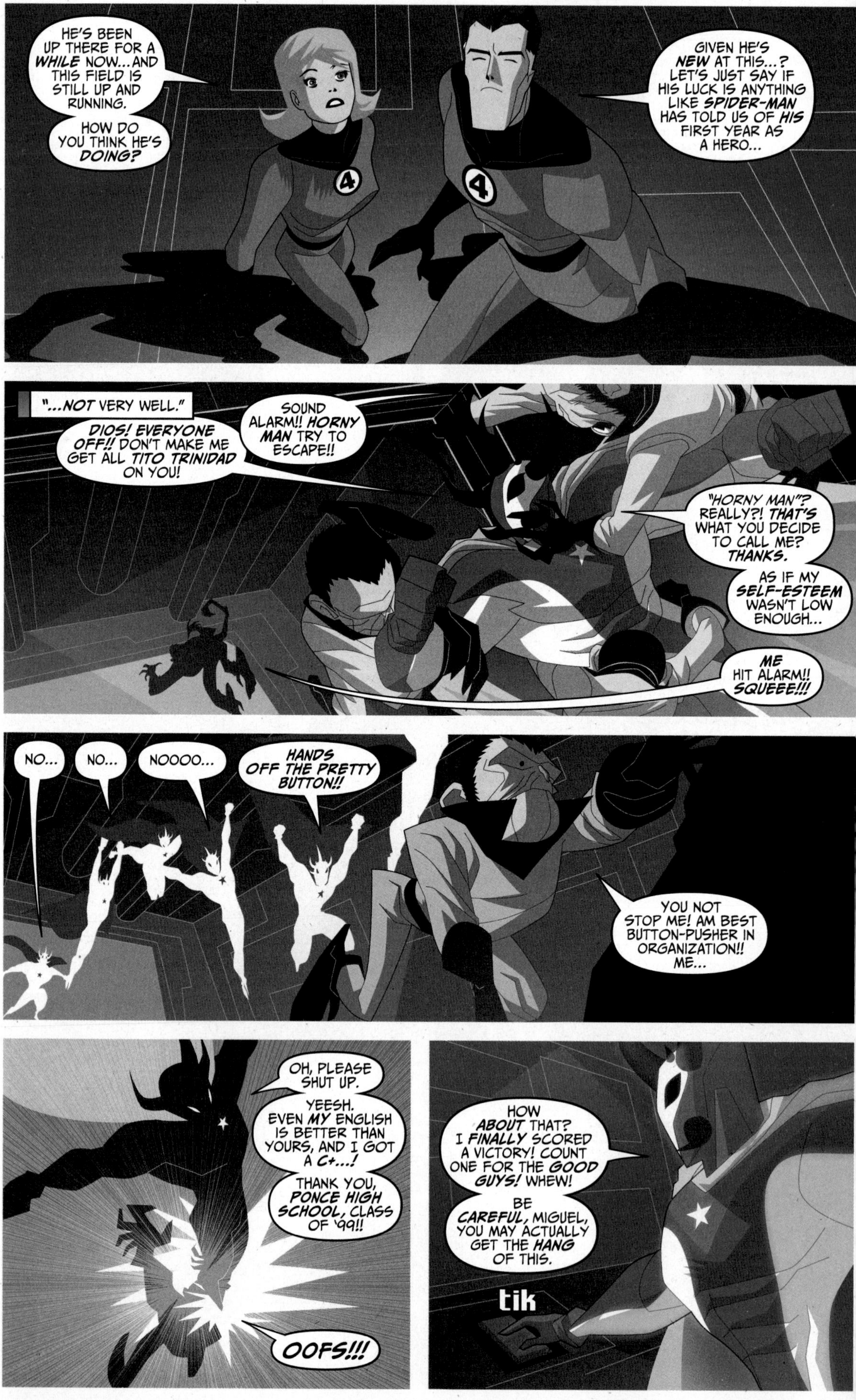

HE'S BEEN UP THERE FOR A WHILE NOW...AND THIS FIELD IS STILL UP AND RUNNING.
HOW DO YOU THINK HE'S DOING?
GIVEN HE'S NEW AT THIS...? LET'S JUST SAY IF HIS LUCK IS ANYTHING LIKE SPIDER-MAN HAS TOLD US OF HIS FIRST YEAR AS A HERO...
"...NOT VERY WELL."
DIOS! EVERYONE OFF!! DON'T MAKE ME GET ALL TITO TRINIDAD ON YOU!
SOUND ALARM!! HORNY MAN TRY TO ESCAPE!!
"HORNY MAN"? REALLY?! THAT'S WHAT YOU DECIDE TO CALL ME? THANKS.
AS IF MY SELF-ESTEEM WASN'T LOW ENOUGH...
ME HIT ALARM!! SQUEEE!!!
NO...
NO...
NOOOO...
HANDS OFF THE PRETTY BUTTON!!
YOU NOT STOP ME! AM BEST BUTTON-PUSHER IN ORGANIZATION!! ME...
OH, PLEASE SHUT UP.
YEESH. EVEN MY ENGLISH IS BETTER THAN YOURS, AND I GOT A C+...!
THANK YOU, PONCE HIGH SCHOOL, CLASS OF '99!!
OOFS!!!
HOW ABOUT THAT? I FINALLY SCORED A VICTORY! COUNT ONE FOR THE GOOD GUYS! WHEW!
BE CAREFUL, MIGUEL, YOU MAY ACTUALLY GET THE HANG OF THIS.
tik

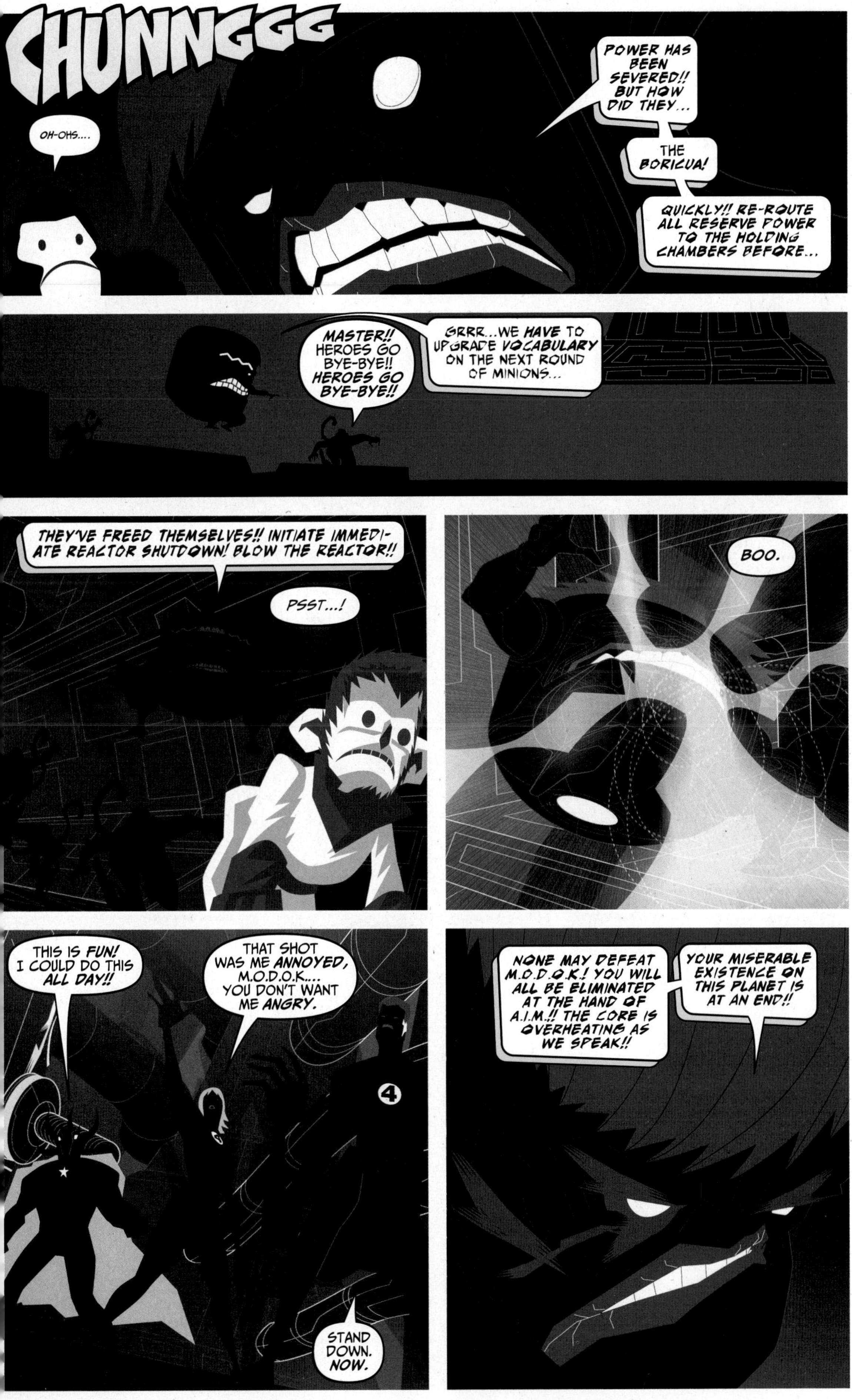
CHUNNGGG
OH-OHS....
POWER HAS BEEN SEVERED!! BUT HOW DID THEY...
THE BORICUA!
QUICKLY!! RE-ROUTE ALL RESERVE POWER TO THE HOLDING CHAMBERS BEFORE...
MASTER!! HEROES GO BYE-BYE!! HEROES GO BYE-BYE!!
GRRR...WE HAVE TO UPGRADE VOCABULARY ON THE NEXT ROUND OF MINIONS...
THEY'VE FREED THEMSELVES!! INITIATE IMMEDIATE REACTOR SHUTDOWN! BLOW THE REACTOR!!
PSST...!
BOO.
THIS IS FUN! I COULD DO THIS ALL DAY!!
THAT SHOT WAS ME ANNOYED, M.O.D.O.K.... YOU DON'T WANT ME ANGRY.
STAND DOWN. NOW.
NONE MAY DEFEAT M.O.D.O.K.! YOU WILL ALL BE ELIMINATED AT THE HAND OF A.I.M.!! THE CORE IS OVERHEATING AS WE SPEAK!!
YOUR MISERABLE EXISTENCE ON THIS PLANET IS AT AN END!!

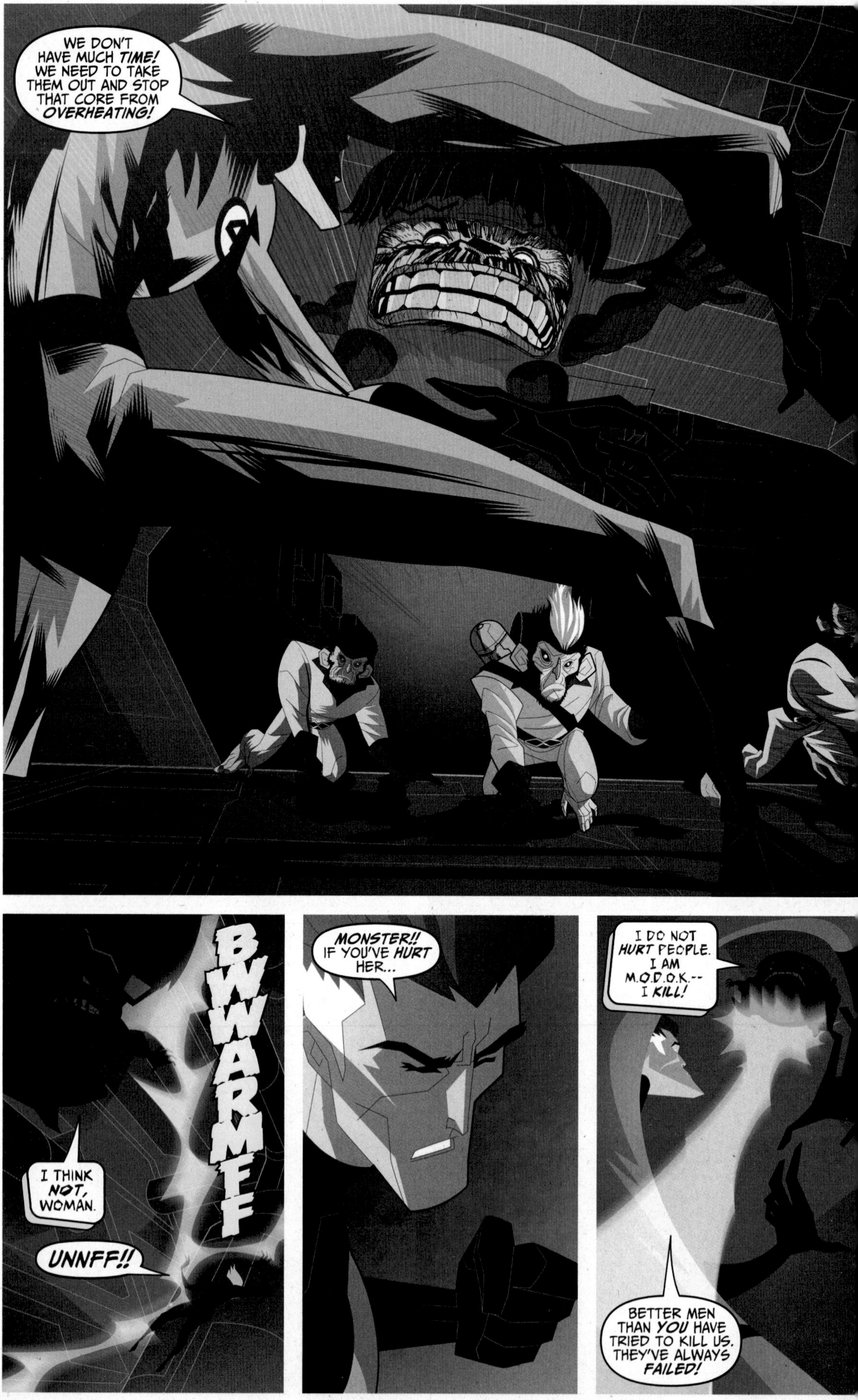
WE DON'T HAVE MUCH TIME! WE NEED TO TAKE THEM OUT AND STOP THAT CORE FROM OVERHEATING!
BWWARMFF
I THINK NOT, WOMAN.
UNNFF!!
MONSTER!! IF YOU'VE HURT HER...
I DO NOT HURT PEOPLE. I AM M.O.D.O.K.-- I KILL!
BETTER MEN THAN YOU HAVE TRIED TO KILL US. THEY'VE ALWAYS FAILED!

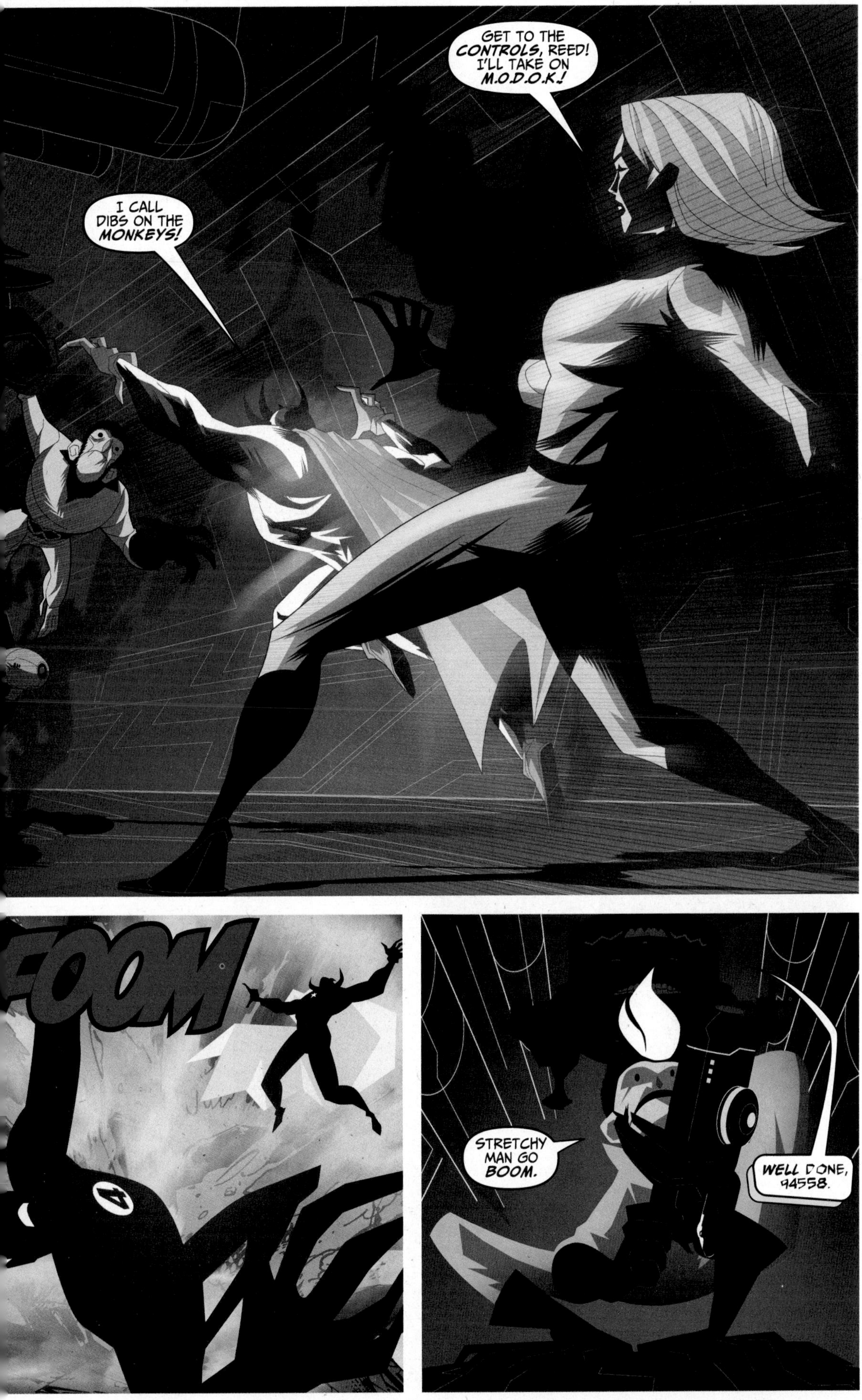
GET TO THE CONTROLS, REED! I'LL TAKE ON M.O.D.O.K.!
I CALL DIBS ON THE MONKEYS!
FOOM
STRETCHY MAN GO BOOM.
WELL DONE, 94558.

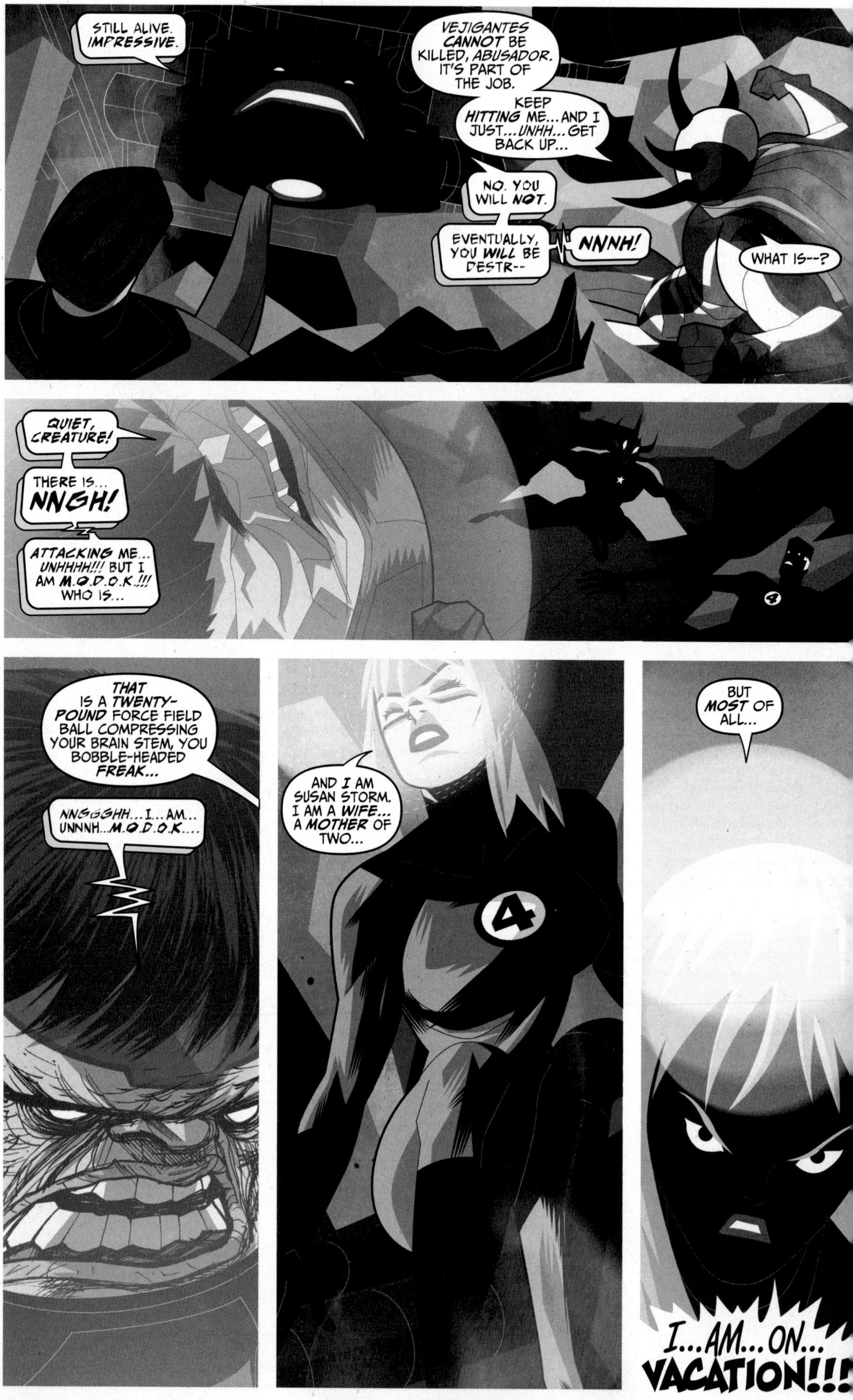
STILL ALIVE. IMPRESSIVE.
VEJIGANTES CANNOT BE KILLED, ABUSADOR. IT'S PART OF THE JOB.
KEEP HITTING ME... AND I JUST... UNHH... GET BACK UP...
NO. YOU WILL NOT.
EVENTUALLY, YOU WILL BE DESTR--
NNNH!
WHAT IS--?
QUIET, CREATURE!
THERE IS... NNGH!
ATTACKING ME... UNHHHH!!! BUT I AM M.O.D.O.K.!!! WHO IS...
THAT IS A TWENTY-POUND FORCE FIELD BALL COMPRESSING YOUR BRAIN STEM, YOU BOBBLE-HEADED FREAK...
NNGGGHH... I... AM... UNNNH... M.O.D.O.K....
AND I AM SUSAN STORM. I AM A WIFE... A MOTHER OF TWO...
BUT MOST OF ALL...
I... AM... ON... VACATION!!!

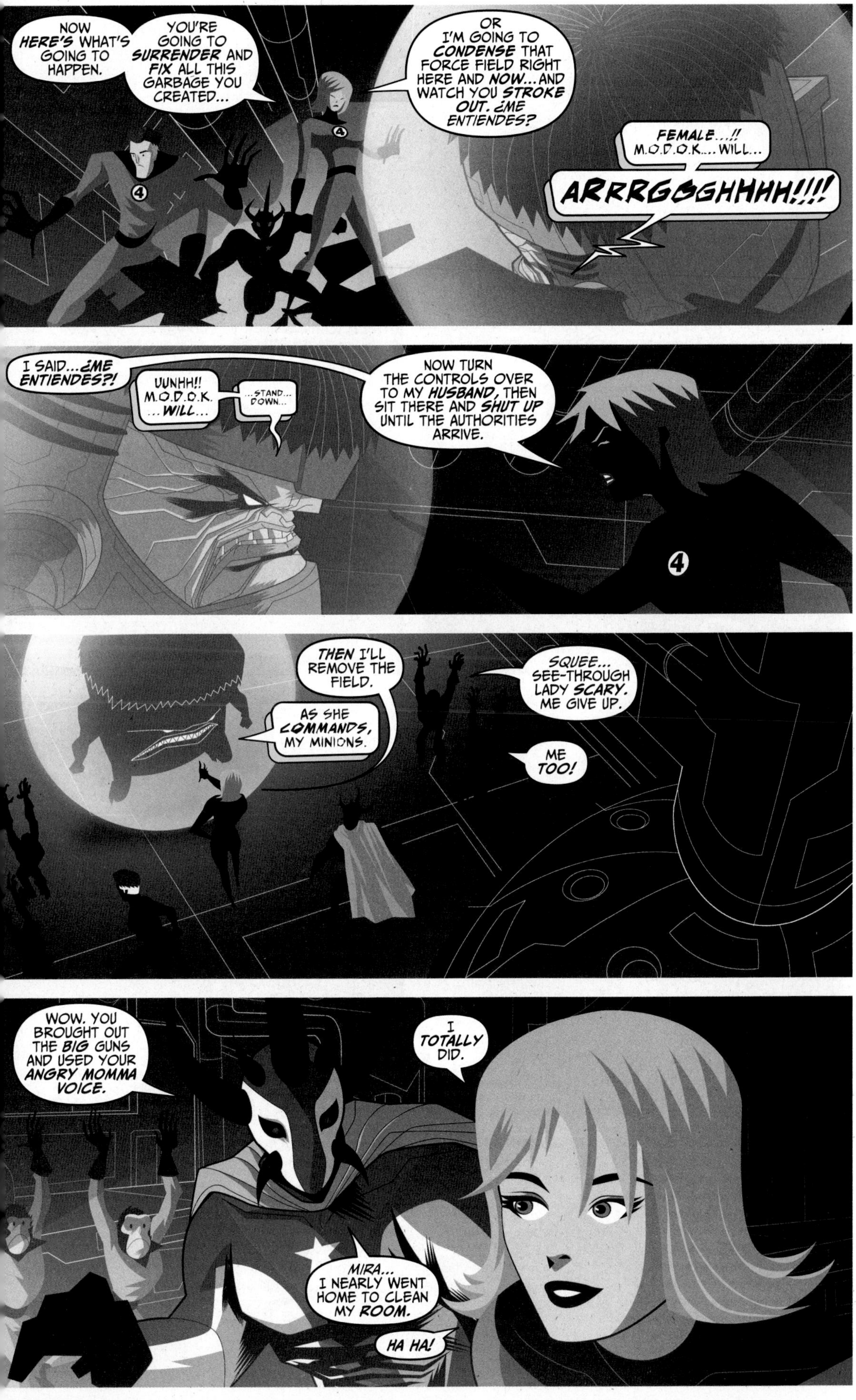
NOW HERE'S WHAT'S GOING TO HAPPEN.
YOU'RE GOING TO SURRENDER AND FIX ALL THIS GARBAGE YOU CREATED...
OR I'M GOING TO CONDENSE THAT FORCE FIELD RIGHT HERE AND NOW...AND WATCH YOU STROKE OUT. ¿ME ENTIENDES?
FEMALE...!! M.O.D.O.K.... WILL...
ARRRGGGHHHH!!!!
I SAID...¿ME ENTIENDES?!
UUNHH!! M.O.D.O.K. ...WILL...
...STAND... DOWN...
NOW TURN THE CONTROLS OVER TO MY HUSBAND, THEN SIT THERE AND SHUT UP UNTIL THE AUTHORITIES ARRIVE.
THEN I'LL REMOVE THE FIELD.
AS SHE COMMANDS, MY MINIONS.
SQUEE... SEE-THROUGH LADY SCARY. ME GIVE UP.
ME TOO!
WOW. YOU BROUGHT OUT THE BIG GUNS AND USED YOUR ANGRY MOMMA VOICE.
I TOTALLY DID.
MIRA... I NEARLY WENT HOME TO CLEAN MY ROOM.
HA HA!

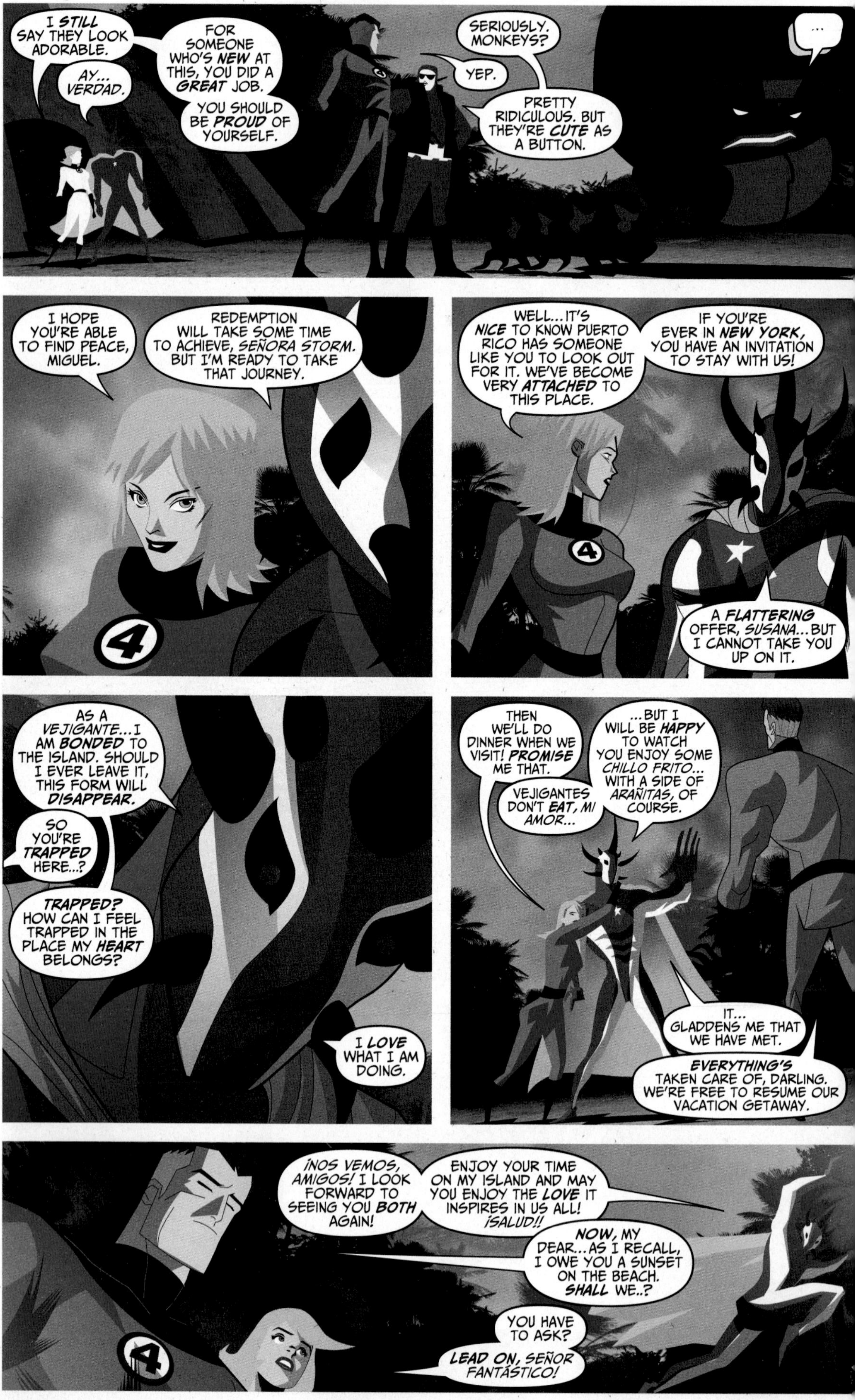
I STILL SAY THEY LOOK ADORABLE.
AY... VERDAD.
FOR SOMEONE WHO'S NEW AT THIS, YOU DID A GREAT JOB.
YOU SHOULD BE PROUD OF YOURSELF.
SERIOUSLY. MONKEYS?
YEP.
PRETTY RIDICULOUS. BUT THEY'RE CUTE AS A BUTTON.
...
I HOPE YOU'RE ABLE TO FIND PEACE, MIGUEL.
REDEMPTION WILL TAKE SOME TIME TO ACHIEVE, SEÑORA STORM. BUT I'M READY TO TAKE THAT JOURNEY.
WELL...IT'S NICE TO KNOW PUERTO RICO HAS SOMEONE LIKE YOU TO LOOK OUT FOR IT. WE'VE BECOME VERY ATTACHED TO THIS PLACE.
IF YOU'RE EVER IN NEW YORK, YOU HAVE AN INVITATION TO STAY WITH US!
A FLATTERING OFFER, SUSANA...BUT I CANNOT TAKE YOU UP ON IT.
AS A VEJIGANTE...I AM BONDED TO THE ISLAND. SHOULD I EVER LEAVE IT, THIS FORM WILL DISAPPEAR.
SO YOU'RE TRAPPED HERE...?
TRAPPED? HOW CAN I FEEL TRAPPED IN THE PLACE MY HEART BELONGS?
I LOVE WHAT I AM DOING.
THEN WE'LL DO DINNER WHEN WE VISIT! PROMISE ME THAT.
VEJIGANTES DON'T EAT, MI AMOR...
...BUT I WILL BE HAPPY TO WATCH YOU ENJOY SOME CHILLO FRITO... WITH A SIDE OF ARAÑITAS, OF COURSE.
IT... GLADDENS ME THAT WE HAVE MET.
EVERYTHING'S TAKEN CARE OF, DARLING. WE'RE FREE TO RESUME OUR VACATION GETAWAY.
¡NOS VEMOS, AMIGOS! I LOOK FORWARD TO SEEING YOU BOTH AGAIN!
ENJOY YOUR TIME ON MY ISLAND AND MAY YOU ENJOY THE LOVE IT INSPIRES IN US ALL! ¡SALUD!!
NOW, MY DEAR...AS I RECALL, I OWE YOU A SUNSET ON THE BEACH. SHALL WE..?
YOU HAVE TO ASK?
LEAD ON, SEÑOR FANTÁSTICO!

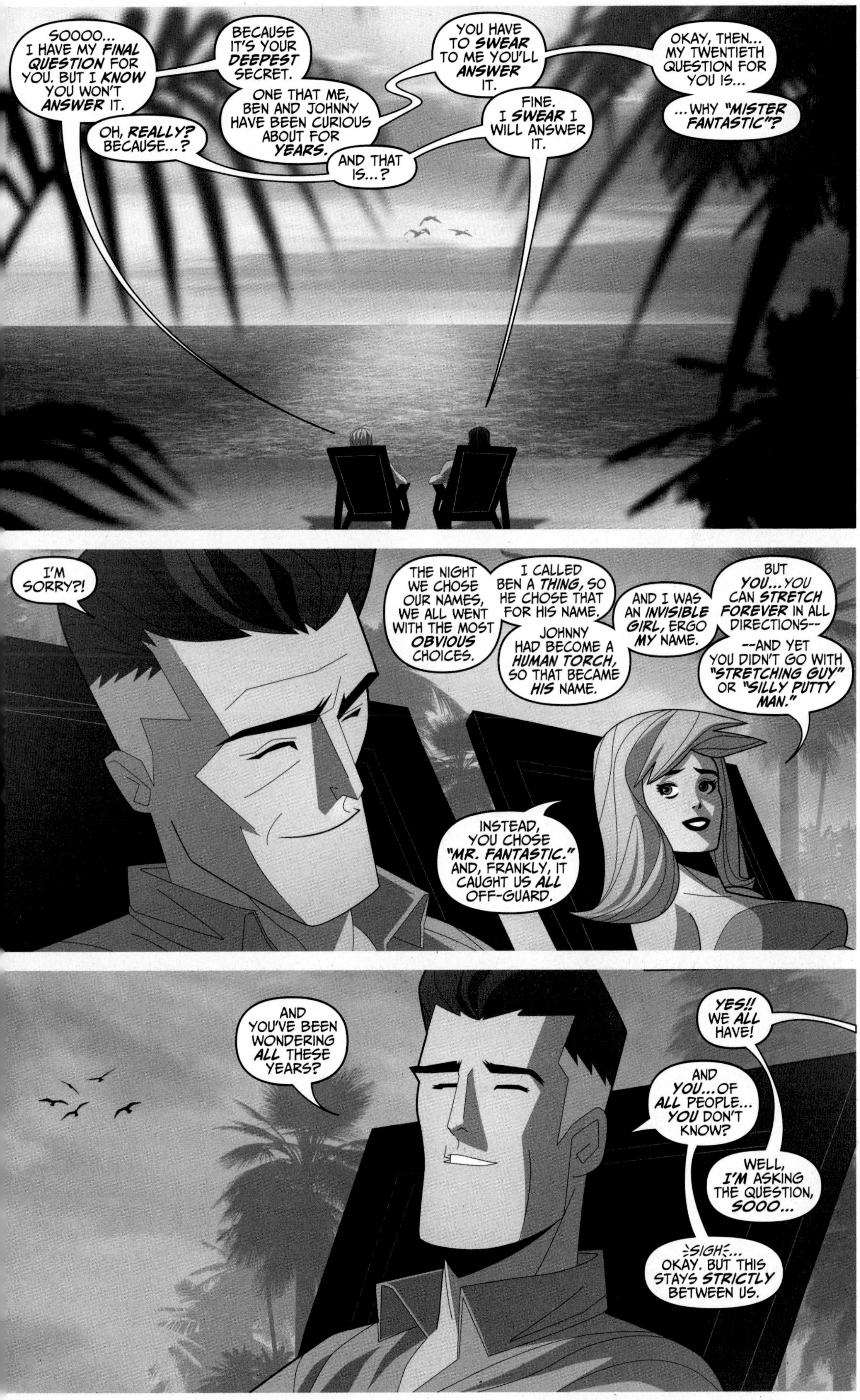
SOOOO... I HAVE MY FINAL QUESTION FOR YOU. BUT I KNOW YOU WON'T ANSWER IT.
OH, REALLY? BECAUSE...?
BECAUSE IT'S YOUR DEEPEST SECRET.
ONE THAT ME, BEN AND JOHNNY HAVE BEEN CURIOUS ABOUT FOR YEARS.
AND THAT IS...?
YOU HAVE TO SWEAR TO ME YOU'LL ANSWER IT.
FINE. I SWEAR I WILL ANSWER IT.
OKAY, THEN... MY TWENTIETH QUESTION FOR YOU IS...
...WHY "MISTER FANTASTIC"?
I'M SORRY?!
THE NIGHT WE CHOSE OUR NAMES, WE ALL WENT WITH THE MOST OBVIOUS CHOICES.
I CALLED BEN A THING, SO HE CHOSE THAT FOR HIS NAME.
JOHNNY HAD BECOME A HUMAN TORCH, SO THAT BECAME HIS NAME.
AND I WAS AN INVISIBLE GIRL, ERGO MY NAME.
BUT YOU...YOU CAN STRETCH FOREVER IN ALL DIRECTIONS--
--AND YET YOU DIDN'T GO WITH "STRETCHING GUY" OR "SILLY PUTTY MAN."
INSTEAD, YOU CHOSE "MR. FANTASTIC." AND, FRANKLY, IT CAUGHT US ALL OFF-GUARD.
AND YOU'VE BEEN WONDERING ALL THESE YEARS?
YES!! WE ALL HAVE!
AND YOU...OF ALL PEOPLE... YOU DON'T KNOW?
WELL, I'M ASKING THE QUESTION, SOOO...
SIGH... OKAY. BUT THIS STAYS STRICTLY BETWEEN US.

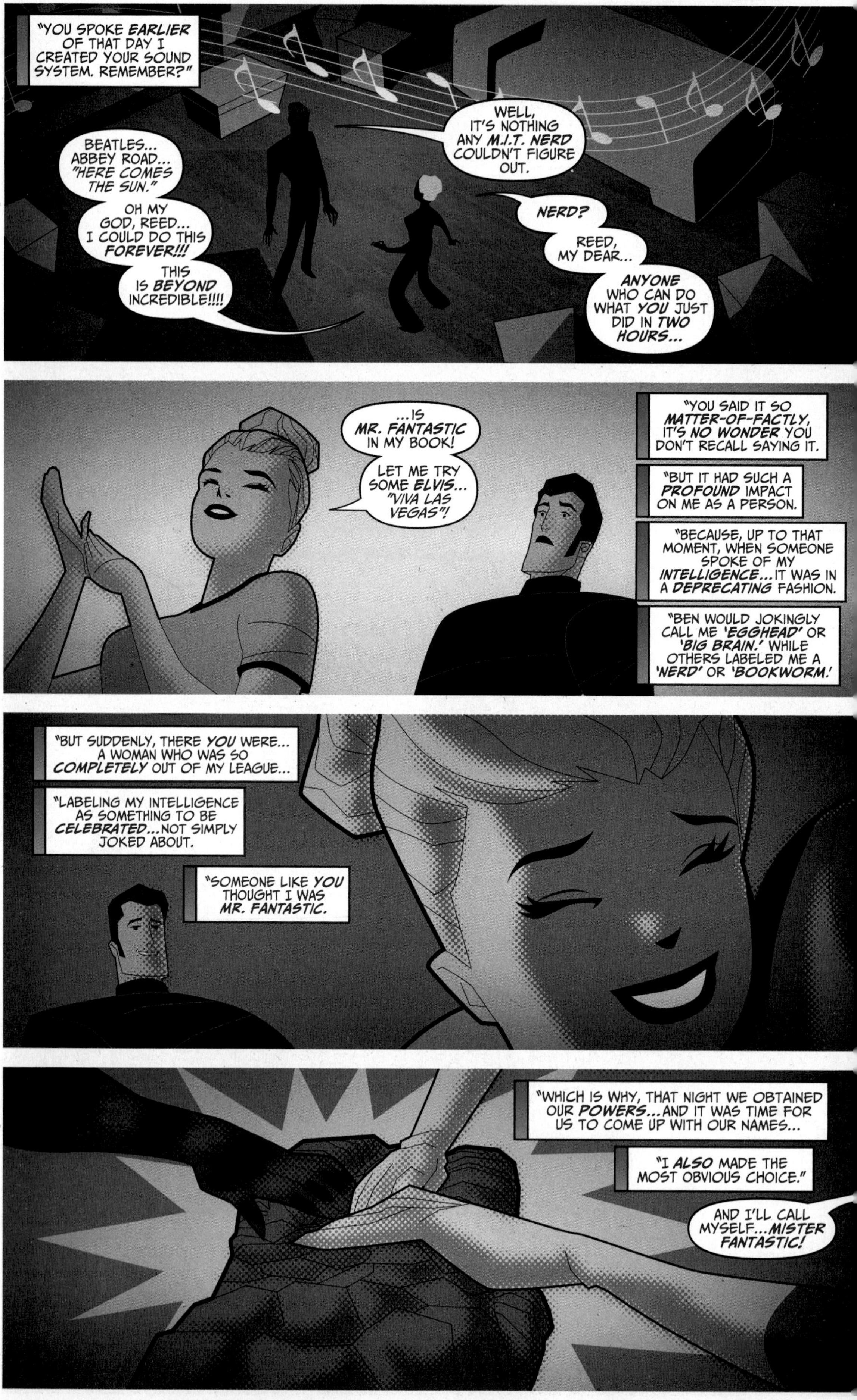
"YOU SPOKE EARLIER OF THAT DAY I CREATED YOUR SOUND SYSTEM. REMEMBER?"
BEATLES... ABBEY ROAD... "HERE COMES THE SUN."
OH MY GOD, REED... I COULD DO THIS FOREVER!!!
THIS IS BEYOND INCREDIBLE!!!!
WELL, IT'S NOTHING ANY M.I.T. NERD COULDN'T FIGURE OUT.
NERD?
REED, MY DEAR...
ANYONE WHO CAN DO WHAT YOU JUST DID IN TWO HOURS...
...IS MR. FANTASTIC IN MY BOOK!
LET ME TRY SOME ELVIS... "VIVA LAS VEGAS"!
"YOU SAID IT SO MATTER-OF-FACTLY, IT'S NO WONDER YOU DON'T RECALL SAYING IT.
"BUT IT HAD SUCH A PROFOUND IMPACT ON ME AS A PERSON.
"BECAUSE, UP TO THAT MOMENT, WHEN SOMEONE SPOKE OF MY INTELLIGENCE... IT WAS IN A DEPRECATING FASHION.
"BEN WOULD JOKINGLY CALL ME 'EGGHEAD' OR 'BIG BRAIN.' WHILE OTHERS LABELED ME A 'NERD' OR 'BOOKWORM.'
"BUT SUDDENLY, THERE YOU WERE... A WOMAN WHO WAS SO COMPLETELY OUT OF MY LEAGUE...
"LABELING MY INTELLIGENCE AS SOMETHING TO BE CELEBRATED... NOT SIMPLY JOKED ABOUT.
"SOMEONE LIKE YOU THOUGHT I WAS MR. FANTASTIC.
"WHICH IS WHY, THAT NIGHT WE OBTAINED OUR POWERS... AND IT WAS TIME FOR US TO COME UP WITH OUR NAMES...
"I ALSO MADE THE MOST OBVIOUS CHOICE."
AND I'LL CALL MYSELF... MISTER FANTASTIC!

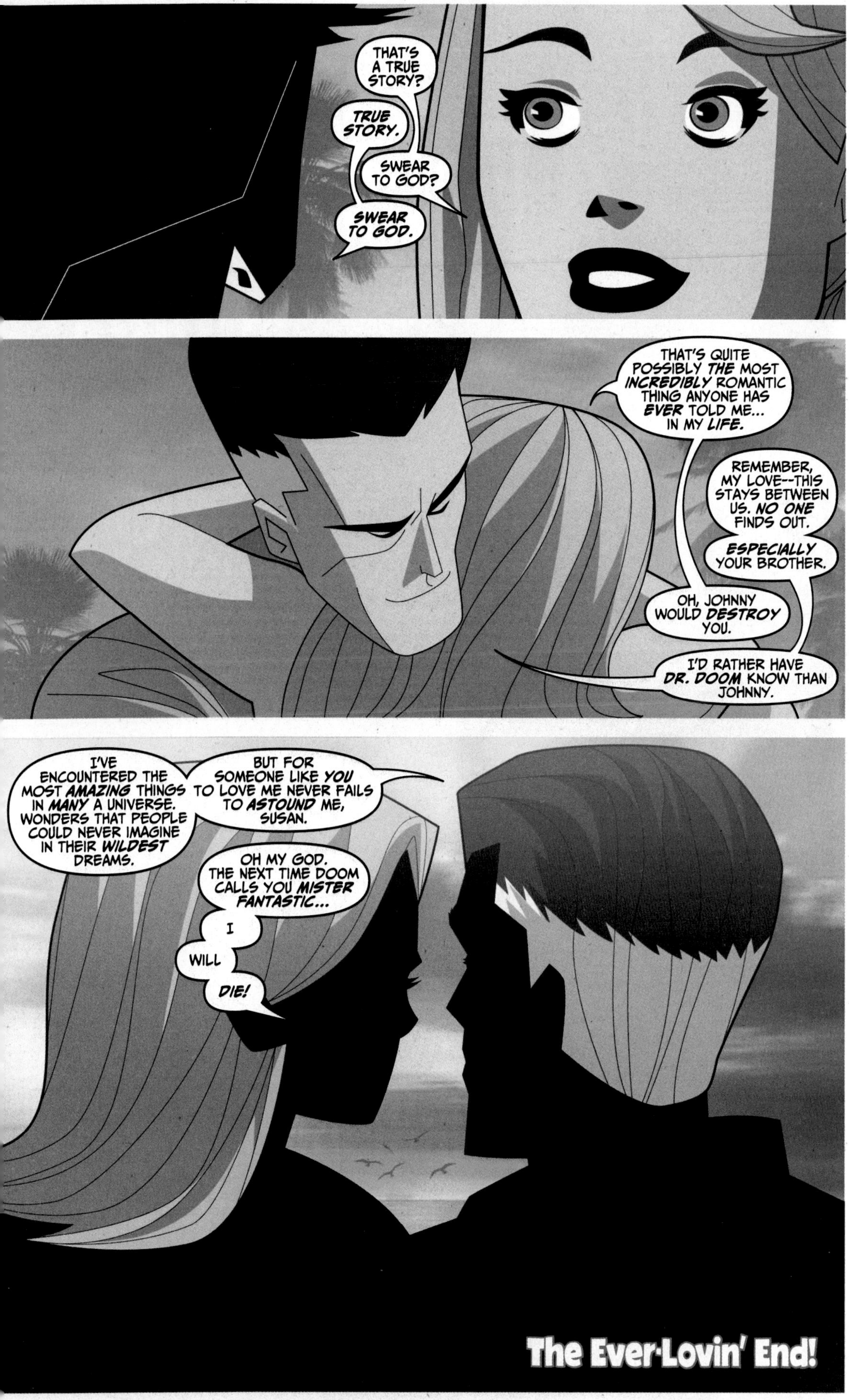
THAT'S A TRUE STORY?
TRUE STORY.
SWEAR TO GOD?
SWEAR TO GOD.
THAT'S QUITE POSSIBLY THE MOST INCREDIBLY ROMANTIC THING ANYONE HAS EVER TOLD ME... IN MY LIFE.
REMEMBER, MY LOVE--THIS STAYS BETWEEN US. NO ONE FINDS OUT.
ESPECIALLY YOUR BROTHER.
OH, JOHNNY WOULD DESTROY YOU.
I'D RATHER HAVE DR. DOOM KNOW THAN JOHNNY.
I'VE ENCOUNTERED THE MOST AMAZING THINGS IN MANY A UNIVERSE. WONDERS THAT PEOPLE COULD NEVER IMAGINE IN THEIR WILDEST DREAMS.
BUT FOR SOMEONE LIKE YOU TO LOVE ME NEVER FAILS TO ASTOUND ME, SUSAN.
OH MY GOD. THE NEXT TIME DOOM CALLS YOU MISTER FANTASTIC...
I
WILL
DIE!
The Ever-Lovin' End!

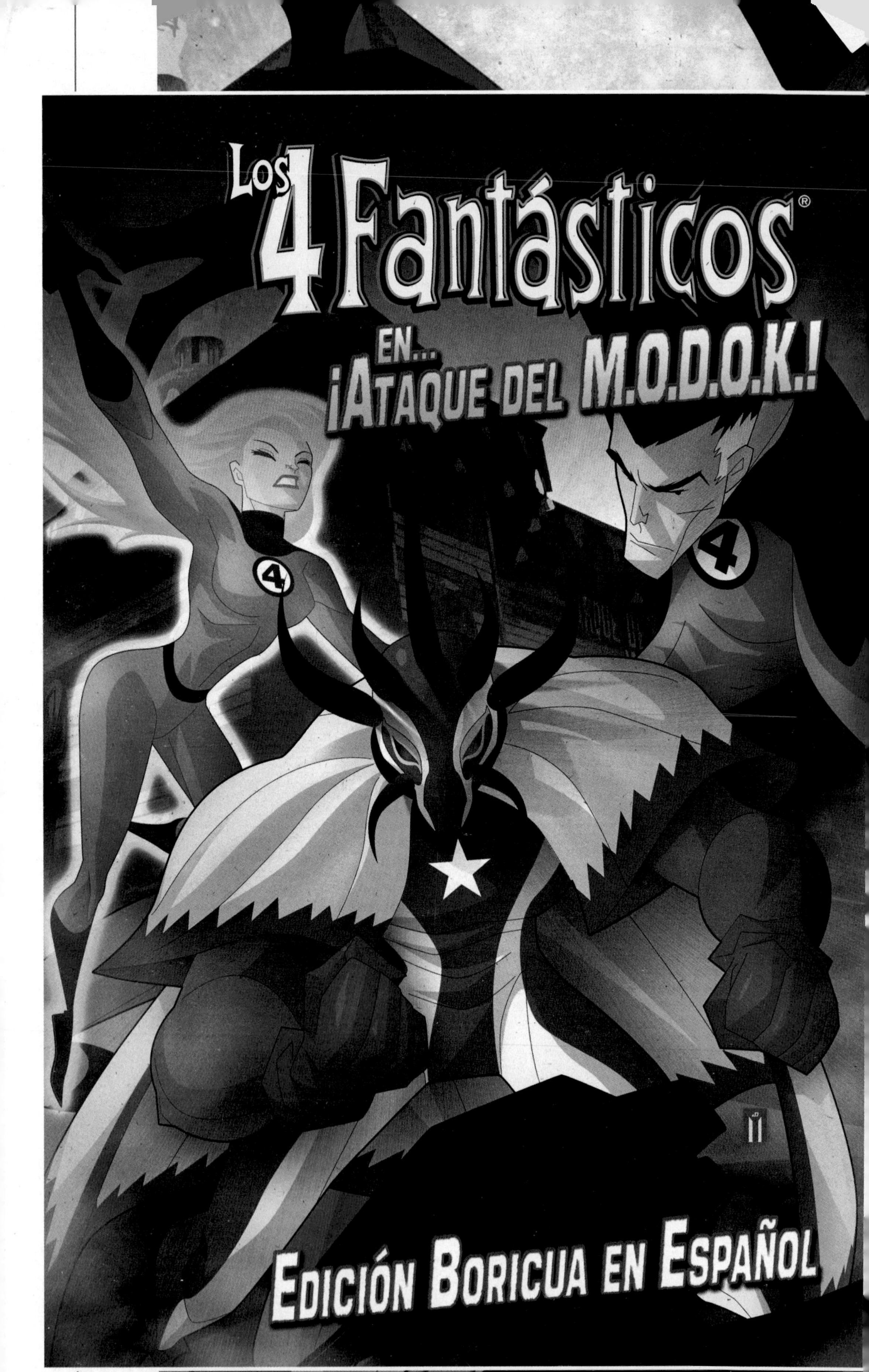
Los 4 Fantásticos®
EN...
¡ATAQUE DEL M.O.D.O.K.!
EDICIÓN BORICUA EN ESPAÑOL

SPANISH-LANGUAGE VARIANT